The Shakespeare Riots

EX LIBRIS

Peter Giordano

NIGEL CLIFF

RANDOM HOUSE

NEW YORK

The
Shakespeare
RIOTS

*Revenge, Drama, and Death
in Nineteenth-Century
America*

Published in the United States by Random House,
an imprint of The Random House Publishing Group,
a division of Random House, Inc., New York.

RANDOM HOUSE and colophon are registered trademarks
of Random House, Inc.

ISBN 978-0-345-48694-3

Library of Congress Cataloging-in-Publication Data
Cliff, Nigel
The Shakespeare riots: revenge, drama, and death
in nineteenth-century America / Nigel Cliff.—1st ed.
p.   cm.
Includes bibliographical references and index.
ISBN 978-0-345-48694-3 (alk. paper)
1. Astor Place Riot, New York, N.Y., 1849. 2. Forrest, Edwin, 1806–1872.
3. Macready, William Charles, 1793–1873. 4. Theater—New York (State)—New York—
History. 5. Shakespeare, William, 1564–1616—Stage history—1800–1950.
6. Shakespeare, William, 1564–1616—Stage history—New York (State)—New York.
7. New York (N.Y.)—Social life and customs—19th century. I. Title.
PN2277.N5C58 2007
792.09747'109034—dc22   2006049139

Printed in the United States of America on acid-free paper

www.atrandom.com

2 4 6 8 9 7 5 3 1

First Edition

Title page: Print by Nathaniel Currier courtesy of the Library of Congress.

Book design by Victoria Wong

To my parents

The theatres of aristocratic nations have always been packed with playgoers who do not belong to the aristocracy. Only at the theatre do the upper classes mingle with the middle and lower classes; only at the theatre do they allow the lower ranks to speak their minds, even if they pay little heed to what they say. . . .

If it is hard for aristocracies to prevent ordinary playgoers from gaining the upper hand, the people will undoubtedly rule the theatres in a country where democratic principles have spread through the laws and customs, where ranks are intermixed, where minds, as well as fortunes, are brought more closely together, and where the upper class has lost, along with its hereditary wealth, its power, its privileges, and its leisure. The tastes and inclinations natural to democratic nations will, therefore, find their first literary expression in the theatre, where we can be sure they will make a violent entry. On the page, aristocratic traditions will be gradually modified in, so to speak, a legal manner. In the theatre, they will be overthrown by riots.

> —ALEXIS DE TOCQUEVILLE, *Democracy in America,*
> Book 2 (1840), Part 1, Chapter XIX

Contents

Prologue

IT BEGAN, STRANGELY, with baseball.

A balmy spring Sunday in New York City, the streets bleached out in the bright light like an overexposed photograph. The year was 1849. Among the crowds pouring down to the breezy Hudson River waterfront, two friends met, touched hats, and strolled along arm in arm. They wore the somber broadcloth coats of professional gentlemen and a conspicuous air of studied nonchalance.

As on every clement Sunday, the docks were crammed with workers itching to get out of town, and as soon as the ferry bell rang the pair slipped smartly forward, thrust their six cents at the ticket booth, jostled on board, and jostled off again near the little hamlet of Hoboken. Still keeping pace with the crowds, they headed down the long path to the Elysian Fields, a popular pleasure garden nestled high above the rocky New Jersey shoreline. Past the turnstile, the meadows and terraces were brisk with promenaders taking the air and picnickers unpacking heaps of beets, sausages, and doughnuts under the trees, but the two men strode straight through, following the crack of hickory on leather to a riverside lawn where, with the brick, smoke, and rigging of Manhattan shimmering in the distance, a most peculiar ball game was in full swing.

Three years earlier the first organized baseball match had been held on this very same spot, but today's gathering was a far cry from the usual genteel Knickerbocker affair. With their sidelocks soaped into glossy puffs, towering stovepipe hats stuck on their heads, and muscular chests glistening beneath unbuttoned red shirts, the players were immediately recognizable as New York's notorious b'hoys. A combustible mix of native rude boys and the mainly Irish immigrants whose swelling numbers had inflected the name that the rest of the city indiscriminately applied to the whole alarming phenomenon, the b'hoys were regularly seen cruising the city streets in great gangs, and their cool impudence and swaggering style had become the badges of America's original youth culture. A big meet was clearly in session, and as the b'hoys lounged around chewing tobacco or loped in relays to the taverns that conveniently lined the pitch, the charier day-trippers steered well clear of the tread of their heavy leather boots. Sometimes gang rivalries dyed the green grass red.[1]

As if by arrangement, the two newcomers ran into an acquaintance who was already watching the game. Together the three approached the b'hoys and engaged their leaders in conversation. The request they made could not have been more unlikely: it concerned two Shakespearean actors. One, an intellectual Englishman called William Charles Macready, was about to arrive in the city; the other, Edwin Forrest, was the first true American star, a national hero and a paladin of democracy to his working-class fans. The two had once been friends, but they had fallen out in spectacularly public style and now were sworn enemies. What, the visitors asked, were the b'hoys willing to do to give Macready an unusually warm reception on his first night on stage? In the heated debate that followed, too many opinions flew out too outspokenly for an agreement to be reached, and long before dusk fell, before the katydids struck up their raspy song and the eight o'clock bell rang to gather the stragglers for the ferry home, the friends left the field knowing there was still work to be done.[2]

Deep in the bricked-in streets of Manhattan the air that week was as acrid as a cheap cigarette. In line with an old Dutch custom, the city's leases expired on the first of May, and Moving Day had wreaked its usual havoc. The sidewalks were piled high with a year's worth of dirt swept out of cellars and yards, ragged bands of prospectors were raking it into choking clouds, and columns of smoke nosed up from the heaps of moldy straw mattresses which provided an annual warm-up for budding neighborhood arsonists.³ Like the ball game, it was the perfect cover for a conspiracy. The Hoboken Two worked their way around the boardinghouses, drinking dens, and dance halls where the gangs gathered, pressing their case on the b'hoys and their bosses, and this time they tried a new line of persuasion. Macready, they explained, had made a speech in which he accused the city's political factions of turning the American public against him and setting "would-be assailants" on his trail. His snide comments, they urged as they slipped printed copies into the b'hoys' hands, could only be construed as a barefaced slur on their sainted Democratic party: surely the idea of an impudent English actor criticizing their politics from the stage was a humiliation not to be endured?

Years of bitter transatlantic disputes, provoked by the still untied ends of Independence and more recent conflicts over America's enlarging sphere of influence, had lifted popular resentment of Britain to an all-time high, and the new ruse, as Andrew Stevens, one of the Hoboken conspirators, later recalled, had a most wonderful effect. On May 7, the day of Macready's first performance, Stevens set out from his Broadway jewelry store and went around town buying up books of theatre tickets on behalf of his new recruits. Clearly someone with deep pockets was behind the operation, because altogether he collected several hundred. He was satisfied, too, that the theatre managers were none the wiser, because he had applied for varying numbers of tickets, between thirty and fifty, at each of the main hotels, and to brush over his tracks even better he commissioned his friends to buy five or ten more apiece. Later in the day, at regular gang hangouts like Billy Brook's barbershop at Doyers Street and Chatham Square, huddles of b'hoys duly showed up to collect their tickets, along with instructions on how to rid the city of the troublesome Englishman.

Further north on Broadway, in the uptown district which stretched for a dozen blocks above Bleecker Street, the bells of the new Grace Church pealed six, the gas jets flared out, and fashionable New York stirred to life. Shimmering silks and pipe-thin pants emerged for their nightly parade along the smart side of America's showpiece avenue: no respectable person would have dreamed of crossing over to the cut-price shilling pavement, because to be seen stumbling among its crockery crates and secondhand furniture was social suicide. The weather had taken a sharp turn for the worse since the meeting at the Fields, but even the piercingly cold wind had failed to belt in the brilliant display, and the crowds pressed on, clutching at hats and scarves, heads bent to the wind, like skaters in a Dutch frost-piece. A crush of four-horse omnibuses and gaudily painted carriages clattered over the granite cobbles, and as night set in, the whole show surged along, past Barnum's museum of grotesques with its dazzling searchlight, past the gaslit windows and marble columns of Stewart's palatial dry goods store, all the way to the last uptown stop, outside the New York Hotel.[4]

A thin, elegant figure dressed in the dark tailcoat and cravat of an English gentleman stepped out of its doors and turned left toward nearby Astor Place. His wavy black hair was graying in late middle age, his large flat face was set with a long irregular nose, a pair of small fleshy lips, and a prominent chin, and though a stern pride shone in his fine blue eyes there was something curiously awkward about the way he walked, as if he were conscious of his limbs parting the air. Even as he made his way under the lanterns flickering in the high stone arches of the Astor Place Theatre, few would have guessed that this passerby in a city of passersby was William Charles Macready, England's greatest actor.

THE NEW THEATRE in Astor Place had been a conversation piece since the day it had opened two years earlier. From the first night the playbills had shocked egalitarian New Yorkers by insisting on a strict dress code—"freshly shaven faces, evening dress, fresh waistcoats, and kid gloves" were the rule—and declaring that unaccompanied women would be turned away. This last stricture was aimed not at respectable society, which would never have dreamed of sending its womenfolk out on their own, but at another class of patrons who, by time-honored custom, plied their trade in the top tier. With their bars, coffee rooms, and smoking lounges, the old playhouses were one-stop places of entertainment, and they also doubled as brothels. Even at the grand new Broadway Theatre—a monster, which held forty-five hundred on its long, riblike benches—a quarter of the seats were set aside for the exclusive use of those regulars euphemistically known as abandoned women. Whores had their own entrance, and up in the gallery, next to the saloon where a plump barmaid served up brandy smashers and deflated doughnuts to an uncomfortable mix of rowdy boys and businessmen who had left their wives and daughters below in the boxes, they transacted their business, adding their cries—"Come, ain't you going to treat, old hoss!"—to the usual chorus of dirty songs and clinking bottles, and the odd full-blown fight.[5] Respectable society had finally had its fill of this outrage to its dignity, and the hundred and fifty aristocratic subscribers to the new theatre in Astor Place had been bent on creating an exclusive temple to propriety—a great drawing room where privilege could parade its wares untroubled by shivery speculation about what was going on above its head.

The dress code had done the trick, but the choice of location left something to be desired. With its serried columns, lofty pediments, and bluff stone walls, the theatre sat like a stern patriarch at the junction of the most showily wealthy and the most fiercely working-class districts of the city. On one side was Broadway and the mansion where John Jacob Astor had lived out his last years: until his death a few months earlier, the sight of the fur-swaddled oligarch being carried down his steps by a retinue of servants and petitioners had been a New York version of the changing of the guard. On the other side was the Bowery. As broad as Broadway but zipped in two by the iron tracks and horse-drawn carriages of the Harlem Rail Road, it was lined for a mile with fruit stalls and roast-chestnut stands, tables of tinny cutlery and faded millinery, and rows of Cheap John shops where smooth salesmen hustled bulk goods from raised platforms to jostling crowds. The Bowery was the entertainment as well as the commercial artery of the down-at-the-heels East Side, and flames smelling of turpentine illuminated glass signs advertising cockpits, rat-baiting arenas, boxing rings, dime museums, bowling alleys, and gambling dens, together with scores of taverns and beer gardens, some of which served firewater through a rubber tube straight from the barrel at three cents a gulp. Above all, though, the Bowery was famed as the favorite stamping ground of the b'hoys and their g'hals. Just as Broadway had its scrupulously dressed dandies with their monocles, polished canes, and lush whiskers, so the b'hoys delighted in nothing more than strutting along their own peacock walk, gussied up with silk cravats knotted jauntily round their necks and bell-bottomed trousers flaring over high-heeled boots in a riotous parody of their snooty neighbors, or flaunting the red flannel shirtsleeves, cone-shaped trousers, and brass medallions of the violently competitive volunteer fire companies of which they formed the core, while the g'hals sent up the latest fashions by dressing in spectacularly clashing colors, necklaces that looked as if they were threaded with Christmas decorations, and hats stuffed with fake fruit. When they sauntered into Astor Place it was as if the Goths were entering Rome.

MACREADY SAT DOWN in his dressing room, set about applying the vermilion-and-carmine to his cheeks, and worried about more pressing matters than a few disgruntled b'hoys.[6] Even now, at fifty-six years of age and the height of his formidable powers, he still felt a crispation of fear at an impending first night, and this was no ordinary first night: it marked the start of his farewell to New York City, twenty-three years after he had first appeared on its stage. The Englishman stationed his dresser outside his door and shut out the noise.

As usual, everything had been left to the last minute. Scene shifters clambered up to the paint room in the rafters and hefted giant flats covered with caverns, castles, and countryside scenes into their grooves. The props man scurried to his den of tricks and pulled fantastical objects from a small hill of lightning bottles and blackened cauldrons, paper snowstorms and dented crowns. On stage the dancers stretched and spun, the extras paced up and down clutching creased notes, and the old hands strolled around dressed as generals, ladies, and porters, breaking off their greetings to try out a favorite line. The conductor glided in and disappeared down a trap door to the band room. In the wings, the prompter consulted his watch, propped his book on a desk studded with bell pulls, and, as a point of professional pride, ordered the perspiring stagehands to rearrange everything. Up front, the manager made a final tour of the pit, which in honor of its newfangled armchairs had been pretentiously renamed the parquette. At the last moment the gasmen darted to light the great chandelier, and the crimson velvet couches, the gilt-and-white latticework, and the sumptuous brocade hangings grudgingly brushed off their daytime shadows. The stage manager peered through the peephole in the curtain and raised his hand to the prompter; just in time, everything was ready for the great event.

The play was *Macbeth,* Macready's trademark. He was expecting a good house: his hairdresser had told him there was a large crowd outside. The curtain bell rang and he heard a huge burst of applause and three cheers go up to Corson Clarke, the actor playing Macduff.[7]

"They mistake him for me," he murmured, and he allowed himself a complacent smile. It did not cross his mind that Clarke was an American—an American, moreover, who had been lent by the sympathetic manager of a rival theatre to assuage the patriotic feelings of Edwin Forrest's fans.

Macready's cue came, his dresser opened the door, and he strode on stage into another storm of applause. He bowed, bowed again; bowed emphatically, but the excitement showed no sign of letting up.

"This is becoming too much," he dryly thought. Then, beneath the applause, he heard the groans and hisses.

Andrew Stevens and his friends had stationed five hundred protestors in every corner of the theatre. From high up in the amphitheatre—the cut-rate balcony squashed in under the roof—one of their proxies, a prizefighter named Bill Wilson, unfurled a white banner. Through the glare of the footlights Macready could just make out the words:

"You Have Been Proved a Liar!" it accused.

A placard swayed up to a cacophony of laughter, cheers, and groans.

"No Apologies—It Is Too Late," this one read.

Macready's supporters were in the majority: the parquette was a sea of waving white handkerchiefs, and several frock-coated figures stood up in the boxes and turned to the amphitheatre.

"Shame! Shame!" they cried.

The b'hoys responded with louder jeers, and a rotten egg cracked at Macready's feet. He pointed to it and smiled contemptuously, perhaps even "with perfect sang-froid and good-humor, reposing in the consciousness of my own truth," as he later boasted to his diary. For several long minutes he stood still and waited, then finally he walked forward to say his piece.

"I feel pain and shame," he began, "which the intelligent and respectable must feel for their country's reputation, and I would instantly resign my engagement rather than encounter such disgraceful conduct." It would have been ammunition to his enemies, if they had heard a word he said.

After a quarter of an hour of mayhem he turned to the actors on stage.

"Go on," he instructed them, and the strangest *Macbeth* in history went on, in pantomime and at helter-skelter pace.

Then the deluge began. Eggs, apples, potatoes and lemons, lumps of wood and an old shoe skidded across the stage. Bottles of asafetida smashed on the boards and stank up the whole house: one mephitic vial soaked Macbeth's kilt. Copper coins pinged off his shield: he picked one up and placed it in his bosom with a gracious bow.

"Boys! Three cheers for Edwin Forrest!" one of the ringleaders called out from the back of the parquette, and Forrest's friends enthusiastically complied.

"Three cheers for Macready!" spluttered a kid-glove swell, to hoots of derision.

Somehow, despite the loud threats to their future livelihoods, the whole cast plowed on: even Lady Macbeth had never been quite so indomitable. Backstage, between scenes, they expressed their sympathy to the star. He received it loftily: "My concern," he replied, "is for the disgrace such people inflict on the character of the country."

During the intermission more society figures stood up in the boxes and tried to reason with the b'hoys.

"When you're done your sermon, we'll go to prayer, old boy!" one Forrestite broke in, aping a hoity-toity accent to roars of laughter.

"Let's have a song first!" another hollered, and several hundred b'hoys blasted out a Methodist hymn, accompanied by stamping and dancing on the chairs.

By the start of the third act, things were getting serious. Up in the amphitheatre, the prizefighter Wilson and his cronies ripped up three seats and sent them crashing onto the stage. George Walling, a young patrolman, stepped in and intercepted another chair while it was still in the grasp of "Butt" Allen, a saloonkeeper, but he was wrestled to the ground and Allen took aim at Macready. The chair thudded two feet from where the actor stood; barely flinching, Macready carried on, though when another seat crashed into the orchestra the musicians dropped their instruments and fled.

Macready's party fought back. "Go on!" one kid-glove shouted: "Don't give up the ship." That was too much for the b'hoys, and they burst out in a chorus of colorful taunts: "Down with the English hog! Take off the Devonshire bull! Huzza for native talent!"

With the calmness that often comes with calamity, Macready bowed one final time and walked over to the stage manager's stall.

"I think I have quite fulfilled my obligations," he observed with as much dignity as he could muster, and he went below to change.

The curtain came tumbling down.

Several of Macready's close friends had been watching from the front with mounting anxiety; now they forced their way to his dressing room and clustered round while he was changing. The consensus was that there would be more trouble in the street: Macready picked up his dirk, decided it might be undignified to defend himself with a toy sword, and set it down.

Outside a crowd was still surging at the front of the theatre. The doors were barricaded, the women in the audience were ushered out through a side entrance, and two actors edged in front of the curtain clutching a placard:

"Mr. Macready Has Left the Theatre," it announced. A cheer burst out from the amphitheatre, and an exultant exodus soon cleared the benches. Long afterward, though, Forrest's fans were seen marching jubilantly through the streets, chanting the witches' chorus from *Macbeth:*

> When shall we three meet again
> In thunder, lightning, or in rain?
> When the hurlyburly's done,
> When the battle's lost and won.

Macready, meanwhile, had made it safely back to his hotel surrounded by his protective huddle of friends. "I was in best spirits," he later persuaded himself, "and we talked over what was to be done." An envoy sent by John Jacob Astor's son urged him to stand firm; more sympathizers stopped in and joined the debate. Late at night, a police officer showed up with a deposition freshly taken from a rioter who had been captured, though since he had sobbed like a baby, the officer sheepishly admitted, he had already been released. Macready retired to his room with the document and set to copying it out, and at last his predicament started to sink in.

"And this is my treatment!" he marveled to his diary. "Being left alone, I begin to feel more seriously the indignities put upon me, and entertain ideas of not going on the stage again." Before he went to sleep, he prayed to do what was right.

By a striking coincidence, Edwin Forrest, Macready's arch rival, had also been playing Macbeth that night, at the Broadway Theatre. Down the great avenue, now thick with the late-night crowd of fancy whores and flash gamblers stumbling out of the bawdy oyster cellars into the red gleams cast by their lamps, his performance was coming to a triumphant end. At one significant moment, he had paused and leveled a look fulgent with meaning at his fans.

"What rhubarb, senna or what purgative drug would scour these English hence?" he hollered.

Four thousand people rose as one, and for several minutes they cheered for America.[8]

THE NEXT DAY Macready had already sent to a steamship to book his passage home when a delegation arrived at his hotel. It was headed by Washington Irving, the elder statesman of American writers. Irving presented Macready with a letter signed by forty-eight of New York's leading citizens, among them Herman Melville, and explained that it was being delivered at that moment to every newspaper office in town. They had heard, the forty-eight wrote, that the outrage in Astor Place was likely to prevent Macready from concluding his farewell engagement. "The undersigned," the letter continued, "take this public method of requesting you to reconsider your decision, and of assuring you that the good sense and respect for order prevailing in this community will sustain you on the subsequent nights of your performances." Macready consulted his sense of propriety and agreed to play Macbeth one more time.

Down on the Bowery, in the close lanes and crowded tenements that were home to the b'hoys and their gangs, a great stir was under way. Forrest's supporters were not about to be outmaneuvered by their self-styled betters, and they saw an unmissable opportunity to demonstrate both their displeasure and their muscle. That Thursday night, as Macready once again set out for Astor Place, he was reassured to see dozens of police officers lining the way. Yet within hours the army had opened fire on thousands of its fellow citizens and William Charles Macready was being hunted through the night by a mob bent on revenge.

BEFORE AMERICAN CULTURAL imperialism there was English cultural imperialism.[9] So, at least, Anglophobes angrily claimed; Americans who were still attached to the Old World countered that English culture dominated the marketplace, in the decades before America had established its own traditions, simply because it gave audiences what they wanted. The stakes were high, because this was no airless ivory-tower argument: to many it seemed inextricably bound up with the question of what sort of nation America would become. *The Shakespeare Riots* is the story of how America struggled to find its own voice between two conflicting identities, and how the contest ended in a bloody riot that shocked the whole nation and forced it to reconsider its most basic beliefs. Yet almost unbelievably, it all started with one man, standing in a Scottish theatre, hissing at another man's performance of Hamlet. The unlikely chain of events that forged tragedy from farce takes us on a journey from the wild American frontier to the decadence of theatre-crazed London, and from the dens of the New York gangs to the mining towns of gold-fevered California. In an age when theatres were the crossroads of a whole society, it brings us to the heart of two countries whose ties were closer to snapping than at any time since. And along the way another story unfolds: the story of Shakespeare's plays, those precious leaves of Elizabethan thought which so entranced the nineteenth century that they were fought over, in frontier saloons no less than in aristocratic salons, with an almost hysterical passion. It was Shakespeare who brought Forrest and Macready together, and it was Shakespeare who tore them apart.

The Shakespeare Riots

CHAPTER I

A Shakespearean Ark

ONE DAY IN the fall of 1814 a traveling actor named Noble Luke Usher presented himself at the door of the theatre in Albany, New York, and offered his services for a few nights; *Macbeth,* he added, was his preferred choice for his debut. Usher was known to have performed in at least three eastern cities and he was engaged on the spot. Soon he had befriended the theatre's stage manager, an Englishman in his mid-forties named Samuel Drake, and confided in him that his real motive in coming to Albany was to engage a company of actors to follow him to Kentucky, where he had three theatres waiting to welcome them. Drake agreed to put the word around and quietly assemble a small group, which he would lead out in the spring. Nothing more was heard of Usher until a letter arrived from his uncle, informing Drake that Noble Luke had died on a ridge of the Allegheny Mountains on his way back to Kentucky and asking whether he was willing to take over the theatres himself. Noble Luke, who had once acted with Edgar Allan Poe's parents, would later be immortalized in "The Fall of the House of Usher." Meanwhile Samuel Drake found himself en route to deepest Kentucky while the ashes of the War of 1812 were still smoldering all around.[1]

The War of 1812 had been muddled together from the almighty mess of the Napoleonic Wars, with a large dash of unfinished business from the American Revolution. The Royal Navy was being ravaged by deserters, many of whom had jumped ship for the better pay and less grisly conditions of the American merchant fleet, and their Admiralty's solution, which proved as gainful as it was tactless, was to board vessels flying the American flag, often when they were barely out of harbor, and haul off every sailor found cowering behind a capstan. In the process, since Britain classed British-born American citizens as British subjects, several thousand American seamen were impressed into military service with the motherland. Several more were cut down in the cannon fire, and the headless corpse of one helmsman was put on display at a New York coffeehouse, a more effective propaganda ploy than any amount of vituperation in the morning papers. When the United States found itself caught up in the Anglo-French trade wars, which cost it nine hundred ships and plunged its industry into recession, the call for action became irresistible. America declared war in June 1812, and marched into Canada, fulfilling a longstanding urge on the part of the hawks in Congress which they had used the dispute as a pretext to satisfy. In 1814 the British burned down the White House, and though Andrew Jackson's forces won an overwhelming victory at New Orleans in January 1815—two weeks after the two countries had signed the Treaty of Ghent, but a month before news of the peace reached American shores—the hostilities ended with neither side having achieved its aims. American public opinion, despite near military disaster, rumbles of secession in New England, and awakened nationalism in Canada, saw things differently: the United States had defended its honor against the mighty British Empire, and national pride was noisily on the march.[2] All in all, it was not the most propitious time for an English impresario to set out for what was then the wildest west.

Drake, like the good pioneer he was, took it all in stride. Early in 1815 he signed up a new recruit, a nineteen-year-old Albany boy named Noah Ludlow, to his fledgling company and sent him on ahead to scout out places to perform along the route. Ludlow, who ran away from home without a word to his family, had set foot on a stage precisely twice in his life, but he had a hunger for the greasepaint. More to the point, Drake had had trouble finding experienced performers who were willing to put their livelihoods—maybe even their lives—on the line in the untamed wilderness they imagined was waiting out west. To be precise, he had found none at all, for the party that finally got under way com-

An American cartoonist gloats over the defeat of the British warship Boxer *by the American frigate* Enterprise *in September 1813. James Madison (right) is clearly getting the better of a blood-gushing King George III.* Courtesy of the Library of Congress.

prised Samuel Drake Senior; his sons, Samuel Junior, Alexander, and James; his daughters, Martha and Julia; a carpenter; the carpenter's wife; and a handyman, along with another runaway novice, the daughter of the innkeeper whose hospitality the Drakes had been enjoying, named Fanny Denny. Like the troupe of the great Vincent Crummles in *Nicholas Nickleby,* whose wife, children, and dog were in the profession and whose chaise-pony went on in *Timour the Tartar,* the Drakes' company was a family affair.

Samuel Senior's plan was to lead his myrmidons by land through New York State, take a boat down the Allegheny River to Pittsburgh, and strike out for Kentucky just as the legislature was returning to Frankfort for its winter session. Off they set, forging ahead for a few days and stopping to perform in any barroom or back room where they could rig up a stage. It was a perilous route—indeed, somewhere in the rough country between Canandaigua and the headwaters of the Allegheny they briefly lost an actress. Between them the company owned two wagons and three horses: most of the little group had to walk, though the foot soldiers took care to maintain their professional dignity by hanging onto the carts until they were out of town, or by getting up at the crack of dawn to make their escape before anyone was awake to see them. The one-horse wagon belonged to Lewis, the carpenter, and its designated role was to bear the substantial weight of his wife. One day Mrs. Lewis was stricken with cramp and heaved herself out to walk for a while. Soon she was lagging behind, and when she failed to appear around a bend Lewis wheeled back and careened up and down the trail, hollering his wife's name. A couple of strangers rode by and sent for a search party, and actors, strangers, and scouts scattered through the woods, carrying burning torches and calling to the misplaced thespian. By the next morning it was generally concluded that she had been eaten by wild animals, but then another stranger rode up and asked if anyone had lost a woman. A joyful reunion was effected; Mrs. Lewis, no doubt pulling herself up in her grandest tragic style, recounted how she had lost her bearings and wandered off into the woods, where she was forced to haul herself up a tree to avoid being eaten by a pack of wolves. After scaring them off with a volley of twigs she had come upon an empty log cabin, where she tucked into a pot of maple sugar with such gusto that she had been sick, at which point a dog had sniffed her in the act and chased her out into the arms of her savior on his horse.

Reading these picaresque tales, as broadly comical as anything in a Henry Fielding novel, it is easy to forget how genuinely dangerous the hardscrabble life of these pioneering actors could be. Fever was rife, the extremes of temperature wreaked havoc with soft constitutions, particularly English ones, and the transportation was bone-rattling at best. As they bumped across the prairies in open wagons, clinging to trunks covered with the skins of circus horses and rubbed so smooth that passengers regularly slid off the side, they must have looked strikingly similar to the strolling players who trudged around England in Shakespeare's time. But their Elizabethan forebears were never called on to cross the frozen Mississippi and watch as their baggage, complete with scenery, props, and the stage curtain, disappeared under a thin patch of ice. That misfortune befell the Jeffersons, another family troupe that followed the Drakes; at the end of their disastrous trek, they were reduced to performing in a pigpen whose regular inhabitants poked their snouts in halfway through and set up a dismal squealing, while a few months later the father of the clan died of yellow fever and his wife, who had once been a popular leading actress, was turned out at the side of a country road, too poor to pay the wagoner for the ride. Theirs was far from the worst fate. In Florida one actor was eaten by wolves, and another troupe was ambushed by Seminole Indians.[3] Most escaped to a nearby fort, but two were captured and cut up into pieces. "The theatrical wardrobe belonging to the company fell into the hands of the Indians, who, dressing themselves up as Romans, Highlanders, and Shakespearean heroes, galloped about in front of the very fort, though well out of gunshot," one of their more fortunate brethren recorded. In the end several of the ambushers were seized, and "as they were robed and decked in the habiliments of Othello, Hamlet, and a host of other Shakespearean characters . . . their identity as the murderers was established, and they were hanged in front of the garrison."[4]

The Drakes plowed on. When they reached the Allegheny they traded their wagons and horses for a broadhorn boat, a small flat-bottomed vessel with wood plank sides and a roof just above head height. Two cabins were partitioned off, one for Drake and his wife, the second for the other three women: the remaining men begged beds or floor space in farmhouses or barns along the banks, or camped around a fire where, after making a show of home comforts with supper, some coffee, a cigar, and a song, they were kept awake by howling wolves. It was a sultry summer, the water was low and sluggish, and little by little they made their way as well as they could, reading, sewing, or getting stone drunk to pass the time. The calm was punctuated by occasional bursts of excitement—one of the company falling overboard from the roof while asleep, an irate shepherd taking potshots at them from the bank after they stole one of his flock, a near fatal encounter with a waterfall after they took the wrong fork in the river—but after several months and plenty more adventures they reached Kentucky and opened right on time. There in the Bluegrass State, at the heart of the frontier, the English troupe quickly became a local institution, though the theatre that Noble Luke Usher had talked up turned out to be nothing more than a cramped room above a brewery.

Yet even in the wake of two British-American wars, what was unusual about the Drakes was their intrepidity, not their nationality: since the prohibition on the immigration of entertainers had been relaxed in the middle of the previous century, actors had become one of England's most reliable, if least official, exports. The trade had been interrupted for a dozen years by the Revolution: during the Stamp Act riots in New York, the Sons of Liberty had turned up in the middle of a performance, chased the audience out through the windows with a barrage of brickbats, sticks, and bottles, and carted the whole theatre off, plank by plank, to stoke a giant bonfire. But, largely thanks to the theatre-mad George Washington, the English influx was soon underway again, and as opportunities expanded in line with the burgeoning population, it turned into a steady flow. New postulants for fame arrived every year, among them real stars like Thomas Cooper, and many more who billed themselves as stars and filled their purses before they were found out as impostors and packed off home, where they passed on the good news about the "easy gullibility of the hospitable Americans."[5] Society, and not just what was left of the third of the population that was still Loyalist in 1776, continued to look to England for its fashions, and genteel actors reaped the benefits. Cooper, a dashing man though an erratic performer—he was famous for forgetting his lines—married the reigning belle of New York society, while Charles Mathews, a suave English comedian, was astonished to find himself treated like an ambassador on a trip to New York: generals, commodores, judges, and merchants left their cards for him, and for his benefit night, the traditional occasion on which the featured performer took the lion's share of the profits, a large party of gentlemen chartered a steamboat to carry them the three hundred miles from Albany and back.[6] For years frustrated patriots and Anglophobes had little choice in the matter: the new country had more pressing things on its mind than establishing its own theatrical tradition, and London remained the undisputed entertainment capital of the English-speaking world. Even by the mid-1830s virtually the entire supporting company, as well as the stars, at New York's Park Theatre, the leading playhouse in the New World, were English imports.[7]

All the competition sent the smaller fry heading for the hills. The Drakes were the first English family to make it out west, but it was left to another clan to take England's penetration of American culture to its most far-fetched lengths.

THE CHAPMANS HAD been well-known theatre folk back home—old William Chapman had once played at Covent Garden's august Theatre Royal alongside the equally grand Mrs. Siddons—but the London stage was hopelessly congested, leaving them constantly on the edge of bankruptcy, so they set out for the great golden yonder. At first William, along with his mother, wife, three sons, two daughters, one daughter-in-law, and a grandson, had followed the usual routes between the eastern cities, but soon they were forced to split up to find engagements, and one trail of work led William to Pittsburgh. Already a sooty black mass of booming capitalism squatting at the strategic point where the Allegheny and Monongahela Rivers join to form the broad trunk of the Ohio, the Smoky City had become the main boatbuilding center, supply station, and embarkation point for travelers setting off down the whole Mississippi system, and as he stood watching the convoys of river traffic wind through the gateway of the west, Chapman had a brainwave.[8]

Several months later, in the late summer of 1831, with the early morning sun slanting through the ancient forests of cypress, maple, and oak, a curious little craft appeared on the great muddy flood of the Mississippi River. To a lumberman leaning over his ax on the distant bank it must have looked as impressive as a twig in a typhoon. A plain white pine raft with a ridge-roofed shack balancing on its back, it was just the sort of thing he would have knocked together himself when he sold his plot of farmland in Cincinnati and floated his family downriver to their new home, mooring up by a patch of pristine forest, chopping down trees and opening a wood yard to feed the insatiate steamboats. Soon, if all went well, he would buy himself a coffle of slaves and become a prosperous planter.

These rough pioneer boats, the waterborne equivalent of the canvas-covered Conestoga wagons that lurched across the prairies, had become grandly known as arks, but the one drawing close that day deserved the name even less than the rest. For one thing it was missing a pen for its family's pigs and chickens, though the shack was a little larger than usual and, whimsically enough, there was a flagpole poking through its roof, with a pennant flying from it. On the pennant a few letters were appliquéd in red, and if the ark had drifted close enough for the woodchopper to read them, he would have looked at the little craft in a whole new light. They spelled the word "Theatre," for this was America's very first showboat.

Putting a theatre on a barge brought three great advantages. It meant an end to paying for acting licenses and room hire, it allowed Chapman to reunite his scattered family, and it gave the troupe a direct line into an untapped and ever growing market. It also had its drawbacks. Hauling the raft against the mighty current was backbreaking work—at every bend they passed the skeletons of boats which had collided in the fog or smashed against the shore—and occasionally they had to fire a round of buckshot to fend off outlaws and pirates. Even in calmer conditions life on board was far from smooth sailing, particularly for the hired help. In 1833 William engaged an eighteen-year-old American named John Banvard as a scene painter. Banvard was not offered a berth, so he rigged himself one underneath the benches in the stage-left box. The back of the box hung out over the river, and as winter set in he realized he had chosen an unfortunate spot. Wide cracks appeared between the unseasoned boards, and every time a steamer paddled by he was drenched with icy water. One day he woke to find his blanket frozen solid, and when he sat up it snapped in two. Conditions had become almost intolerable when, halfway to New Orleans, Chapman informed his young painter that he had run out of money and was unable to pay him. Apparently Banvard was undaunted by his showboat baptism, because he quit Chapman's employ, assembled his own troupe, and converted another primitive flatboat into his own copycat theatre. It did not last long. The boat ran aground; the cast ran out of money and food and then came down with malaria. They continued to perform, stopping to vomit over the side, until a knife fight brought an officer of the law on board, and when he fell through a trap door, broke his neck, and died, the company finally scattered.[9]

Yet for all its privations, showboating's payoff was plain to see. The rivers were jammed with giant rafts of newly felled lumber, manned by crews of two dozen men living in crude wigwams on the lashed-together logs, and with flatboats of every size, each worked by half a dozen hands. Riverside hamlets like Vicksburg and Memphis had sprung up from a solitary log cabin and a curl of blue smoke and were booming into strate-

gic trading towns. Farther south, the prairies had been tamed into plan-
tations and the water shimmered with the white columns of airy new
mansions. Like the alluvial flood that nourished the great groves of cotton trees, the river had washed down rich pickings for its hardy actors.

The Chapmans' craft became an institution on the Ohio and the
Mississippi. Since there was no competition, it was usually called the
Floating Theatre, though it was also dubbed Chapman's Ark. Each season the family set out from Pittsburgh, getting under way at three in
the morning to beat the headwinds; they tied up at every landing that
could muster an audience, paraded around town blowing a trumpet to
announce the play, and worked their way the eighteen hundred miles
downriver to New Orleans. There, like the tradesmen who drifted
alongside them, they sold their boat for timber and started back up-
stream, at first overland and then, as business improved, by paddle
steamer, where they shared the hurricane deck with freshly paid merchants who jangled their pockets and traded insults and the occasional
pistol shot with the next wave of boatmen going south.[10] Back in Pittsburgh they built a brand-new theatre and started all over again.

The early arks were undoubtedly creaky places to watch a play—a
few rough benches for a pit, as the orchestra seating was still known, lit
by a barrel hoop jammed with tallow candles that dripped throughout
the evening—and more than once the action ground to a halt while
William's sons played tug-of-war with a catfish over the side. Yet wherever the Chapmans moored, audiences made their way by foot, wagon, or
mule and paid fifty cents, a sack of potatoes, or a side of bacon to cross
the gangplank. The venture was such a hit that after a few seasons the
Chapmans bought a steamer, hired a crew, and ushered in the golden age
of the showboats; soon even a full-sized floating circus was a familiar
sight on the Mississippi, complete with seats for three thousand spectators, cabins for a hundred employees, stables for fifty horses, a twelve-
piece brass band, and a full-sized pipe organ. As the wedding-cake giants
swept along, they towered over the minnowy newcomers, who were still
starting out with a few boards and a box of props; among the latter were
the long-suffering Jeffersons, who rigged up a backdrop painted with a
palace scene for a sail, staged practice sword fights on deck, and lent
credibility to the rumor that their barge was a mobile lunatic asylum.[11]

Today that world of sunshine and shadows, dreamy with images of the slow-flowing river silvered by the harvest moon, plagued by gamblers and scourged by slavery, seems overwhelmingly, quintessentially American. But like the rest of the American entertainment business, it was an English monopoly first. If that seems incongruous, even stranger was the name that kept appearing at the top of the Chapmans' bills: William Shakespeare.

SHAKESPEARE WAS READ in America before he was performed there. His plays crept onto the stage in the middle of the eighteenth century, though sometimes they had to be tricked out as moral dissertations to sneak past the Mrs. Grundys who guarded the nation's virtues; in the Puritan north they were treated as public nuisances, on a level with bullbaiting and cockfighting, as late as 1792, when the sheriff of Boston shut down the city's first performances. Even Americans who knew their Shakespeare tended to have little time for the theatre. In 1786, three years after the Treaty of Paris brought an end to the Revolutionary War, John Adams and Thomas Jefferson went on a joint pilgrimage to the Bard's birthplace in Stratford-upon-Avon: and yet the two future presidents regarded Shakespeare as a teacher of morals and rhetoric to be read in the study, not as a playwright whose characters were meant to be seen on the stage. Once again it was George Washington, never much of a reader, who proved the unlikely champion of English drama; under the first president's patronage, paying homage to Shakespeare at the playhouse became a social obligation among the beau monde of the seaboard cities.

Shakespeare was one thing in the east, but something quite different was clearly at work in what was then the far west. By the early nineteenth century, the great movement of pioneers rumbling across the Allegheny Mountains into the Mississippi basin had staked out a new America, a vast wilderness settled in large part by Europeans fleeing economic hardship and political despotism, driven by a fierce libertarianism, nursing a hard-learned loathing of privilege and an impatience with tradition. Their standard-bearer was Andrew Jackson, the hero of New Orleans, a sporadically educated boy from the backwoods, a dueler and brawler, a fierce Anglophobe, and, by 1829, an unprecedentedly populist president. The west had left England far behind: even to adopt the English-style manners and speech of an easterner laid a frontiersman open to ridicule. Yet every time the Drakes and Chapmans played Shakespeare, horsemen rode up wearing Spanish hats and cavalry boots, and plantation workers walked miles into town, and if the theatre was full they might hire a farmer's cart, push it against the wall, stand on top, and watch through a window. Altogether Shakespeare accounted for nearly a quarter of the plays performed in America during the nineteenth century, and he was by far the most popular playwright on the frontier.[12] What was going on?

It may be hard to imagine today, but Shakespeare was in the blood of the west from the start. When the twenty-five-year-old Alexis de Tocqueville toured America in the 1830s he was astonished to find the Bard in "the recesses of the forests of the New World. . . . There is hardly a pioneer's hut," he marveled, "that does not contain a few odd volumes of Shakespeare. I remember reading the feudal drama of *Henry V* for the first time in a log cabin."[13] Peregrinating actors rumbled past mountain peaks, canyons, mines, and whole towns named after the Bard and his characters. They sailed on Shakespeare packets and steamers and rode down Main Streets boasting Shakespeare Saloons plastered with advertisements for Shakespeare almanacs and Shakespeare patent medicines. They checked into the Shakespeare Hotel and turned up at the theatre to discover that at least a few townsfolk knew the plays better than themselves, and could shout out the prompts to prove it. Sometimes, with a swagger or more often a shy murmur, a local would ask to try his hand at playing a favorite character, and he would throw a spangled cloak over his boots, pistols, and spurs, scrub on some whiskers with burnt cork, and go on as Shylock or Richard III to the roar of his friends.

One source of America's newfound familiarity with the Bard was the schoolroom. The growing patchwork of private academies and common schools, and even the traveling elocutionists who crisscrossed the west, taught the craft of public speaking by drilling their pupils to declaim passages from the plays—alongside another book, published in the year Shakespeare retired from the stage, which sustained America's conversance with his language: the King James Bible. For many, the great soliloquies became the stuff of everyday speech. When Mark Twain wrote about his years as an apprentice pilot on a Mississippi steamboat, one of his most vivid memories was of his master's passion for the Bard. "He would read Shakespeare to me," he recalled, "not just casually, but by the hour, when it was his watch, and I was steering. . . . He did not use the book, and did not need to; he knew his Shakespeare as well as Euclid ever knew his multiplication table."[14]*

Shakespeare's language was familiar for another reason. Like the Elizabethans who thrilled to Queen Bess's speech to the troops at Tilbury, nineteenth-century Americans were in love with oratory. Words, as a largely Protestant country knew well, were the most powerful weapons in the world—they could rouse pilgrims to cross an ocean, could inspire a revolution, and could change the course of a continent—but it was the theatricality of great public speechmaking that really set America alight. In 1830 the nation was glued for weeks to the states' rights debates between Daniel Webster and Robert Hayne: Webster's oratory was hailed as godlike, and he was captured full-flow in acres of popular paintings. Americans drank in the barnstorming sermons of Henry Ward Beecher, who was known as the Shakespeare of the pulpit, even though he used his platform to inveigh against the shady morals of the stage. On the frontier, acting and public speaking were even more closely linked: many revivalist preachers started out as strolling actors, then switched sides and burst out in frenzied hallelujahs against their histrionic competitors. Just as oratory was theatrical, the theatre was a showcase for oratory, and when an actor strode to the lip of the stage to declaim the rhetorical set pieces— the great soliloquies that turn rhetoric inward onto identity, or Mark Antony's world-changing funeral speech for Caesar, or any scene involving Richard III, who self-consciously sets out to "play the orator"—and launched into the climactic line like a singer holding a high note, the audience turned a connoisseur's ear to his delivery.[15]

Shakespeare was revered as a seer and a prophet, the master spirit of Anglophone civilization, but his plays were also the stuff of log-cabin

---

* Twain again remembered the Mississippi's thirst for Shakespeare in *Huckleberry Finn*: the phony duke and king who inveigle their way onto Huck's raft settle on playing the sword fight from *Richard III* and the balcony scene from *Romeo and Juliet* as the surest way to raise some cash. They also pretend to be English: the duke's playbills announce him as "the world-renowned Shakespearean tragedian, Garrick the Younger of Drury Lane" (Chapter 20).

wisdom, the staple of schoolboy speechifying, and above all the stock-in-trade of popular drama. With one or at most two theatres in all but the biggest cities, men and women of every class went to the same shows and watched the same medley of "legitimate" plays and the skits and songs, farces and acrobatic displays that were served up as after-pieces or entr'actes, and no one thought of removing Shakespeare to a separate category called Culture. The boxes wept and cheered at his stories, the pit shouted its opinions as vehemently as the groundlings at the Globe, and the gallery roared like the crowd at a soccer match and shied rotten vegetables at maladroit actors. Some spectators became so wrapped up in the action that they forgot they were watching a play at all. In Albany a canal boatman was enraged by Iago's scheming: "You damned lying scoundrel!" he roared as he rose to his feet, "I would like to get hold of you after the show and wring your infernal neck!"[16]

Only a few sensitive souls saw anything untoward in all this. In 1828 the English traveler Fanny Trollope went to the playhouse in Cincinnati to watch Alexander Drake and his wife perform.* Mrs. Trollope took one look at the men with their shirtsleeves tucked up to their shoulders, spitting or lying down on the benches with their heels thrown above their heads; she sniffed the reek of whisky and onions, listened to the cries and foot-thumping, and pitied the poor actors their miserable working conditions.[17] One man's high spirits was another woman's "contempt for the decencies of life, certainly more than unusually revolting," as Fanny grimaced; Shakespeare would have understood the denizens of the gallery and pit rather better, and in return, his new American audience paid him a compliment that was lost on Mrs. Trollope's sense of propriety, and would be lost, too, on a century of later theatregoers.[18]

His plays, the settlers saw, were too vital to be mired in respectability. Shakespeare's imagination might have spanned the world, his ear might have caught the legion tones of life, but the country boy from the English Midlands was also wild, vulgar, and bloody; his goriest scenes, the eye gougings, child murders, and wife suffocations, were too much even for

---

* Alexander's wife was none other than Fanny Denny, the young runaway who had joined the Drakes' first tour: she was now married to her old manager's son and established as America's first native-born leading actress.

frontiersmen and were banished offstage or whisked behind a curtain. His writing was rooted in the countryside and its folklore, its witches, monsters, and spirits; throughout the plays, the daily rhythms of shepherds, fleeces, and feed, of foot soldiers, gravediggers, and pimps, of merchants, markets, and hard-won lives, act as a check on the elevated stories of lords, ladies, and kings. *Macbeth* has its drunken porter; *King Lear* finds its heart in a hovel on a storm-torn heath. Puncturing it all were the clowning and songs, the cross-dressing and obscene punning, the men turned into asses and the fools wielding pig's bladders—the mayhem of the country fair, parlayed into sophisticated entertainment. That far at least, the popular taste for Shakespeare could be easily explained.[19]

Yet there was something much deeper that attracted frontier audiences to Shakespeare, and it was this. The American west was an earthshaking experiment in building a new society from the ground up, and its pioneers were faced with fundamental questions. How far could individual freedom be cultivated before it started to encroach on the rights of others? To what extent would the human propensity for evil unmask itself if unchecked by laws? Unlike any other playwright, Shakespeare seemed to offer answers—or, at least, to raise the questions—in stories that went to the heart of human passions and allowed his audiences to judge their world against the worlds of the man they venerated as its wisest mind. Before long, the plays had become so ingrained in everyday thought that a newspaper report of a domestic assault, a gunfight between rival land claimants, or a dispute among heirs was scarcely complete without a reference to *Othello, Macbeth,* or *King Lear.*

That was why the plays that most struck a chord with the new America were the great tragedies, in which Shakespeare pushed his source material to the limits of human conflict, in which Macbeth and Lear warn about the perils of ambition and the price of guilt, generational conflict, and the complacency of power, and Hamlet struggles to keep the flame of moral integrity alive in a noisome world. Helpfully, none were set in England apart from *Lear,* and *Lear* is swaddled in an ahistoric mist. The most popular play of all, *Richard III,* was certainly English, but Shakespeare had turned the historical Richard into the arch stage villain long before theatrical tradition completed the process, and he was played as an irredeemable monster, a dire warning against political tyranny.

In these plays the pioneers found stories that were as radical and amplified, as copious and ebullient, as their own lives. Risking all in a wild, perilous world, they responded to the force and vigor of characters struggling with raw passions, with jealousy, envy, and revenge, with pride, ambition, insecurity, split loyalties, and love. Struggling with the loss of old religious certainties, too. America, like Shakespeare, was a child of the Reformation, and the Second Great Awakening of the early nineteenth century ushered in a religious upheaval that was hardly less confusing (though a lot less vicious) than the credal turmoil of Elizabethan England. Struggling with the great unknown, as well, because Shakespeare lived in an age of exploration, the time of the great adventurers and the earliest settlement of America, when the English language was twisting to find words for new and unspoken things. Shakespeare, the country boy who started writing for a theatre on the outskirts of society, was the voice of that thirst for discovery, and the exuberance of the frontiersman's language had more than a little in common with his outreaching Elizabethan tongue. Both were young and free, robust but flexible, coarsely seasoned and continually expanding to encompass a brave new world.

Above all else, the western settlers were individuals—Bunyanesque individuals who subdued a continent to carve out a space of their own—and they could turn to the Bard for an affirmation of their creed. His greatest characters, dreamed up during the epochal shift from the mysteries of the Catholic mass to the vernacular Bible, were unlike anything else on the stage: they had a tumbling, questioning inner life that made them inconsistent, human, and real, and they came to seem like friends to whom you could turn for advice. For all his weird sisters and star-crossed lovers, Shakespeare took modern man and dashed him against himself and his world, not against the gods and the fates. Men, insists Caesar, not the stars, are masters of their destinies; blaming the heavens for our disasters, says Edmund, is a way to worm out of responsibility for our actions. We make our world ourselves, for good or ill; our character and choices determine our fortunes: the message that America found in the plays dovetailed with the founding stories of the new nation. They were epically human plays for an epically human world.

Shakespeare had become American. America had not become Shakespearean: that would be a claim too far, even if anyone had known what America, so backbendingly attracted to the twin poles of freedom and order, really was. But if he was not quite the marrow and sinews of the new country, he was substantially its voice and its conscience. "Literature, philosophy, and thought are Shakspearized," said Ralph Waldo Emerson. "His mind is the horizon beyond which at present we do not see. Our ears are educated to music by his rhythm."[20] Crucially, he was also one of the few things that the vast sweep of the country had in common; his plays became the property of every class and community from Indiana to New England. James Fenimore Cooper called him the great author of America and declared that Americans had just as good a right as the English to claim him for their countryman.[21] Some went further: the New World, they insisted, embodied the Bard's spirit better than his own country. America itself, many came to believe, was the ark in which the true Shakespeare would be saved.

Shakespeare's sway over American life was unquestioned, but the monopoly that English actors held on performing his plays was about to meet its first and most decisive challenge.

CHAPTER 2

The Western Star

EDWIN FORREST WAS a poster child for Jacksonian America. He was born in Philadelphia on March 9, 1806, to a Scottish father and a mother of German descent. His father, William, had emigrated from Midlothian, just south of Edinburgh, in his early twenties, and set up as a shopkeeper. When the shop failed he became a peddler of Scottish fabrics, a roving occupation which did not comport with the views of his new wife's devout family, and instead he took up a position as a runner for a bank. He was hardworking but careworn and unsuccessful, and when he died of consumption in 1819 he left his widow with a mountain of debts. More hardship was in store for the penurious Rebecca. In 1822 Edwin's eldest brother, Lorman, tired of his trade as a tanner and currier and ran away to seek adventure on the high seas. He sailed on board a patriot privateer bound for South America—Edwin, who was complicit in his deception of their mother, thought it was a glorious caper and wished he could have gone himself—and was never heard from again.[1]

Young Ned, the seventh of eight children, was a weak and sickly boy.[2] He was thin and pale, easily given to crying, with a forward stoop to his chest and shoulders that marked him out as consumptive. Yet he was already showing signs of the stubborn resolve that would thread throughout his life. One day he overheard his father worrying that he would never reach his majority; shortly afterward, the circus passed through town, and Edwin decided there was no good reason why he should not be as powerfully built as the riders and acrobats. He started imitating their gymnastic routines, climbing ropes, leaping bars, walking on his hands, throwing somersaults, and, when he could find a sparring partner, wrestling. Within a few years he was proudly throwing back his shoulders and thrusting out his muscular chest. "Early in life I took a great deal of exercise and made myself what I am, a Hercules," he later recalled.[3] He was not exaggerating. His legs were like Greek columns. "What an enormous man he is," the actress Fanny Kemble marveled when she first saw him on stage.[4]

If Forrest was not a born strongman, he was a born actor. As a seven-year-old he would go home after the Sunday sermon, stand on a chair, and reel off the address in an uncanny takeoff of the minister's hellfire style. His father began to think of educating him for the clergy. After dinner, at his brother's tannery, he would be lifted onto the leather-dressing table and repeat his act to a hearty round of applause. Between the ages of five and thirteen he was sent for a short spell each year to the local school, where he won prizes for declaiming speeches while dressed in a checkered harlequin's costume run up by his sisters, complete with a mask and wooden dagger, though he could never resist crowning the recitation with a burst of somersaults. Soon the playground dubbed him the Schoolboy Spouter.

Ned was already addicted to performing. He joined an amateur acting society and spent his free hours in its woodshed clubhouse, where he played to the town's boys in return for an apple or a handful of raisins. The rest of the time he sidled around the local theatres, especially the South Street, where the Washington Box, resplendent with the seal of the United States, was preserved in memory of the time, a generation earlier, when the first president had attended in state.[5] For a boy who was already a fierce patriot, this was a sacred place, and it was at the South Street, at the age of eleven, that he first appeared on stage.[6]

It was an inauspicious debut for the future giant of the American theatre. The curtain was due to rise in a couple of hours, an actress was missing, and the manager was starting to panic when he saw Ned playing marbles by the stage door and recalled his talent for spouting. In desperation he offered him the role: a female captive in a Turkish prison. There was no time to learn the lines, but that was a minor detail: he could recline on a couch and hide the script at his side. The costume seemed more of a dilemma: no problem, said Ned, he had often tried on his sister's dresses and they fitted very well, though they were a little short in the skirt. That was easy, the manager replied: he could cover his feet with a shawl.

"But what about my hair?" Ned asked. A solution was found by cutting off the horsetail from a cavalry helmet, and the manager suggested he borrow a drape or pillowcase from home and pin it around his head for a turban. And so all obstacles were swept away.

"That's first-rate," young Ned concluded, "and now I am engaged, and will be on hand for sure."

Night came, the curtain rose on *Rudolph, or the Robbers of Calabria*, and Ned, as Rosalia de Borgia, was revealed in his horsehair wig, his homemade turban, and his calf-skimming dress, lying prone on his prison couch. There was only one flaw in the scheme: the tallow candles that served for footlights were too dim for him to make out the script. His first speech was a soliloquy, so he made it up, but then another character appeared and the dialogue became embarrassingly one-sided. Ned looked around, noticed that the lamps at the side of the stage were brighter than the footlights, jumped out of bed, and ran toward the wings. Since the promised shawl had been provided he had not bothered to take off his boots and thick woolen stockings, and while he was still peering at the page a shrill voice burst out from the pit:

"That's Ned Forrest—twig his Germantown stockings and his boots!"

The audience broke out in a confused ripple of laughter, hissing, and applause. Rosalia threw down her script, ran to the footlights, and shook her fist at the whistleblower.

"Bill Jones!" she cried, "I'll lick you like the devil the first time I catch you on the street—remember that!"

The drama mavens in the audience were less tickled than Ned's classmates. "Turn him out! Off! Off!" they shouted, and a heavy hand clasped the novice's shoulders and hauled him off the stage. But Ned refused to let his debut end with such indignity. He waited until the interval between the play and the farce—the programmed one—that followed, and while the stage was dark, the orchestra playing, the actors changing, and the manager buried in a mug of ale at a nearby beer shop, he ran home, grabbed his Harlequin dress and mask, tore back to the theatre, and rang the prompter's bell. The curtain rose on Ned Forrest reciting his prize-winning school speech. Dead, baffled silence met him at first, then a smattering of applause, and when he went somersaulting around the stage he was rewarded with a chorus of cheers that lasted until the manager turned up, gave him a good rattle, and sent him flying through the door.

Ned was not disheartened. At the ship's chandlers where he had been established on his father's death, his employer kept coming across him conning Shakespeare in a corner or declaiming a soliloquy to the back office. "Did you ever know a play-actor to get rich?" he chided him, wagging a greasy finger.[7] The young man's break soon came, when he walked into a demonstration of the euphoric effects of laughing gas. Ned stepped up, volunteered to try the experiment, inhaled deeply, and launched into a speech from *Richard III* with such force and ardor that he won himself a patron and a proper debut, at the grand Walnut Street Theatre.

It was 1820, and he was just fourteen. The audience was startled by the prodigy's precocious self-possession, his refined elocution, and his strong and melodious voice. A more talented newcomer had never appeared before the town, one critic enthused, and another presciently hoped that the lovers of native talent would support the young man who showed such early proofs of genius.[8] Still only fifteen, Forrest rented the theatre on Prune Street for a night and played Richard III, this time without the aid of gas.[9] His next step was to seek an audience with the great Thomas Cooper. With the true maverick's optimism, Forrest expected to be signed up as a leading man on the spot, but Cooper, who had suffered through a long apprenticeship like every English star, warned him not to trust to his amateur triumphs and advised him to seek out a modest position in which he could practice his craft. Forrest smelled a foreign rat: "When one knows how to read, he needs not to learn his letters," the cocksure boy shot back.[10]

Cooper's advice, though, was sound. There were limited openings on the crowded eastern stages, and Forrest's letters to managers in New Orleans and Charleston fell on equally deaf ears. One day in 1822, the proprietors of the theatres in Pittsburgh, Lexington, and Cincinnati called in town seeking actors to perform on their rural circuit, and with his rejections fresh in his mind Forrest signed up to play wherever and whatever he was asked for eight dollars a week. He rushed to say good-bye to his childhood acting club, his brother's tannery, and his father's grave, he summoned up the courage to take leave of his beloved mother, who was inconsolable at his unrighteous choice of profession, and after brushing away a few tears with his sleeve he set out with a few keep-sakes and clothes, a dictionary, a Bible, and an edition of Shakespeare, to learn his trade in the west.

IN A COUNTRY whose total population was only ten million, traveling actors crossed each other's paths in the strangest places. So it was that in 1820, five years after they had battled their way to Kentucky, old Samuel Drake's two eldest sons arrived in Vincennes, Indiana, to play a summer season and there ran into a familiar face from Albany. The face belonged to a young runaway named Sol Smith, and it was under his unlikely tutelage that Edwin Forrest would later become a star.

Smith was born in a log cabin built on land granted to his father, a fifer at Bunker Hill, but by the age of fourteen he had been pressed into service as a clerk in his brother's Albany store. Like his fellow townsman Noah Ludlow, he was dazzled by the footlights, and while Ludlow was heading out of town to scout for the Drakes, the younger Sol loitered around the stage door and befriended the actors who had declined to go hare-and-hounding in Kentucky. Sol's brothers heartily disapproved of his habit and banned him from going near the theatre, so every night he knotted together his sheets and blankets, let himself down from his bedroom window onto the roof of a hen coop, tiptoed through an obstacle course of old barrels and piles of wood, scaled a fence, and went on stage as an unpaid extra. One night, having daubed his cheeks with burnt cork to play the swarthy accomplice of a criminal magician called Three-Fingered Jack, he forgot to wash before going home, which put an end to his theatrical aspirations for a time. In 1817 he was left truly bereft when the theatre was converted into a church, and Sol bundled up his few possessions and headed off in pursuit of his theatrical friends.[11]

His reception was less enthusiastic than he had anticipated. The manager promised him a debut—in the important part of a waiter—and promptly skipped town with his cast in hot pursuit, leaving the sixteen-year-old Smith to settle their bill for two weeks' board, lodging, and ale. He sold his two best coats and a vest, paid the landlord, and trudged off toward Saratoga, where he was reduced to hauling stones for fifty cents a day. After three weeks with scarcely any bread to eat he wrote home begging to be allowed to return, but the next day his brothers replied, peremptorily refusing to receive him. The day after, they relented and sent for him, but Sol was already on the move. He hiked through the country, eking out a living as a farmhand, and ended up in Pittsburgh, where he paid for the essentials—a round at the tavern and a ticket for the pit—and was left without a cent to his name. A year or two later he trekked on to Cincinnati, where he clerked in one of his brother's expanding chain of stores, studied the law, and taught a psalmody class two nights a week. He soon grew restless and set out for Vincennes, where he took up a position as a compositor in a printing office. That was where he ran into the Drakes and at last found himself a bona fide actor, on a salary of six dollars a week. There were six others in the company—in a play about Pizarro, Sol impersonated the whole Spanish army, the High Priest of the Sun, a blind man, a guard, and half a dozen other characters—and soon even that modest number was reduced when they went for a communal dip in the Wabash River and one of the troupe was swept away.*

When the season was over, Sol retreated to Cincinnati, married a soprano, established a singing school in Newport, Kentucky, and, having forgotten about that, a newspaper in Cincinnati a week later. He called the paper the *Independent Press,* and undoubtedly it retailed no opinions but Sol's own. He began by borrowing a wheelbarrow, buying some metal type on credit, and pushing the barrow full of type

---

* At ten feet by eight, the stage for *Pizarro* was as diminutive as the company. Smith subsequently performed on a two-foot-deep hotel landing shared with passing guests, in a carpenter's shop, and on a table outside the window of a room that had only enough space for the audience. One night potatoes stood in for candlesticks; another night there were no lights at all and the company performed in the dark (Sol Smith, *Theatrical Management in the West and South for Thirty Years* [New York, 1868], 45, 90–92, 108).

to the local printing office, where he compacted to work the machines himself. On Sundays he played the organ in the local church, and when the preacher launched into his sermon he slipped away and pressed out the first page, returning in time to blast out the Hallelujah Chorus for the closing voluntary. For once Sol stayed put for a couple of years, and he was still editing his paper when, in the winter of 1823, a ragtag company of actors arrived to reopen the Cincinnati Theatre. Among them was Edwin Forrest.

FORREST WAS LOST. Long journeys by foot, flatboat, and wagon, ending at theatres with leaking roofs where the audience put up umbrellas on rainy nights, were not calculated to bring out the best in a green teenager, even one whose manly physique, resonant voice, and twinkling black eyes had already won him a keen and almost exclusively female following. In Cincinnati, he played Othello for the first time, and it was clear to Sol Smith that he hardly knew the text: he was visibly crestfallen, and much more comfortable dancing in *Little Red Riding Hood* or singing comic songs between the acts. Yet as soon as the play was over, Sol rushed back to his office, put on his critic's hat, and composed a piece in which he prophesized future greatness for the awkward young actor. He was roundly laughed at for his trouble. He would spoil the lad, his fellow editors scoffed: Ned was a clever boy, certainly, but everyone knew that stars were English, not American.

That was precisely what had quickened Smith's pulse. By now Sol was a confirmed westerner, and he was filled with the new land's optimism and democratic fire. His little newspaper was among the first in Ohio to campaign for Andrew Jackson for president, and he saw an equally radical prospect in Forrest: the glimmerings of the first autochthonous American star. This was no trifling matter: the English theatre towered over America's cultural landscape, and to topple it, or at the very least infiltrate it, would supply potent proof that the New World was a match for the Old on the artistic as well as the political stage. Even better, a truly American theatre could shake off the shackles of British taste and allow the nation to forge its own style. The military war was won: the war for true independence, for the country's emerging self-image, had barely begun, and American culture was there for the defining. What was needed was an actor as big and bold as the west itself, and Sol was convinced that Forrest was just the rebel for the job.

As an older man of twenty-two, Smith decided to take Forrest under his wing, and after chiding him for trifling away his time he made him write directly to New Orleans for an engagement. This time Forrest was signed up, but he lost his nerve and ran away to the circus, and there he might have stayed if Sol had not found him out and paid a visit to the big top. "There was Ned in all his glory, surrounded by riders, tumblers, and grooms," Smith later recalled. "He was a little abashed at seeing me, but putting a good face on the matter, he said he had made up his mind not to go to New Orleans. . . . To convince me of his ability to sustain his new line of business, he turned a couple of flip-flops on the spot."[12] It took a good deal of hard lecturing before Smith persuaded him to change course, but finally Forrest tiptoed onto a steamboat and went south.

NOTHING HAD PREPARED the young actor for the Crescent City. Standing on the levee that kept out the great sweep of the Mississippi, he looked on as sailing packets, steamboats, rafts, and arks wedged themselves in as far as the eye could see. Planters, deckhands, and stevedores swarmed the streets, staking cotton fortunes at faro tables or meager salaries at dockside gambling dens, or falling for the soft voices, loose limbs, and fiery eyes in the plush bordellos. Society was still dominated by the proud French and Spanish families who had first settled Louisiana, and at first sight the city looked like a little slice of Europe in the swamps. On closer acquaintance with its unsleeping dock life, its impassioned Creole and southern spirit, its balls lit up by the beauty of the famous quadroons and ringed by their mothers scrutinizing every change of partner from their divans along the walls, it seemed like nowhere else on earth. It was intoxicating, and part of its mystique was the danger that lurked just under its serenity. Without warning, violence would rear up and throw a shadow over the delicate glitter—and just as quickly, the shadow would slide away. The English actor George Vandenhoff was equally captivated by the city's chiaroscuro charms. In the immense barrooms, he marveled, where thousands gathered at a time, "high words would be heard at one end; a scuffle, perhaps; a general clearing took place for a moment, a pistol-shot or two were fired, a body was carried out, the lookers-on closed up again, and the matter was forgotten." At the balls, the orderly movement of a quadrille or a waltz might be broken by a quick and fatal stab

> that left some much-coveted damsel unpartnered for a moment; but the music scarcely stops, the waters join, the half-uttered compliment is taken up again, the half-told anecdote is concluded, the interrupted laughter rings livelier, louder than before . . . eyes sparkle, feet twinkle, white shoulders shine beneath a thousand lamps, swelling bosoms heave, and pant, and sigh, as triumph, love, or envy moves them; and gay cavaliers flit about, pouring volleys of quick-winged compliments, or shooting feathered darts of passionate admiration, till the ears of the fair tingle again; and one is bewildered by the many-tongued accents, that make the ball-room a Babel of confused delight.[13]

Forrest was seventeen when he made his debut, on February 4, 1824, at the American Theatre, so named to distinguish it from the French. His attractions were soon the talk of the parlors. Here was a new celebrity to amuse even jaded New Orleans—a fresh-faced, muscular young man with eager eyes and a charmingly naïve manner, and yet with a jolt of half-felt distinction throbbing in his veins. Women smiled and sent him notes and flowers, and he steadily slept his way through the town. Yet Forrest soon became aware that he was too refractory to be good at social niceties; and, too proud to be a novelty, he turned his back on the brilliant drawing rooms, the elaborate conventions, and the strangely brittle languor of southern society and sought out the other New Orleans, the defluxion of wild pioneers from across the west whom the mighty Mississippi funneled to the city. Forrest headed down to the lawless docks and befriended a gentleman gambler and duelist, a retired colonel with a weakness for the horses, a steamboat captain who was famous for having once pulled an entire brothel into the river when one of his deckhands complained of his reception, and a soft-spoken adventurer called James Bowie who invented the knife which bears his name and wielded it with unrivaled skill in countless fights to the death. He hung around at cockpits and casinos, bare-knuckle fights and bars, and the racecourses where everyone from the governor to the lowliest boatman went armed, and Bowie presented him with his favorite blade—a long, ugly thing whose secret was in the handle, braided with steel so that it wouldn't slip through a fist slicked with blood.

In turn, his friends crowded his performances, and suddenly Forrest found himself thriving in the element that Sol Smith had urged him to make his own. His new audience loved nothing more than hearing him let out a hair-raising yell or watching him hotdog across the stage, and he started playing up to the crowds. Soon the theatre was packed every night, right to the top of the gallery where, particularly when he was playing Shakespeare, free blacks filled every seat in their railed-off area—railed off from the quadroons, who refused to mix with those of pure African blood.* This was something new: an American actor, independent, self-reliant, proud of his natural prowess, frank, manly, passionate, untutored, a little rough; here, for the first time, was an actor who was one of them.

It was here that Forrest became the first homegrown American star, and it was here, too, that his amour propre grew apace. So much unaccustomed celebrity was enough to swell a head much older than Ned's, and on top of the tendency he had shown since childhood to burst out with a fierce, implacable rage against anyone he thought had wronged him, he had now adopted the ferocious honor code of his new friends and sworn that he would never be bested. One day he stormed out of the theatre rather than accept a minor part from the English manager Caldwell, who was growing envious of his young recruit, and when they both fell in love with the same actress, a twenty-year-old beauty from Charleston named Jane Placide, Forrest challenged his manager to a duel. Caldwell refused to accept, and an outraged Ned had a Card, a formal statement,

---

* "The playgoing portion of our negro population feel more interest in, and go in greater numbers to see, the plays of Shakespeare represented on the stage, than any other class of dramatic performance," the New Orleans *Picayune* reported on March 14, 1844. African Americans' enthusiasm for Shakespeare was not restricted to the south: in New York the African Grove Theatre, where whites were relegated to a roped-off section at the back, showcased black actors playing the Bard, though its star, Ira Aldridge, fled the United States for European fame after the theatre was repeatedly attacked by white mobs.

printed up and pinned prominently around town. "Whereas James H. Caldwell has wronged and insulted me, and refused me the satisfaction of a gentleman, I hereby denounce him as a scoundrel and post him as a coward," it blustered.[14]

That was the end of New Orleans for Forrest, and almost the end of his career. Among his dockside associates he had become closest of all to Push-ma-ta-ha, a chief of the Choctaw tribe and a powerful orator who claimed he was the result of an immaculate conception. On the same day he issued his Card, Forrest ran away to live with the tribe. They smoked, danced, and sang together, and hunted on their shrinking lands, and Ned felt more strongly rooted than ever in the soil of the west. That sentimental attachment never left him. At his lowest point, in the summer of 1823, when he had been living in a dilapidated cottage in Newport, Kentucky, wearing his landlady's clothes because his own were too grubby and gathering corn from the fields to take home and cook, he had settled under a spreading oak tree, pulled out his well-thumbed volume of Shakespeare, and read a speech from the second part of *Henry IV*:

> Oh God! that one might read the book of Fate,
> And see the revolution of the times
> Make mountains level, and the continent,
> Weary of solid firmness, melt itself
> Into the sea! and, other times, to see
> The beachy girdle of the ocean
> Too wide for Neptune's hips; how chances mock,
> And changes fill the cup of alteration
> With divers liquors! O, if this were seen,
> The happiest youth—viewing his progress through,
> What perils past, what crosses to ensue—
> Would shut the book, and sit him down and die.[15]

As his head sank on his chest and he mused on Shakespeare's melancholy lines, the penniless young man felt how immense his task was to him, and yet how insignificant it could seem if he lost his self-belief. Perhaps, he desperately thought, he should shut the book on his dreams and his life. Yet poetry, or at least simile, had entered his soul, because when he looked up he saw a sturdy vine that had been torn off the tree and rerooted itself along the ground. When even a poor plant could adapt to its forsaken world, he thought, surely it would be shameful for a fine specimen like himself to succumb. Twenty years later he bought the whole wood: he renamed it Forrest Hill and owned it till his death.

After his sojourn among the Choctaw, Forrest recovered his pride and sailed home to Philadelphia. He was now twenty, and he firmly expected fame to be waiting on his next move. But the grandstanding that had thrilled his New Orleans friends was still too broad for the east, and again he felt suddenly, sickeningly, out of his depth. A fellow actor recalled that the young man could scarcely muster the courage to enter the greenroom at one theatre where several leading lights were gathered.[16] For months he patched together engagements playing supporting roles, until one took him to Albany, where Edmund Kean, the greatest superstar of all, had arrived during an American tour.

Kean was in a different class from any actor Forrest had seen, and though he was English, his roots were even humbler than the American's. To the eager young aspirant, their meeting was a revelation.

EDMUND KEAN WAS Romanticism in motion. He was the illegitimate son of a failed actress who hawked cheap goods, and sometimes herself, along the mean streets of east London; his likely father threw himself off a roof when Kean was three, and the young boy was brought up by his uncle's mistress, a bit player named Charlotte Tidswell. Charlotte had great ambitions for her clever, high-spirited charge: she put him on stage as an opera Cupid at three, a pantomime imp at four, and the last goblin in the row in *Macbeth* at five, and set him to memorizing Shakespeare as soon as he could read. Much of Edmund's early life, though, was spent on the street. He disappeared for days on end and roamed around inns and fairground booths, where he tumbled, clowned, danced the hornpipe, and reeled off speeches in a precocious takeoff of the stars. The frantic Charlotte locked him up in the attic, but somehow he always escaped; in desperation she clamped a brass collar around his neck and stamped it with her address and instructions to return him home. At fifteen he left for good and trudged between provincial stages for ten hard years, ten years during which he became an alcoholic, drinking to overcome his natural shyness and frustrated ambition, raving vaingloriously in taverns, and getting into countless brawls. In 1808 he married an actress nine years his senior: too poor to take the coach, they walked from town to town with their two children on their backs, selling their clothes and finally their dog, playing at any country theatre that would pay their way. Eventually Kean was spotted and signed to Drury Lane, one of the two great London theatres, which was on the verge of bankruptcy and desperate for a new attraction. Less than a month after his elder son had died for lack of medical attention, he turned up at the stage door, a little man with dark curly hair, eagle eyes, and a voice as rough as a hackney coachman's, his costume in a paper parcel under his arm, a grubby white greatcoat hiding his thread-bare clothes, and was received with barely suppressed sneers. His debut was repeatedly delayed; when he was finally announced as Shylock the rehearsals were insultingly slovenly, and more than one of his fellow actors disdained to turn up at all.

And yet his debut was the most unexpected triumph in the history of the theatre. As soon as Kean stepped on stage, spitting hate and wielding a butcher's knife, shockingly different from the grotesque, shambling Jew of stage tradition, the age of the stately John Kemble, the reigning king of the English theatre, was over. Kemble's style, a series of brilliant effects that never ruffled his clothes or his composure, was as formal and picturesque as eighteenth-century landscape painting. But Kean was living in the age of Constable and Turner, of proto-impressionism, of stormy seas and restlessly scudding skies, and Kemble was suddenly open to the charge that Constable leveled at the previous generation of artists, of running after pictures and seeking the truth secondhand. The nature of perception and the perception of nature had shifted: Wordsworth and Coleridge had buried Augustan wit under Romantic earth, and, said Coleridge, to watch Kean was like reading Shakespeare by flashes of lightning. Alienation and violent passion were his forte: his performances were thrillingly mercurial, skidding from white-hot anger to plaintive remorse, "scarcely giving you time to think but ravishing your wonder, and carrying you along with his impetuous rush and change of expression," one actor said.[17] They were the products of his own turbulent nature, and his nature was of his time. Kean threw away the tragic stilts, reached into his wild, affectionate heart, and found Shakespeare's great characters already there, waiting to be stormed.

Physically and temperamentally, Forrest could not have been more unlike Kean: he had a robustness and an ingenuousness that marked him out for heroic roles. But Kean showed Forrest that a great Shakespearean actor did not have to be steeped in the timeworn traditions associated with the English stage: instead he could follow the dictates of his own nature. Perhaps, Forrest thought, the Bard of Avon could be transformed into something distinctively American: a new Shakespeare, played with a skill that matched the best England could offer, but with all the fire and energy of the west.

Forrest set to work and reemerged in triumph, and within months he was engaged to open the brand-new Bowery Theatre in New York City, a three-thousand-seat marvel resplendent with Doric columns, crimson curtains, and boxes painted the color of apple blossom, which was being built on the site of an old tavern and a clutch of abattoirs.

Perhaps the anticipation was too much. Forrest arrived in New York, a stranger without friends, while the Bowery was still heavily under construction, and again depression stole over him. He bought a bottle of arsenic at a pharmacy, pretending he needed it to kill rats, and almost drank it. But fate, or a friend, stepped in one more time. An actor approached him as he was sitting, brooding, under the awning outside his hotel; banking on the novelty value of the storied young man, he asked Forrest to play Othello for his benefit night at the grand old Park Theatre. Forrest closeted himself in his room and pored over the play. Novelty or not, the audience for the benefit night was thin, and in a box Charles Gilfert, the manager of the Bowery, sat fiddling severely with his snuffbox, wondering whether his gamble would pay off. He soon knew the answer. A stir went through the Park Theatre when the newcomer with the magnificent physique walked calmly onto the stage. His sweet, deep voice sent backs shooting up straight, his steady possession of his character wove its spell, and finally, when

Othello's pent-up anguish burst out in a thunderous peal of passion, the whole audience rose to its feet and cheered. Gilfert's snuffbox fell through his fingers.

"By heaven, he has made a hit!" he cried out loud.[18]

Soon Forrest reprised his Othello at the Bowery; this time, with expectations soaring, he was painfully stage shy, but he rallied in time and, by the end of the play, New York was convinced that a great new talent was in its midst. Like a giant, the astonished critics wrote, the young Hercules had bounded to the front of his profession in a single leap: an American by birth, education, and feeling, he had formed a distinctively new school of acting from the study of nature and the dictates of his own exuberant energy. "The history of the stage," one writer boldly stated, "affords no parallel to such a precocity of histrionic talent, and it is a proud distinction for an American actor, in the first year of manhood, to be deemed worthy, by enlightened audiences, to succeed the greatest tragedian of the age."[19] The tragedian the writer was referring to was Edmund Kean.

From that night Forrest was billed as "The Native Tragedian," and professionally he never looked back. Yet success never drove away his susceptibility to black bouts of depression, and he wrote to his unfortunate mother to tell her—to tell someone—that he was deadeningly tired of life. "The terrible reflection haunts me in spite of myself," he bleakly scrawled, "and were it not for you and the girls I should not shrink to try the unsearchable depths of eternity."[20] His childhood weakness also came back to taunt him, and soon after his New York triumph he began to suffer from excruciating attacks. One day after dinner, he collapsed on the floor, complaining of pains shooting through his heart; a copious bleeding seemed to bring some relief, but over the next days the stabbing spread to his legs and head, and he struggled to get through his performances with a liberal lacing of brandy and ether.

Forrest weathered the bouts of pain, and when he was reengaged he set his price, not at the eight hundred dollars a year at which he had been hired, but at the unprecedented sum, for an American actor, of two hundred dollars a night, at least four thousand dollars in today's money.[21] He was just twenty-one; within two years he had earned enough to pay off his father's debts and to buy a house for his mother and sisters and settle a generous endowment on them. Few among his thousands of new fans failed to realize what they had witnessed: nothing less than a defining moment in the birth of American culture.

Among the audience one night during that first season was an Englishman thirteen years older than Forrest. He sat erect and observant in a box and surveyed the scene with envy, for he had been struggling for years against what seemed like the terminal decline of the English stage.

———— ⊗ ————

CHAPTER 3

Rogues and Vagabonds

O N SEPTEMBER 18, 1809, seventeen years before Edwin Forrest's triumph in New York, the grand opening of London's theatrical season collapsed into a spectacular brawl. The weeks of mayhem
that followed turned on the same question as the Astor Place riot: Just
who controlled the national stage?

Throughout the day, a huge crowd had been gathering outside the
new Theatre Royal, Covent Garden. The old theatre had burnt down a
year before, as theatres regularly did in an age of candlelight and erratic pyrotechnic effects, with the loss of more than twenty lives.
While the new building was still swaddled in scaffolding, London's
other great playhouse, the Theatre Royal in Drury Lane, had also gone
up in flames. Since the old acting patents, which dated back to the
Restoration, restricted the so-called legitimate drama—proper, full-
length, nonmusical plays—to the two royal theatres, that left Covent
Garden the sole place to watch a play in a city of more than a million
people.[1] A few days earlier, the covers had come off, exposing a vast
stone façade, two hundred and twenty feet long, towering above the
huddled houses and market stalls of the district from which the theatre
took its name. Turning into Bow Street, the rubberneckers were put
firmly in their place by a Doric portico, modeled after the Parthenon,
and boasting the biggest columns in Europe. On one side Shakespeare's egg-smooth head nodded its blessing from a niche; on the
other, Milton performed the same tutelary role. It was every inch a

temple dedicated to the dramatic arts—and yet, as the liveried attendants drew the bolts and the crowd shouldered the doors back on their hinges, reverence was the last thing in the air.

Inside the grand entrance hall, with its stone staircases and red porphyry pillars gleaming against white-veined marble walls, the ticket sellers dished out admissions like dealers in a bubble company at the new Stock Exchange. Within minutes the pit and gallery were full; three quarters of the crowd, perhaps six thousand people, were shut outside, where they were cut into wedges by boxholders barreling along in their carriages. At seven o'clock the national anthem struck up and John Philip Kemble strode in front of the curtain, dressed as Macbeth.

Given the curse that had long ago attached itself to Shakespeare's story of ambition prompted by darkness to ruin, it was an intrepid choice at the least. *Macbeth* was known as the Scottish play, because even to speak its name was enough to invoke the black magic of the weird sisters and compel all sorts of long-winded recantations. Leaving the theatre, swearing, and spinning around three times was the favored purgative; variations included spitting over your shoulder, petitioning Shakespeare while quoting Hamlet, or just cursing like crazy. As superstitions went, this one had an impressive track record. The first Lady Macbeth, the leading boy actor of Shakespeare's company in 1606, supposedly died on the opening night, leaving Shakespeare to don drag and finish the part. James I, whom the play was designed to flatter, hated it and banned it for several years. In Amsterdam, one Macbeth switched a stage dagger for a real one and killed not just King Duncan but the actor playing him. Troops were called in one night in 1721 when the actors started attacking the audience with their swords. Just the year before, Covent Garden had opened its season with the black-natured thing, and seven nights later the theatre went up in smoke. Macbeth himself, though—the brave general steeled to regicide despite his better self, the antihero who discovers that might without right breeds self-doubt, and self-doubt breeds brute force—was too magnificent a gift for any leading actor to pass up. Kemble, like Macready, chose *Macbeth* to mark the great nights of his career, and Kemble, like Macready, would pay the price.

He had barely opened his mouth when the uproar started. "Off!

Off!" the audience chanted. Hisses, hoots, and curses drowned out the play, one man in a box howled like a hound on a scent, and the tumult carried on long after the curtain had fallen. Two magistrates were summoned to read the Riot Act; the Bow Street Runners, the constables whose headquarters were down the road, carted away a few token troublemakers and inflamed things more. "No police in a theatre!" the pit and gallery bellowed, and they kept on shouting until two o'clock in the morning, when they burst out in a valedictory chorus of "God Save the King" and "Rule, Britannia," and went home.[2]

Kemble had committed three cardinal sins in the eyes of his patrons—or his masters, as they preferred to term themselves. He had been saddled with huge debts from the reconstruction and had raised the price of admission to help cover his costs. At the same time he had turned the third tier into a row of private boxes, which, he hoped, would be rented by leading families for the season—though the real business of the boxes, with their separate staircase, lockable antechambers, commodious couches, and watchful keepers, was an open secret—while the topmost level of the relatively roomy old gallery had been replaced by a squash of seats that were so hemmed in by the roof arches that the protestors complained they were no better than pigeonholes, a point they made vividly by releasing real pigeons from the rafters. Kemble's third mistake was to engage Angelica Catalani, the leading prima donna of the age, at a vast weekly salary. Mme. Catalani was married to a French officer and Napoleonic France was at the height of its power; earlier that year, a ravaged Austria had been forced to join the continental trade embargo against Britain. On the second night a new chant went up: "God Save the King—no Foreigners—no Catalani—no Kemble!" As the rioters dug in their heels Catalani's name was abbreviated to Madame Cat and mutated into Nasty Pussy, while Kemble was denounced as a papist. Catalani was paid off and took her peerless voice to Ireland; the whole unpleasant episode was a foretaste of how easily xenophobia and theatrical disputes could become entwined.

In contrast to the Astor Place disaster, the defining feature of the Old Price riots, as they quickly became known, was longevity, not bloodshed. After three or four weeks, the first acts of the main play were just about audible to the few supporters who bothered to turn up, but at half-price—the point in the four- or five-hour-long program when newcomers were admitted to watch the end of the first play and the late show of skits, songs, melodramas, and farces—the town piled in bedecked with hats and medals, fans and handkerchiefs, waistcoats and caps, bearing printed placards and painted banners, all of which prominently displayed the letters "O.P.," and set up a racket with bugles, whistles and bells, frying pans, gridirons and tongs, fifes and rattles, and anything else that made a noise. The protestors' next innovation was to improvise a dance: the routine was to scream "O.P." as loudly as possible, make a quarter turn, and beat time by stamping or banging a stick against the seats, all with an air of infuriating mock gravity. When that grew stale, races were held along the benches; a few days later the benches were pushed aside and gymnastic displays, sword fights, and wrestling matches kept everyone's eyes off the stage.

The performers persevered, as Macready would later, but barely a word was heard. The newspapers took sides; the conservative press murmured about barricades and revolutions. Outside the theatre, O.P. graffiti appeared on walls, and children and newsboys cried out the slogan in the streets. Each night several rioters were arrested and a small troop of soldiers assembled, though at a safe distance and more for show than action. The authorities were genuinely perplexed about what they should do. Since theatres were both privately owned business premises and publicly licensed gathering places, they operated in a strange legal no-man's-land, and the relationship between actors and spectators had always been regulated by custom. Everyone agreed that the audience had an inalienable right to hoot an objectionable play or performer off the stage: the idea that dissatisfied ticket holders should slip out or suffer in silence until the end was ridiculous. Besides, the theatres provided a useful safety valve for public feeling, which was well worth a few bruised thespian egos. There were presumably some limits beyond which crowd action could not be tolerated, but no one quite knew what they were, and the only obvious recourse, to declare the theatre closed, would amount to an unfair restraint of trade and a capitulation to the mob.

The standoff continued. In case of a surprise attack on their home, Kemble's wife took to keeping ladders by her windows—one night a deputation shattered them with stones—and Kemble himself, with un-

In this print by George Cruikshank, fighters hired by John Kemble, led by the Jewish champion boxer Daniel Mendoza, wreak havoc in the pit of the Theatre Royal, Drury Lane, during the Old Price Riots of 1809.

erringly bad judgment, planted dozens of prizewinning pugilists among the audience and instructed them to clobber the troublemakers. Defiant sham fights were staged nightly in the auditorium; fruit, hats, shoes, coins, sticks, and the occasional chunk of bench landed on the stage, and self-appointed orators urged resolve on the crowd. The sixtieth night was marked with an O.P. ball—thrown, to show who was in charge, in the theatre itself—during which several people were knocked out for real.

That was as far as the violence went. Like the Astor Place rioters, the O.P. protestors saw themselves as patriots, determined to preserve the tradition of access for all to the theatres, the great meeting places of the town, against fancy continental notions of elite culture. But, unlike their successors, they had no real personal malice or antiestablishment bias, no enemy who was threatening their national culture, and certainly no appetite for revolution. Crucially, they were also united across class divisions: lawyers and merchants, carpenters and shoemakers, clerks and warehousemen all joined in the fun. A few days after the ball, Kemble finally apologized and capitulated to his critics on virtually every count; a few weeks later, in a spirit of triumphalism masquerading as reconciliation, the ringleaders invited him to a banquet which, putting the best face on abject deference, he attended.

The riots had lasted for sixty-seven nights. On the second night a sixteen-year-old boy had taken his seat to watch his first London play. For several weeks he looked on as Britain's leading actors plied their trade to empty rows, with only the banging of a few box doors and the bawls of drunken ushers for company, and then heard them shouted into silence. Actors, he saw, were public servants, and disaster was always a catcall, a hiss, or a rotten apple away. It was a cruel trick of history that William Charles Macready's introduction to the national stage in one country, and his farewell to it in another, were ruined by the two most famous theatre riots in the English-speaking world.

MACREADY WAS NEVER meant to be an actor, though his mother and father both were. William McCready, a jaunty but irascible upholsterer's son from Dublin, had run away to England, where he married a young actress of modest talents but respectable connections and served ten years on stage at Covent Garden as a Walking Gentleman, a line of work that required a lot of standing in the background and little else.* Pride finally galvanized him into action, and he quit London for the shabbier but infinitely more self-important life of a regional theatre manager. A little retinue of flesh and spirits followed in his wake: three children had died in infancy, but three had survived—two girls, and William Charles, who was born in 1793.

At first the new enterprise thrived. Admiral Nelson, taking a break from the Napoleonic Wars during the short-lived peace of Amiens, commanded a performance in Birmingham and arrived in state with his mistress, Emma Hamilton, on his arm. John Kemble and his sister, the incomparable Sarah Siddons, journeyed from London to lend their empyrean presence, for a hefty fee. By 1803 the manager was secure enough to enroll his son at a reputable public school, and from there, it was planned, he would progress to Oxford, the bar, and the respectable middle class.

---

* His son changed the spelling of the family name to the grander Macready when he made his London debut; at the same time he started using both his given names to distinguish himself further from his father.

McCready was far from the first actor to wish his son well clear of the stage. The old taboo against performers was not just upheld by common prejudice: it was enshrined in centuries of law. The statutory ostracism dated back to the 1572 Act for the Punishment of Vagabonds, which sent Shakespeare and his contemporaries scurrying for the cover of royal patronage. It became briefly redundant during the Commonwealth, but only because the Roundheads, one of whom called actors "the very dregs of men; the shame, the blemish of our English Nation . . . the very instruments of sinne and Satan," not to mention unholy dogs, filthy swine, and uncircumcised Philistines of "more than Sodomiticall uncleannesse," ordered the theatres pulled down and all actors apprehended and publicly whipped.³ It was brushed up under Queen Anne, and it was hammered into irrefutability by George II and his prime minister Robert Walpole, who for years were sent reeling by a barrage of slanders lobbed at them from the London stage in the guise of plays, many the products of Henry Fielding's joyously scabrous mind, though not the most notorious of all, a raucously mocking and provokingly anonymous piece of sedition called *A Vision of the Golden Rump,* which suggested that the royal bowels were struck from solid gold and could be evacuated only with the aid of an enema administered by the queen.

The most famous provision of Walpole's 1737 act was to fix in law the lord chamberlain's powers of censorship—powers that were not finally abolished until 1968. Like most attempts at censorship, this one had an effect both calamitous and electrifying. On the one hand most of the minor theatres, the homes of the outlawed radical writers, promptly shut down, and the drama went into a century-and-a-half-long tailspin out of which it was only briefly lifted by the fresh gloss given to classical comedy by the Irish wit of Sheridan and Goldsmith. On the other hand, Fielding turned to writing fiction, thereby more or less giving birth to the modern English novel. Writers, however, were harder to shoot than their mouthpieces, and so the act's framers indulged in a piece of shameless scapegoating. Doubts had crept in over the years, they noted, about whether actors might have become a shade more socially acceptable than before. Not any longer. "Be it declared and enacted by the King's most excellent Majesty," the law thundered, by and with the advice and consent of the Lords Spiritual and Temporal, and Commons, in this present Parliament assembled, and by the authority of the same, that from and after the twenty-fourth day of June, one thousand, seven hundred and thirty seven, every person who shall, for hire, gain or reward, act, represent or perform, or cause to be acted, represented or performed any interlude, tragedy, comedy, opera, play, farce or other entertainment of the stage, or any part or parts therein, in case such person shall not have any legal settlement in the place where the same shall be acted, represented or performed without authority by virtue of letters patent from His Majesty, his heirs, successors or predecessors, or without licence from the Lord Chamberlain of His Majesty's household for the time being, shall be deemed to be a rogue and a vagabond within the intent and meaning of the said recited Act, and shall be liable and subject to all such penalties and punishments, and by such methods of conviction as are inflicted on or appointed by the said Act for the punishment of rogues and vagabonds who shall be found wandering, begging and misordering themselves, within the intent and meaning of the said recited Act.

The establishment was not about to be terrorized by a few jumped-up players, those all too visible Lords of Misrule—or, worse, exposers and ridiculers of misrule—and it was determined to put them back in their box.

Four years after the act was passed David Garrick strode onto the stage and tore up the rulebook. Garrick, the first actor to be called a star, was also the first to be admired not just as a figure of fashion but as a gentleman-scholar, and his secret weapon was Shakespeare. For several decades after the Restoration, when the courtly fashion was for everything French, Shakespeare's punning rustics and running metaphors had gone out of style, but by the 1730s tastes had started to swing back.*

---

* "It is a play of itself the worst that ever I heard," Samuel Pepys wrote of *Romeo and Juliet* in 1662, adding a few months later that *A Midsummer Night's Dream* was "the most insipid ridiculous play that I ever saw in my life," and the next year that *Twelfth Night* was "a silly play" (*Diary*, March 1, September 29, 1662; January 6, 1663). Ben Jonson enjoyed greater critical prestige than Shakespeare; Beaumont and Fletcher's refined romances were more popular on the stage.

Sturdy Elizabethan adventurers, not simpering Restoration roués, looked like real Englishmen again, and Shakespeare was enshrined as the natural genius of a heroic age. Pressure groups like the Shakespeare Ladies' Club campaigned to erect a monument to the national poet in Westminster Abbey and encourage more performances of his plays, but it was Garrick who was the real prophet of Bardolatry: Boswell called him the colorist of Shakespeare's soul and declared he had reacquainted the nation with the inestimable riches of its own stage, "in possessing so illustrious a dramatic author with such amazing variety and wonderful excellence as Shakespeare."[4]

In 1769, in a belated celebration of the bicentenary of Shakespeare's birth, Garrick threw a Jubilee extravaganza in Stratford-upon-Avon—three days of parades, concerts, dinners, masked balls, races, and fireworks, which climaxed with the actor's own ode, delivered in a purpose-built rotunda to the accompaniment of an orchestra and choir. In true British fashion, the festivities were washed out by torrential rain, but by then Bardolatry was already established as nothing short of a national religion.[5] Middle England had discovered its image in the plays: empirical, pragmatic, resolute, ironic, gruffly eloquent, quietly sentimental, a touch melancholic. They might be set in Venice or Rome, their truths might be universal, but somehow, it seemed, you had to be English to understand them. The point was loudly made in Garrick's *Jubilee,* the stage version of his washed-out extravaganza, in which Frenchmen, Italians, and even Irishmen were excluded from the festivities because they were incapable of appreciating them, and it was heard with increasing frequency as nationalism mounted through the Revolutionary and Napoleonic Wars.* After Garrick the prestige of the English theatre was firmly tied to the nation's newly discovered pride in its greatest writer, and for a few golden decades the playhouses were at the center of the nation's life. England's leading men and leading ladies were no longer just actors:

---

* Conversely, Voltaire retracted his former admiration for Shakespeare and called his plays a pile of dung, and as late as 1822 an English production of *Othello* was forced off the Parisian stage with shouts of "À bas Shakespeare! C'est un lieutenant de Wellington!" (Jonathan Bate, *The Genius of Shakespeare* [London, 1997], 230).

they were Shakespearean actors, celebrants of the faith, and the stately Kemble and the spellbinding Siddons, who turned down immoral parts and censored lines she considered beneath her dignity, picked up the torch of respectability and carried it into the nineteenth century.

Garrick, Kemble, and Siddons, though, were the exceptions to the rule, the select few who kept their heads above the tide of decorum; beneath them, there shelved away layers of deepening murk. Drunkenness was one recurrent problem, even among the higher ranks. George Frederick Cooke, a startlingly talented actor who drank himself onto the stage and drank his way off again, was renowned for his ability to stagger from the pub to the theatre and put on an impressive show, though sometimes he tottered around in a stupor and insulted the audience, frequently he failed to show up at all, and more than once he disappeared for several months—on one occasion, or so he later claimed, having enlisted as an ensign during the American Revolution. Then there was the whiff of vice that still hung around the stage door. A century and a half after pretty, witty Nell Gwyn, the fabled orange-seller and likely child prostitute, had made the leap from the stage to the royal four-poster, the standing of actresses had gradually improved: a growing number earned themselves a healthy independence, while others became the wives of titled bigwigs instead of making do with being their mistresses or, worse, the victims of their abductions and rapes. Yet, to many minds, an actress and a whore were still one and the same thing: both rouged up and exhibited themselves for money.

Down in the depths of the profession, the reflected glory of the new stars shone dimly at best. At the main London playhouses, separate greenrooms were provided for the higher and inferior orders, one tricked out in damask and crystal for the ten-pound-a-weekers, the other, a bare-boards closet, for the lower-paid actors, dancers, and pantomimists and the rest of the "little people," who really were called the little people. Only a handful who started in one group progressed to the other; perhaps only one in a hundred actors made it through the hallowed doors of the great London theatres at all. At the provincial theatres a guinea a week and a handful of candle ends was a decent wage for a supporting actor, out of which he had to find the means of purchasing and maintaining an extensive wardrobe.* Away from the playhouses, the road led to inn yards, where a few tallow candles were stuck on hoops for lighting and a platform was knocked together in the street on which the talent paraded in costume, illuminated by pans of noxious smoking grease, to tempt passersby inside. At the very bottom of the profession, in the penny gaffs and fairground booths, many subsisted on a starvation wage, sidestepped the law, shifted to avoid the workhouse, and, with alarming regularity, ended up among the suicide statistics. All in all, it was hardly surprising that few parents contemplated the notion of their children going on the stage with anything less than sheer terror.

ENGLISH PUBLIC SCHOOLS in the early nineteenth century were not the preserve of the aristocracy, who were privately educated at home. They were middle-class institutions run on tough love, and Rugby, where William McCready sent his son, was no exception. A few years earlier a battalion of boys had blown off the headmaster's door with gunpowder and made a bonfire of the furniture and books in the schoolroom, then retreated to a moated island on the grounds and pulled up the drawbridge; the standoff only ended when the Riot Act was read and soldiers waded through the water with drawn swords. Macabre legends cobwebbed the place, and they tended to be true. Months before Macready arrived, one boy was tortured and left with second-degree burns; another was expelled, despite having just lost his father, for refusing to name the older boy who had sent him to steal some twigs so he could be thrashed. A lowly impresario's son was prime meat, and the ten-year-old boy shook with fear as the coach rolled him to the doors.

To his relief, after the first wretched year of bullying and fagging and tearful letters home, he found his feet among the gentlemen's sons. Public school was not so different from the theatre—regimentation before the scenes, anarchy behind—and, far from being ribbed for the

---

* Feathers, hats, ruffs, collars, boots, shoes, swords, belts, sashes, pantaloons, fleshings, sandals, wigs, stockings, buckles, and breeches were the basic minimum for men, while women needed endless styles and colors of dresses, robes, draperies, points, trimmings, hats, shoes, and accessories.

gypsy glamour dancing on his father's profession, he found that his ability to procure costumes for the older boys' plays proved a handy insurance policy.* He was rewarded with girls' parts, then with manly leads, and he was discovered to have a startling way with words, which earned him pride of place on Speech Day. As he rose slowly from his seat, a deep hush fell upon the assembly; he was aware of every creak of his shoes as he walked to the center of the room. For the first time, he thrilled to the power of caressing an audience in the crease of his voice, and fifty years later he still recalled the feeling of conscious pride.[6]

The boy had a rare and wonderful talent, his housemaster wrote to McCready: "Such a combination of fine figure, expression, countenance, elegance and propriety of action, modulation of voice, and most complete power of representation I have formed an idea of, perhaps, but have never before met with," he marveled—though, he added, he was aware that this news might not be altogether welcome.[7] He need not have worried: the idea of treading the boards had never crossed young William's mind. One day, while he was kicking a ball around in the schoolyard, the headmaster called him over and asked what profession his father had chosen for him. He was intended for the law, he replied.

"Have you not thought of your father's profession?" the old man asked.

"No, sir."

"Should you not like it?"

"No, sir, I should wish to go to the bar."

"Are you quite certain you should not wish to go on the stage?"

"Quite certain, sir; I very much dislike it, and the thought of it."[8]

He always did. He was born into the acting profession and roundly educated out of it. He was a gentleman-scholar by training and inclination; dressing up in costumes was fine for school plays, but it was hardly a dignified calling for a grown man, and the chaotic, unruly intimacy of the theatre seemed like a vision of pandemonium to his well-trained mind. Yet in 1808, with several terms still to go at school, Macready joined the family firm.

---

* In one letter, he sent home for a red petticoat, a blue bedgown, a point-lace apron, a frilly mobcap and pairs of mittens, yellow stockings, and high-heeled shoes.

His father was bankrupt. William's school bills had been piling up unpaid, and with the stubborn pride and stern self-discipline that would define his life—and perhaps with half a thought to the thrill of that Speech Day—the young man made up his mind. Christina, his beloved mother, had died five years earlier, at thirty-eight, following his elder sister to an untimely grave, and his father was alone with his failure. In helping him out for a while, William would curtail the expense of his education, and perhaps he could even improve the family fortunes. The elder McCready made a halfhearted attempt to demur; William shut his schoolbooks, set about memorizing the usual juvenile parts, and learned to fence. He was still only fifteen, and he had no idea of the plunge his social status had just taken. Within a few months he discovered that he could be challenged to a duel by a drunk soldier whom he had asked to leave the theatre, and then be refused satisfaction on the grounds that he was not a gentleman. In status-obsessed England, where snobbery was a creed, it was a vital distinction. The law, the church, the army, and the navy gave a man the rank of gentleman, and however outrageously he behaved he could still be received at court; an actor had to earn his standing by his conduct and bearing, and yet however distinguished he became, he was shut out from the sacred precincts for life.

McCready went into hiding to avoid arrest for debt, the family's furniture was sold, and when there were no dodges left William had the dismal task of accompanying his father to the sheriff's office, where the elder McCready surrendered himself and was marched to prison. When he saw his father taken captive, the proud young man burst into tears; the equally fiery McCready bit his lip and brusquely dismissed his son.

William found himself in charge of a company of unpaid and mutinous actors, and he set to work. After improving the takings at one theatre, he paid off the outstanding rent, closed it down, and pawned his pocket watch to buy passage for himself and three of the actors to join the other family troupe. A day into the journey, on a wet and windy Christmas morning, an innkeeper refused his last banknote, insinuating that it was forged, and despite the youthful manager's protestations that he was a respectable gentleman, the actors were forced to pawn their watches to pay for a fresh team of horses. For months he pressed on, putting what improvements he could into effect at each stop on the circuit, falling head over heels for a new actress, and rattling away in floods of tears.

Mr. William, as his employees now called him—there were perquisites to being a manager's son, not least when the manager was in prison—had no intention of staying in the family business for long, especially now that he witnessed its shortcomings first hand. Theatres still ran on the stock system, which entailed keeping several dozen plays permanently on the books and throwing together regular new attractions, usually in a mad panic, to satisfy the demand for variety; and while the breadth of the repertoire made the country circuits fertile proving grounds for talent, it also encouraged a production-line approach to acting. One actor claimed that the amount of study piled up on novices was a regular cause of brain fever, but even when that awful end was eluded the work was genuinely taxing.[9] "A country actor in a small company, and aspiring to a first-rate situation, will invariably have to study about *five hundred lines per diem*," warned Rede's *Guide to the Stage,* a popular contemporary handbook: "This will occupy the possessor of a good memory about six hours—his duties at the theatre embrace four more in the morning for rehearsal, and about five at night; here are fifteen hours devoted to labor alone, to say nothing of the time required to study the character, after the mere attainment of the words."[10] The character was generally not studied, and the hard-pressed actor fell back on the received methods of signaling emotions. Rede spelled them out. "The ten Dramatic Passions," he explained, "are *Love, Joy, Grief, Fear, Anger, Pity, Scorn, Hatred, Jealousy,* and *Wonder.*" Joy "is expressed by clapping of hands and exulting looks; the eyes are opened wide, and on some occasions raised to heaven; the countenance is smiling, not composedly, but with features aggravated; the voice rises, from time to time, to very high tones. . . . *Grief,* sudden and violent, expresses itself by beating the head or forehead, tearing the hair, and catching the breath, as if choking; also by screaming, weeping, stamping, lifting the eyes from time to time to heaven, and hurrying backwards and forwards." In fact, trying to be too clever was positively dangerous: "A straining after originality has been the ruin of many actors," Rede warned, and in any case, he reasoned, there were really only half a dozen disputed readings, mostly of odd lines from Shakespeare.

All in all, a good leg for dancing and an elegant thrust with a sword were prized attributes, while an education was strictly optional. "I could mention two individuals, now walking the first green-rooms of our national theatres, who actually could not read until they had been sometime on the stage," Rede added, no doubt reassuring anyone who had got that far that he or she already had a head start.[11]

Macready had higher aspirations, and his enterprise prospered. After a few months the elder McCready won his release, and his son could no longer put off the night of his own great test. His debut was fixed in the part of Romeo: a tragedy, of course, not only because it suited the serious young man but because the Tragedian, the interpreter of Shakespeare's greatest characters, towered over the other ranks of the theatre.*

In the usual way, to guard against failure, Macready was billed not by name but as "A young gentleman, his first appearance on any stage." He still nearly lost his nerve when he saw the playbills pasted up around town, but he studied day and night and finally he had every gesture and intonation off by heart. It was just as well. He stepped into the glare of the lights, a curly-haired, chubby-cheeked teenager dressed in tight white satin with purple slashes, a frilly ruff, a flowery sash, a pair of dancing pumps, and a giant plumed hat, and was struck with a hopeless case of stage fright. The theatre swam, everything was misty, and he listened to his lines as if they were being spoken far away from the strange little space in which he was trapped. Then he heard something new: applause, growing louder and louder, and he felt himself coming back into focus and growing into a bigger, better version of himself. When the curtain fell and his friends swarmed onto the stage, pumped his hand, and asked how he felt, he replied in a rush of relief that he would like to act it all over again.[12]

---

* In order to stop the stock system from collapsing into chaos, the profession relied on a sort of institutionalized typecasting, whereby everyone apart from the general factotums specialized in a particular line of work. In a large theatre, the Tragedian might be followed by specialists in Light Comedy and Eccentrics, Old Men, Low Comedy, Irish Characters, and Heavy Business, together with a Juvenile Lead, a Country Boy, and one or more Gentlemen Fops. Actresses were divided into equally strict categories, including Fine Ladies, Singing Chambermaids, and Old and Heavy Women. The Walking Ladies and Gentlemen and the General Utility players, the jills and jacks of all trades, were at the back of the parade; only the supernumeraries, the extras who were often hired from the local stage-door throng for the night, showed them any respect, and that was by no means a given.

The young actor became a popular attraction for the family company. In many ways it was the perfect training: after a few years he had played at least seventy-four parts alongside some of the greatest stars of the day, including his idol Mrs. Siddons, then on her retirement tour, who sent him so dizzy with terror that he was struck dumb on stage.[13]* But friction was growing between father and son. William was mortified by his father's fondness for crowd-pleasing animal acts, and he was convinced the older man's notions of acting were hopelessly out of date. McCready, like every manager, was a despot by trade: he was not about to be crossed by his own son, and he habitually slapped him down in public. "God's blood!" he would shout, "you fool, William!" There were only three ways to respond: cave in, argue back, or leave home. Deference was not in Macready's nature, but the family temper was, and when the arguments got out of control—William, his father screamed, was a talentless good-for-nothing who would never be able to support himself—he deserted to the theatre in Bath. The fashionable spa town, still the winter resort of London society, was a recognized stepping-stone to the capital, and cautiously—for his whole life was now riding on the outcome—Macready edged his way toward the great city.

ON SEPTEMBER 16, 1816, the young man who had never dreamed of being an actor grasped his costar by the hand and dashed onto the stage of the Theatre Royal, Covent Garden. The soaring scale of the auditorium hit him first: with space for nearly three thousand, it was twice as big as anywhere else he had performed. Four tiers of cream, pink, and gold boxes curved away, glinting like the bars of a great gilded cage; a hanging wall of faces stared back at him, their expectant expressions thrown into deep relief by the forty glass chandeliers that kept the auditorium ablaze. One face, conspicuous in a private box, belonged to the great Edmund Kean. An alarming sound came from the front row: a snigger, as if someone were making fun of the figure cut by the newcomer. He did look faintly ridiculous: his face was still fleshy,

* By the last scene he recovered enough that she raised her hands and clapped loudly from the wings. "Bravo, sir, bravo!" she called out, and on her last evening she sent for him. "You are in the right way," she said as he shakily entered her room, "but remember what I say, study, study, study, and do not marry until you are thirty" (*Reminiscences*, I. 53–57).

*Macready, aged twenty-
eight, as Macbeth in an
1821 painting by George
Clint.* V&A Images/
Theatre Museum.

his lips budlike and pursed, his nose large and shiny with sweat, his eyes sunken, though gleaming with intelligence and energy. The role chosen for his debut was Orestes, in a translation of Racine's *Andromaque,* and his corkscrew wig, fluttering hairband, and satiny knee-skimming toga hardly helped.

The moment of danger passed: the rest of the audience applauded warmly and settled into a watchful silence. Again came the dry mouth, the shallow breath, the throbbing heart and dazzled vision; again an outbreak of applause restored his self-possession, and by the end, as he sank into the arms of the actor whom he had held onto for courage seemingly hours before and heard the audience burst into prolonged cheers, he knew the crisis was over. He found his way back to his new lodgings and ran over the day's events—the jolts of the hackney coach as it rumbled to the theatre like a hurdle taking him to the gallows, the silent routine of dressing and the heart-chilling cry of the call-boy, the official rap at the dressing-room door and the long walk to the stage, then the clamor of congratulations that enveloped him on the much shorter walk back—and felt as if he were slowly awakening from a horrible dream. As if to prove it, he hardly slept at all that night, for there was one more ordeal to be undergone. Early in the morning he dressed and waited for the papers, and as he tore at the pages he must have wondered what to make of the reviews. Hazlitt, the greatest critic of the age, was greatest in his praise. "We have not the slightest hesitation in saying," he pronounced, "that Mr. Macready is by far the best tragic actor that has come out in our remembrance, with the exception of Mr. Kean."[14] Not everyone agreed: *The Times* sniffily allowed him only "a certain amount of ability" backed up by "a large quantity of vocal and brachial force."[15] But even the most positive reviews were shot through with glancing doubts. The problem was his appearance. "Mr. Macready is one of the plainest and most awkwardly-made men that ever trod the stage," the *News* baldly declared: for one thing, his nose was untragically retroussé.[16]

London got used to the odd-looking newcomer. But knowing he was no good at looking statuesque, he overcompensated by winding his body into his characters with such concentrated effort that for years he was typecast as the stage villain in a string of trashy melodramas.*

Melodrama was born of Gothicism, Britain's decades-long fascination with a fantasy medieval world of dungeons and dark lords.† By the end of the eighteenth century, when Ann Radcliffe perfected the archetypal Gothic novel—aristocratic villains stalking virtuous damsels through haunted and preferably ruined mansions—and Matthew Lewis added another jolt of sensationalism with stories of Satanism and incestuous rape, the craze had spread to the stage, where it launched a vogue for stylized acting backed by soaring music and spectacular visual effects. Gothic drama hit an all-time low with Charles Maturin's wildly depraved *Fredolfo,* in which Macready was forced to play the snarling vil-

---

* That Macready's looks were unimposing was not for want of trying: after long rehearsals of *Henry V* he was seen walking about the stage for hours with "his cuisses on his thighs," but all to no avail, for on the night, a fellow actor said, he tossed and tumbled like a hog in armor. As to fencing, the same actor declared, "he handled a foil like a pitchfork; but the glamour of his genius blinded his auditors to these blemishes" (John Coleman, *Fifty Years of an Actor's Life* [London, 1904], I. 50).

† Gothicism, depending on which way you look at it, was a product of either Enlightenment arrogance or Enlightenment anxiety—a titillating ride into a tyrannical, superstitious past from the vantage point of secure modernity, or a rejection of the triumph of rationalism, Wordsworth's meddling intellect.

lain to an audience that first laughed and then howled its single performance into condign obscurity, but already playwrights had begun experimenting with topical versions of similarly lurid stories. One, *The Castle of Paluzzi, or the Extorted Oath,* was tantalizingly billed as a dramatization of "some of the interesting facts in a recent Trial on the Continent"; the trial, in which a cabal of murderers had been convicted on the evidence of a brothel keeper, was the talk of the town, and the play was rushed out to capitalize on its currency. To Macready, who had long since realized his mistake and was exasperated with lashing himself into displays of ferocious passion, desperate revenge, hardened triumph, and bitter chuckling, it was the dregs of a distasteful cup.

Almost without exception, the bad guys of melodrama were decadent aristocrats or, as time went on, rapacious rent collectors and factory owners, because the new genre appealed strongly to lower-middle-class artisans and the working classes, and hardly at all to the educated elite. That hardly mattered, for the latter had largely abandoned the theatres in any case.

MACREADY HAD MADE his debut at the height of the Regency, the decade when the future George IV ruled in the name of his sporadically mad father and "Beau" Brummel earned everyone's gratitude by inventing a loop that went under the shoe to keep the set of a gentleman's trouser leg wrinkle-free.

Adam Smith, a few decades earlier, had identified two norms of morality in English society: one, strict and austere, that was clung to by the respectable "common people" who knew that one slip from the straight and narrow would be their ruin; the other, awash with "luxury, wanton and even disorderly mirth, the pursuit of pleasure to some degree of intemperance, the breach of chastity, at least in one of the two sexes," that was the privilege of the rich and titled.[17] By the time of the Regency, leisured hedonism was taking its last, decadent gasp, and for London's young bucks the latest craze was for slumming it. To the disgust of their parents, who at least had gambled away their fortunes in respectable settings, they slouched down the streets, toothpicks stuck between teeth, knuckles crammed into coat pockets, throwing down wads of their inheritance at bare-knuckle bouts, cockpits, or monkey fights; at night they piled into the seediest parts of town, drinking, swearing, and singing smutty songs, and in the morning, according to *Life in London,* a wildly popular sketchbook of Regency society, you were not the genuine article unless you made sure to weave out of your drinking den, "reel about like a rake of the first magnitude, insult all you meet, knock down an old woman or two, break a few windows, stagger to another tavern for a fresh supply of the juice of the grape, and finish your glorious frolic in being sent home in a hackney-coach, senseless, speechless, and motionless, more like a beast than a rational intelligent human being."[18] It was especially provocative behavior at a time when real slums—the word was coined during the Regency—were starting to scar the city. Two of the worst, the St. Giles Rookery and the confluence of noxious alleys known as the Seven Dials, vast tangles of overhanging houses, patched with rags and paper, undermined by thieves' escape routes, stuffed with thirty or sixty men, women, and children to a room, teetering across dank dead-end yards like piles of old crates in an abandoned warehouse, were right on the edge of the West End, a world where solid doors opened in solid walls to let out elegant figures who galloped in carriages between brightly lit ballrooms.

It was unfortunate for the acting profession that Covent Garden, the chaotic market district where the two national theatres stood a hundred yards apart, was the focus of the rakes' rough pleasures. They were not so much interested in the stage—though they took a languid pleasure in annoying actors by coughing loudly during poignant speeches and applauding at the wrong moment—as in what surrounded it. The alleys, bagnios, and brothels around the theatres were thick with *grandes horizontales* and half-tipsy whores—if you somehow failed to find one, there were guidebooks, complete with price lists and appendices of special skills, to help out—and so were the playhouses themselves. Soliciting in the stalls was nothing new, but it had become endemic. Fancy courtesans held court in their boxes, and at nine o'clock, when the shops shut and half-price was called, streetwalkers hurried across Waterloo Bridge and piled through the doors. "Throngs of prostitutes and men of every station crowd into the theatres; the women go wherever they please, will even sit next to you if there is a seat, nearly asphyxiating you with the smell of gin they exhale with every breath," the French writer Flora Tristan objected in her journal, adding that they received men in the foyer as if in their own drawing rooms.[19] Cash-hungry theatre managers, far from dissuading the trade, had taken to pushing free passes under brothel doors, and the fame of the madams who prowled up and down, handing out business cards and keeping a beady eye on their charges' jewels, spread far and wide. Jehangeer Nowrojee and Hirjeebhoy Merwanjee, two shipbuilders from Bombay who spent two and a half years in London delving into the mysteries of steam power, cautioned their compatriots that more than a cup of coffee could be procured in the saloons at Covent Garden:

> for here, at the half price, are to be found swarms of well-dressed, highly-painted, but unhappy females, who, having lost their virtue, resort, as a means of maintenance, to the saloons of theatres, and with much wantonness endeavour to draw young men into the snares of vice and misery of which they themselves have been the victims. We do think this very discreditable to be allowed.[20]

So did many locals. The middle classes had caught another strong dose of Evangelicalism, and once again the theatres were firmly in their sights.* With so many aristos rampaging around town, it was wildly unfair that anyone noticed a few murky affairs backstage; but, as usual, actors, having no status but plenty of visibility, were easier targets than aristocrats and certainly than royals. Hannah More, the most prolific Evangelical writer of the age, had once been a playwright herself, but

---

* They had never really been out of them. In the early eighteenth century, a network of Societies for the Reformation of Manners planted self-appointed moral guardians along the benches to tot up profanities as ammunition for prosecutions, though since the informers were effectively paid on commission it was not unknown, one contemporary noted, for them to "pick harmless words out of Plays, to indict the Players and squeeze twenty Pound a Week out of them, if they can, for their exposing Pride, Vanity, Hypocrisie, Usury, Oppression, Cheating, and other darling Vices of the Master Reformers" (Thomas Brown, *The Works of Mr. Thomas Brown* [London, 1715], II. 55–56). In 1757, in the middle of Garrick's reign, one anonymous pamphleteer volunteered, under the title *The Actors' Scourge,* that actors were "the most profligate wretches, and the vilest vermine, that hell ever vomited out; . . . the filth and garbage of the earth, the scum and stain of human nature, the excrements and refuse of all mankind, the pests and plagues of human society, the debauchees of men's mind and morals," and in the latter part of the century reform movements found a willing audience in George III, who has been called the first middle-class monarch. Shakespeare was not always above the fray: in an age when regular theatregoers might see a blockbuster like *Macbeth* dozens of times, stage-haters were convinced that it hardened them to murder.

she changed horses and exhorted the upper classes to set an example to the poor by shunning the snares of the stage. A few obliged. When Harriot Mellon, the daughter of strolling players, retired from Drury Lane to marry the banker Thomas Coutts, then in his mid-eighties and the richest commoner in England, and subsequently the Duke of St. Albans, a descendant of the natural son of Charles II by Nell Gwyn who was twenty-two years her junior, she was so determined not to dip back into her past that she would deign to communicate with her old theatrical acquaintances only via a messenger from a separate room; though like More, she perhaps had more need than most to distance herself.[21]* By the early nineteenth century More's point had been won, if not entirely in the way she envisaged, and the world of fashion, when it left its drawing rooms and increasingly late dinner tables at all, drifted away from the theatres to the fancy Italian Opera House, where prostitutes, along with frock coats, colored trousers, and boots, were banned.

The result of these shifts in the fashionable and moral codes was a downward spiral in the social composition of the audiences at the two great playhouses. English theatres had always been noisy, rowdy places which thrived on a tantalizing sense of barely controlled mayhem—a tradition that made the courtly theatres on the Continent look prim in comparison, and which the American stage had inherited. Now the lucrative boxes emptied out, prices fell, the remaining theatregoers grew more unruly, and respectable types were scared off in still larger numbers. Foreign visitors were astounded to find butchers, barbers, and shoemakers lounging in the pit and journeymen, apprentices, bargemen, laundresses, domestic servants, and chimney sweeps packed into the gallery, and they were positively astonished at their antics. In 1826 Prince Pückler-Muskau, a Silesian traveler, garden designer, and serial marriage proposer, went to watch Macready in *Macbeth;* despite the fine acting, he puzzled, "the interest was generally so slight, the noise and mischief so incessant that it is difficult to understand how such distin-

---

* Harriot's scrupulousness was all the more self-denying since for all her exorbitant wealth she hankered after her old way of life. The theatre crowd, she wrote, were all "fun, frolic, and vivacity," and for all their improvidence they were far more full of life than the "weary, stale, flat, and unprofitable" circles in which she now moved. "Why," she added, "we might as well be in the treadmill, as toiling in the stupid, monotonous round of what they call pleasure, but which is, in fact, very cheerless and heavy work" (Sandra Richards, *The Rise of the English Actress* [London, 1993], 61).

guished artists can form themselves with so brutal, indifferent, and ignorant an audience."[22] Jehangeer Nowrojee and Hirjeebhoy Merwanjee were equally discomposed by the whistling and yelling from the gallery at Drury Lane. "We have to recommend to our countrymen," they advised,

> should any of them on their visit to England desire to see the Theatres in London, always to go to the boxes, which are frequented by a respectable class of people . . . but never for the sake of economy go either to the pit or gallery of any of them . . . because these places are always resorted to by the humbler classes, as well as by rogues, thieves, and pick-pockets, and should a stranger happen to be there, he is often teased and insulted with gross and abusive language by these fellows, besides he could not see much of the performances. . . .

"And here," they added, "we would inform our countrymen that the majority of the lower orders in England are very rude in their manners and behaviour towards strangers, whom they do not like to see in their own country."[23]

The inability to see, or hear, much of the performances was the crux of the problem. In a misguided attempt to retain their monopoly in the teeth of an exploding population, the patent theatres had grown out of control. Up by the roof of Covent Garden, or Drury Lane with its thirty-six hundred seats, a quarter of the audience was virtually oblivious to what was happening on stage. The only way to see anything from the back benches was to stand up, and standing up in the gallery was not a safe move. Even from the front of the gallery you could barely make out what was going on, and in order to get a good seat on a Saturday night, when the city's workers had been paid and could stay out late, groups of friends lined up early, rushed at the doors the instant they opened, jostled up the dimly lit stairs, and jumped over the benches, where they stripped to their shirtsleeves, hung their bonnets, shawls, and coats on the railing, unwrapped parcels of food, and wiped stone bottles of porter on their sleeves and passed them along the row. Before long, though, perspiring in the heat, dizzy from the gas fumes rising up from below, and as closely imbricated as tiles on a roof, strangers would start to resent being pressed up against each other, squabbles would break out, and the rest of the play went to pieces.

Yet what kept them coming was their sheer love for the theatre. A ticket for the full evening cost about the same as the standard four-pound loaf of bread, which lasted a laborer for a week: there was "many a hungry belly and ragged back," one journalist noted, "among the host of the unwashed in the upper or one shilling galleries of Drury Lane or Covent Garden."[24] On Sunday morning, when the barbers' shops in the working-class districts were packed with men waiting in their best Sunday outfit of drab corduroy trousers, blue coats, and yellow waist-coats for their weekly shave, criticism of the previous night's drama dominated the conversation.

"Have you seen this 'ere new piece?" one customer would ask, point-ing to an advertisement in a paper while his face was being lathered.

"No," his neighbor would reply, after downing one of the medicinal "revivers" which were dispensed under the counter and bore a surpris-ing resemblance to sweetened, spiced rum. "What sort of piece is it?"[25] And a third customer would chime in with an extensive review, even if he had to make up the bits he had missed.

Other times, the talk was of the latest Shakespeare: even in the gallery, there were always aficionados of the Bard who urgently shushed the noisemakers when a great speech was coming up. More typical of the new audience, though, was Charley, a hardworking newspaperboy who lived off St. Martin's Lane in Covent Garden and whose views on the theatre were recorded by the engineer Charles Manby Smith:

He looks upon the drama, which he calls the "drawmer," as the grandest of all our institutions, and he has very original ideas on the subject of plays and acting. He knows, as he says, lots of tragic speeches, and spouts them to [his brother] Billy as they lie awake in bed, sometimes dropping off to sleep in the middle of a solilo-quy. . . . He knows of course that *Hamlet* is "first-rate," and *Macbeth* the same; but his sympathies go with that little pig-tailed tar in the shiny hat . . . who, hitching up his canvas trousers with one hand, and shaking a short, dumpy cutlass in the other, hacks and hews his way through a whole regiment of red-coats, who surprise him in the smuggler's cave, and gets clear off, leaving half of his adversaries dead on the stage.[26]

"Love and murder suits us best, sir . . . of *Hamlet* we can make neither end nor side; and nine out of ten of us—ay far more than that—would like it to be confined to the ghost scenes, and the funeral, and the killing at the last," a prosperous costermonger who went to the theatre or the dances three times a week told the journalist Henry Mayhew.[27]

Sensational, escapist melodrama, which apart from anything else was easier to follow from the gallery, had begun to subsidize Shakespeare. A comparison with America is revealing. During the 1820–21 season at the Park Theatre in New York, then a city of around 125,000, Shakespeare was played thirty-seven times. In London, a city of more than a million, his plays were performed forty-eight times at Covent Garden, and that figure included seventeen outings of a wretched operetta based on *Twelfth Night,* eleven repetitions of *The Enchanted Isle,* Dryden and Davenant's almost unrecognizable version of *The Tempest,* with some new songs and dialogue added for good measure, and one performance of *Katherine and Petruchio, by Mr. and Mrs. Charles Kemble,* an equally bastardized version of *The Taming of the Shrew.* The next year at Covent Garden brought fourteen nights of more or less recognizable Shakespeare plays, plus twenty-nine of an operetta based on *The Two Gentlemen of Verona.* At Drury Lane, the only other place in London where Shakespeare could be legally performed the year round, the 1820–21 season saw Shakespeare's plays staged just eleven times, and that in a year when the theatre, exceptionally, was kept open for a full twelve months. Just as Britain's great Shakespeare revival was on its last legs, America had adopted the Bard.

MACREADY WAS MORTIFIED, but there was nowhere else for him to turn. Numerous so-called minor theatres had sprung up over the decades to serve the burgeoning city, but under the old patents any actor who opened his mouth in them unaccompanied by music was liable to be hauled before the magistrates. Competition for the leading roles at Covent Garden had turned that establishment into a snakepit of conniving factions, while over at Drury Lane Edmund Kean was the

An earlier rivalry over Shakespeare: In this cartoon from 1814, two actors costumed as Richard III are tearing Shakespeare apart in their struggle to claim him as their own. "Murder! Murder!" cries the Bard. On the left is Edmund Kean, then the new star of Drury Lane, while on the right is Charles Young, the leading tragedian at Covent Garden during Macready's first years there; their respective theatres are shown behind them. Despite his diminished drawing power, Shakespeare was still the great test for a leading actor.
Courtesy of the Library of Congress.

undisputed king and the Wolves, his infamous fan club, had vowed to hound out of town anyone who challenged him. In any case, Drury Lane had already decided that Macready's price was too high. Byron, who was on the board, snorted when he was told that Macready was a highly moral young man: "Ha! then, I suppose he asks five pounds a week more for his morality," the poet retorted.[28]

"Where then was the place for me?" Macready agonized. "I should have better weighed all this before! It now became apparent I had made my venture too soon."[29] The answer came quicker than he could have hoped. A series of marriages, illnesses, and feuds suddenly left Covent Garden shorn of its stars; in desperation, the manager risked everything on his last remaining name, and Macready had the sickening experience of walking out of his lodgings one morning and finding himself announced in Richard III, Kean's most famous role.

Kean had made his London debut just two years before Macready, but his reputation was so fearsome that few dared take him on. Failure had already hobbled several challengers, and the Wolves, Macready had no doubt, were on his scent. "In the present temper of the public mind," *The Morning Chronicle* explained after the event, "warm and enthusiastic as it is in admiration of Mr. Kean's admirable performance, there was no middle point between disgrace and glory. Mr. Macready's professional reputation was, in fact, at stake."[30]

There was only one thing to do. Kean had known better than to compete with Kemble on his stately terms: to win London to his side, he had had to overturn Kemble's whole school of acting. Macready knew he had to do the same. He could never match Kean's innate genius, but he could follow his own instincts as Kean had followed his. Suddenly he saw the way forward: not Kemble's educated artistry, not Kean's flashes of insight, but a new style of acting, stripped of artifice, as natural as was consistent with the poetry of the text, in the service of characters who were psychologically plausible, based on close study, and kept at every moment in contact with a coherent reading of the play.* It was an approach to which his education and earnest, exacting nature had led him, but to pull it off he had to throw away all his training— the singsong declamation his father had taught him, the elaborate gestures of melodrama—and he set himself on a course of practice, which he would keep up for the rest of his career. Every day he lay down on the floor or backed up against a wall, bandaged his arms, and worked himself up into a frenzy while forcing himself to keep stock still. He made himself whisper bursts of rage; he set up three large mirrors in his room, limned out his character, watched to make sure he wasn't striking a pose, and trained himself to flash passion from his eyes without moving a muscle.

The night finally came. For days he had fluttered between hope and fear; now he threw his whole effort into what seemed a life-and-death struggle. He was transparently nervous, his self-possession deserted him once again, yet he was hardly finished when the pit shot to its feet and waved handkerchiefs and hats for minutes on end. In one night he

---

* To us Macready would appear old-fashioned—there was a sentimentality and sententiousness about him that still savored of the eighteenth century—but his innovations and self-discipline brought him closer to modern acting than any of his predecessors or peers.

had saved the great theatre: the treasury was reopened and the actors were paid.

All of a sudden, Macready was at the head of his profession. Pamphlets were published comparing his Richard with Kean's—one was a ridiculous forty pages long—and from that day he was billed as "The Eminent Tragedian." Offers flooded in from the regions; his life between London engagements became a sleepless whirl of carriages, mail coaches, and post-chaises. After five years at Covent Garden, he reengaged at the theatre's highest salary; security, finally, seemed to be within his grasp.

Yet the theatre, as Macready knew well, was a fickle mistress, and his new style, seemingly subdued next to his rivals' fireworks, was still a minority taste. For two frustrating seasons he was virtually banished from the stage by another vogue for gaudy spectacle; then he got enmeshed in a power struggle at Covent Garden and found himself sidelined and threatened with a cut in salary. He dashed off letters that talked of disgraces and breaches of promise, issued a pamphlet that set out his grievances in petty detail, and finally resigned in a fit of pique. He was soon snapped up by Robert Elliston, the manager of Drury Lane, and there his troubles really started.

NO PLACE IN the history of the theatre was more infamous than Drury Lane in 1823. Elliston was a handsome, educated, and accomplished actor whose reign had begun promisingly, but bad habits had gotten the worse of him. He was particularly notorious for his early application of the casting couch. One teenage actress, the daughter of a respectable shoemaker from the Isle of Wight whom he inveigled up to London with promises of an engagement, became pregnant by him after a night in Soho Square and was shunned by her friends. Elliston, who was busy working his way through his wife's fortune, refused to acknowledge her and she ended up in the workhouse, where her baby boy died of suffocation after she lay on him, out of distraction or desperation, in the middle of the night. Unconscionably, anticipating legal trouble, Elliston tried to blacken her character, and he promised to reward anyone who would come up to London and dish some dirt on the mother of his dead child.[31]

That was the nastiest episode, but Elliston and his star Edmund Kean were such a lethal combination that James Winston, the acting manager at Drury Lane, felt it safest to write large chunks of his diary in code. "Kean requested the rehearsal might not be till twelve as he should get drunk that night—said he had frequently three women to stroke during performances and that two waited while the other was served. . . . That night he had one woman (Smith) though he was much infected," ran one entry.[32] There was much more of the same, usually involving Elliston, Kean, and Alfred Bunn, the stage manager, getting blind drunk, climbing on tables, kicking each other, and letting rip with a string of choice epithets. "Shitwig" was a favorite. Elliston was often absent; Bunn was missing half the time as well, and more often than not he was found sleeping off his hangover on the manager's sofa.

Macready was not a killjoy. He was fond of a drink, he had a loose tongue after a good dinner, and he was a frequent visitor at the establishment of the Count d'Orsay and Lady Blessington, one of the more notorious ménages of the period. But he was painfully aware that he was required to hold himself to a higher standard than other public figures if he was to retain his personal reputation; besides, even if he had not been an actor, his nature would have been out of kilter with the lurid Regency whirl. He could be spectacularly unworldly: at one dinner he was cringingly embarrassed by talk of Byron's sex life. "I am not formed for the world's vain pleasures," he worried after another party; "they must be substantial ones of feeling, thought or sense to hold me captive."[33] At Drury Lane he must have felt like a eunuch in a harem, but it was Kean's spectacular shenanigans that he found hardest to swallow, partly because his behavior played into the theatre baiters' hands, partly because, he admitted to a colleague, he knew what a magnificent actor the beast was. Kean's womanizing was now on the same grand scale as his drinking, and in 1824, a few months after Macready joined Drury Lane, the beast was finally caught with his pants down. A city alderman by the unfortunate name of Cox sued him for criminal conversation, the old euphemism for adultery, and as soon as the trial got under way the prosecution unfurled eighty of the actor's letters which had been found in Mrs. Cox's bureau. *Cox vs. Kean* was a gift to the scandal sheets, and the case became a national obsession. Dirty songs, ballads, pamphlets, and caricatures recycled the lurid revelations, and even the *Times* waded in and lashed the adulterer daily. Kean, it thundered, had "advanced many steps in profligacy beyond the most profligate of his sisters and brethren of the stage"; his offense was "aggravated by the most shocking circumstances of indecency, perfidy, brutality, obscenity, and hypocrisy," and he deserved to be hanged.[34] Genius or not, he was a vulgar upstart whose effrontery had provoked fashionable society, which liked to keep a monopoly on bad behavior, and society took its revenge.

In January 1825, after losing the case, Kean reappeared at Drury Lane, defying the advice of the home secretary, Robert Peel, to postpone the engagement on the grounds of likely riot. Twelve thousand protestors tried to push through the doors: almost without exception they were men—for women, in sympathy with Kean's estranged wife, had shunned him. Hardly a line was heard amid the catcalls, hisses, and bawdy quotes from his letters, and at the end his attempts to speak were thwarted by a hail of missiles. The fracas went on for a week: card games were played in the pit, banners were unfurled, and orange peel and rotten eggs rained down, and though there was a lull when he threatened to retire, the trouble reared up again when he went on tour. After one particularly bad night in Greenock, where Kean had arrived drunk on the morning steamer, downed a gallon of whisky before breakfast with the porters who carried his luggage from the dock, and then started on another bottle in the afternoon, he threw his fur coat over his costume, made a show of going to lie down in his room, escaped through a window to a nearby bar, and sent word to his dresser to hire a pair of boatmen to row them to the island of Bute. Away they sailed, Kean singing, reeling off Shakespeare, and toasting the moon, until they beached in the morning and the greatest actor in the English-speaking world strode up the pebbles, still dressed as King Richard, and poured two speechless customs officers a glass of Scotch.[35] When he finally returned to Drury Lane he would disappear for days on end, just as he had as a boy, and then show up fast asleep in his greatcoat on his dressing room couch, his eyes bloodshot, his face bloated and blotched. He started bringing women to the theatre all day and night. " 'Send me Lewis or the other woman. I must have a fuck, and then I shall do,' " Winston recorded as his condition for going on one night. "He had it. They let him sleep till about six, when they awoke him, dressed him, and he acted but was not very sober. After the play [we] got him to supper . . . and got him to a bedroom and locked him up till the morning."[36]

Macready had been hired to act opposite Kean, but he had not been on stage with him once, because the great star had become gripped with paranoia that the younger man would usurp his throne. Twice Kean ran away from the theatre with a doctor's certificate rather than take on the contest—the first time, he went to Scotland, the second to France—and once again Macready was kept out of the limelight.

Worse was to come. By 1825, Elliston was losing vast sums of money, and in quick succession he lashed out at his actors, landed himself with actions for assault, challenged a shareholder to a duel, reduced himself to imbecility with brandy, and ended up in the Rules of the King's Bench Prison as a debtor. Even Kean had him arrested for nonpayment.* Within months, a stock market crash and banking panic had brought widespread hardship to Britain, and the theatres were half empty.

Macready set sail for America.

For six months he played a profitable season as the English star at the Park Theatre in New York, with equally happy side trips to Boston, Baltimore, and Philadelphia. He was warmly welcomed by the East Coast intelligentsia, he was pleasantly surprised to find the taste for Shakespeare flourishing, and he began to think that being an actor in America was a more respectable condition than it was back home.

Edwin Forrest was making his debut just as Macready arrived, and the Englishman duly set out to scrutinize the new star.[37]

"A new theatre in the Bowery, a low quarter of the city, was opened during my sojourn in New York," he later recorded. "It was handsome and commodious; but its locality was an objection insuperable to the fashion of the place." Forrest was playing Mark Antony in *Julius Caesar*. "The 'Bowery lads,' as they were termed, made great account of him," Macready wrote, "and he certainly was possessed of remarkable qualifications. His figure was good, though perhaps a little too heavy; his face might be considered handsome, his voice excellent; he was gifted with extraordinary strength of limb, to which he omitted no opportunity of

---

* Years earlier, Kean had also had Macready's father arrested for defaulting on his salary.

giving prominence." Forrest had clearly received only the commonest education, he added, but his readings showed strong discernment and a good intellect; he was energetic, "and was altogether distinguished by powers that under proper direction might be productive of great effect." The young American made a strong enough impression for Macready to seek him out another night, though a second viewing left him less impressed. "His performance," he decided, "was marked by vehemence and rude force that told upon his hearers; but of pathos . . . there was not the slightest touch, and it was evident he had not rightly understood some passages in his text."

"My observation upon him was not hastily pronounced," Macready later reassured himself. "My impression was that, possessed of natural requisites in no ordinary degree, he might, under careful discipline, confidently look forward to eminence in his profession. If he would give himself up to a severe study of his art, and improve himself by the practice he could obtain before the audiences of the principal theatres in Great Britain, those of Edinburgh, Liverpool, Glasgow, Birmingham, Manchester, &c . . . he might make himself a first-rate actor. But to such a course of self-denying training I was certain he never would submit, as its necessity would not be made apparent to him. The injudicious and ignorant flattery, and the factious applause of his supporters in low-priced theatres, would fill his purse, would blind him to his deficiency in taste and judgment, and satisfy his vanity, confirming his self-opinion of attained perfection."[38]

Despite his condescending gasconade and his vaunting faith in the meliority of the English stage, Macready had a point, however much his zeal for the hard-knocks school of English provincial training smacked of special pleading. If he had traveled beyond the drawing rooms of the East Coast he might have understood America a little better and been a little less glib, but it was inconceivable to the Englishman that this young American, thirteen years his junior, could ever challenge him for his tin crown.

CHAPTER 4

Boxing Mac and Hot Cross Bunn

WILLIAM CHARLES MACREADY woke late on the morning of his fortieth birthday. A burnt-out candle sat accusingly by his pillow; one of the trashy romantic novels to which he was guiltily addicted lay open by his hand. Shame seized him for wasting the whole night—had he read till five, or six?—on such unseemly, debasing stuff.

He quickly got up, began to dress, and almost started when he remembered the season his life had reached. Anxious thoughts set in. "What has my life been? a betrayal of a great trust, an abuse of great abilities!" he brooded magniloquently.[1]

Macready went downstairs and basked in the sight of his wife playing with their two young children. He had first met Catherine—she was called Kitty then—when she was nine, and had promptly reduced her to tears: she had stood in for a child actor at the last minute, and he had roundly scolded her for being unprepared. Five years later he ran into her on stage again; this time he was struck by her spirited intelligence, almost as much as her willingness to take his instructions. Catherine's parents were penniless theatre folk, and Macready wrote to his father casually asking whether he had space on his books for the whole family: the father was a damned hick, he admitted, though a good set painter, and the mother "a *female hick*—or hickess" who was only fit to deliver messages, but the girl was highly promising.[2] McCready obliged, and his son continued to take an unusual interest in his young protégée. Paternalism led to friendship, friendship to love, and Macready started writing to Catherine every day in his dual role as suitor and tutor, alternating affectionate sentiments with homework to improve her mind, and taking care to excise indelicate passages from her set texts. When the news reached him that her father and brother had drowned in a shipwreck, he found himself unable to bear the thought of leaving her undefended in a provincial playhouse, and after an exchange of ardent letters they were engaged. Macready immediately insisted that Catherine leave the stage, and he set out with his sister Letitia to remove her to London.

Letitia idolized her older brother, and an unmistakable look of contempt swept her face as she took Catherine's hand. There was complete silence. Macready sat between them in the carriage, one looking one way, the other the other, and felt it was the most wretched day of his life. As soon as they arrived home, Letitia ran to her room and threw herself on her bed in floods of tears. She was utterly disappointed in his choice, she told her brother; he had led her to expect so much more. Of course he had to go through with the wedding, but surely he could postpone it and give his child bride time to improve in her studies. Catherine swallowed her pride, restrained herself from telling Macready to stand up to his fond, priggish sister, and quietly acquiesced. Henceforth she had two tutors and progressed at double speed, or perhaps her gentle charm soothed the stern Letitia. "Not only in acquirement from study but even in outward appearance did my dear pupil confirm by most delightful evidence the opinion I had always maintained of her wonderful aptness of improvement," Macready pedagogically exulted, and a year after the painful trip they were married.[3] Catherine was barely nineteen, Macready thirty-one: Mrs. Siddons had told him not to marry until he was thirty, and if his sister had not intervened he would have been right on cue.

After prayers and breakfast, he turned over a few pages of Cicero and Homer—he had started rereading the classics to prepare for his son's education—then stole out into the garden and breathed in the sweet, sharp country air. Three years earlier, when Catherine was expecting their firstborn, he had rented a large, comfortable farmhouse in Elstree, a village a dozen miles west of Drury Lane, and it had become his idyll and his refuge. Every day he could get away he took the stagecoach home, turned his back on the city with its gilded guardsmen and plumed grandes dames, and played the gentleman farmer, busying himself with supervising the little harvest, buying a new cow, rowing on the reservoir, lying on the grass, and passing languid, happy days in a world of respectable peace.

Catherine was devoted to him. He had been courted by women of fortune—an earl's daughter among them, the rumors said—but he was too proud to stomach being kept as an aristocratic pet, and whatever the world said, he was constantly thankful for his choice.⁴ His adoption of a career had been out of his hands and so, more often than not, was its progress, but his family was all his own. He continued to plan his wife's studies—the *Iliad* and Burke's *On the Sublime* were one week's task—and, having formed her mind, he found it easy on his temper. Catherine became rather brilliant: soon he was practicing in front of her and absorbing her criticism. He doted on his children, too, though he could be a stern taskmaster. Above all, he was determined to succeed where his father had failed: he would earn an independence for his family and keep them well clear of the dreaded profession of acting. "I had rather see one of my children dead than on the stage," he told young men who applied to him for a position; they usually left very quickly and, he was certain, very grateful for his advice.⁵

It was a happy thought, or perhaps an awareness of his faults, that led Macready to install his family on a toy farm: happy for him, and happy for them, because the moment he stepped into the coach and set off for the theatre, this strange man, austere and emotional, gifted and insecure, morbidly sensitive and monstrously egotistical, turned the other aspect of his Janus face to the world.

MACREADY HAD GROWN to hate the business of acting with a vengeance. On his return from America, he had found it impossible to secure a London engagement, and he spent several years tramping around the provinces, only stopping in town to order a dress or a new beard or to scribble pages of heavily underlined instructions to the next set of managers, before wedging himself into the corner of another coach swaying on its springs between dingy lodgings run by landladies who sniffed at his profession and drafty dressing rooms whose dank smell he tried to mask with liberal dousings of perfume.⁶ At each stop he laughed a hollow laugh at the tinsel glamour of the stage and the bald reality behind it, then took a deep breath and went down to rehearse the actors. Most were scarcely on nodding terms with their parts, while the old hands resented being hectored by the London star whose income was a large multiple of theirs and trod sullenly through his long and explosive rehearsals. "Stand—er—er—still!" he barked like a tyrannical schoolmaster in the eccentrically hesitant manner he had developed, and he chalked a mark or banged a nail in the stage to mark the precise spot. "Keep your—er—er—eye on me, sir!" he hissed repeatedly during a nervous newcomer's speeches, in between denouncing another actor who was trying to strike a scene-stealing pose and confusing a third so much that he stood snuffling and wiping his nose.

At night he would come back after a pork chop and a quick rest at his lodgings to find, more often than not, half the cast stone drunk. Firmly shutting his door and trying to sink into character, he would stride out the moment the bell rang, a picture of furious concentration, and stand in the wings, muttering under his breath to get into voice or shaking a ladder to work himself up to the right pitch of anger. When things went well, he forgot himself and seemed to become his character: sometimes he got so carried away that he swore, involuntarily and audibly, at stage villains, or shook the breath out of them, and more than one actor who missed a parry in a sword fight received a cut to his head. (In one instance a serious wound resulted in a suit for assault.) Even during love scenes, he nearly wrenched several actresses' arms out of their sockets and bruised them black and blue: one of his stage lovers was so fed up with having her hair pulled that she studded it with pins. But when something jolted him out of his reverie, Macready lost his character as quickly as his temper. There was usually something: a carpenter slapping him on the back while he was coughing himself into voice, his wig catching fire, or a party of drunk butchers in the gallery. One night a barely literate props man misread the word "map" and Macready, enthroned in state as King Lear, was handed a curly white mop with which to divide his kingdom. In one theatre, a prompter went mad and was carried away in a straitjacket minutes before the curtain went up; a dresser ran off with Macready's purse, gold watch, and rings in another; and in a third he lost all his earnings when the box office was robbed. Mostly, though, he found fault with his supporting cast: every night actors entered from the wrong side, missed their cues, and cut him up by garbling their speeches, and at the end, perspiring and out of humor, he would throw himself on the couch in his dressing room, issue the dreaded summons, and administer a series of stern rebukes. "What a calling is this!" he despaired after one night of pratfalls. "How deeply I feel the degradation of belonging to it. . . . This is the profession which the vulgar envy, and the proud seem justified in despising! I come from each night's performance wearied and incapacitated in body, and sunk and languid in mind; compelled to be a party to the blunders, the ignorance, and wanton buffoonery which, as to-night, degrade the poor art I am labouring in."[7] Perhaps, he thought, he would have been happier if his education had been on a level with his situation.

Years on the road spent hawking around his talent like a dyspeptic salesman had worn him down, and his tongue became the scourge and terror of the country theatres. "Beast! Beast of hell!" he hissed at the slightest mistake. He could not help it, and he detested himself for it. "Oh, my temper! my temper!" he exclaimed to his diary, which he started writing with rampant honesty in 1833: "how truly unhappy—even to sometimes growing indifferent about existence—does this morose and impatient temper make me! These theatres have brought it on in its early offensiveness."[8] He feared and therefore despised his audience: they were, he fumed, dull, insensitive, and brutal, and he was sure they preferred the grinding, roaring, and grimacing of country actors to his meticulous impersonations. He loathed his fellow actors even more: they were, he burst out in uncontrolled anathemas, quacks, coxcombs, and humbugs, contemptible blackguards, vile reptilian things and wretched biped beasts, trash, liars, ignorant, impertinent, disgusting, conceited, vulgar, and vain. He was mortified to find himself in the same profession as fame-seekers like "Romeo" Coates, an eccentric amateur who played his namesake in a costume glittering with diamond buttons and drove around in a showy carriage adorned with a gilded crest of a crowing cock and the motto "While I Live I'll Crow."* "What

---

* Coates was so pleased with the ironic applause that met his death scene one night at Drury Lane that he spread his handkerchief on the stage and died all over again.

are players?" Macready asked himself, and he had the answer. "The re-fuse of trades, discarded servants; in short, idle persons from every low stage of society. . . . They are low men, of low extraction, uneducated, and unrestrained in their naked baseness by any moral or gentlemanly feeling."[9] If he could, he ranted, he would have a police officer stationed at his funeral to throw the lot of them out.

Macready soon perceived that he was not wildly popular in the profession. They thought he was a stiff, self-centered snob: the only play he could stomach, they said, was a monologue performed by himself. It is easy to despise a man who despises his own great talent, particularly when he makes no effort to conceal his disdain from his less gifted peers; harder to feel sorry for him, though some did. His detractors were also right to complain that his insecurities could betray him into hypocrisy: Macready was not above gloating over his competitors' failures, while in the same breath lamenting the dearth of talent in the profession. "I am abused, libeled, and an object of persecution because I do not make friends of actors!" he discovered to his seeming astonishment.[10]

Nor did he win any prizes for popularity outside the profession. He was not the first actor to find that hoisting himself above the crowd made him an easy target for abuse: John Kemble and Mrs. Siddons had also suffered from being seen as unapproachable. "The mob must have their idol upon familiar terms," a contemporary observed: "the privilege of calling them, behind their backs, 'Old Sall Siddons,' and 'Black Jack,' was not sufficient; they must meet them at the Harp or Finche's, or the Coal-hole, as they could . . . 'Neddy Kean,' or they were not content: they therefore looked up to their splendid talent with awe for its sublimity, with wonder at its attainment, and with envy at the feeling distance at which, by comparison, it placed themselves; and, in consequence, the vulgar public worshipped and hated them."[11] Kean might be a boozehound, but at least that meant you ran into him in the Coal Hole, the lair of the Wolves.

Kean and Macready were driven by different demons. Kean's was the fear of being unprepossessing, which drove him to perform and to drink; Macready's was his obsession with his social status. He did not have enough insouciance to shrug off an insult—on greeting him, some thoroughgoing snobs would extend their index finger for him to shake—and even when he was invited to fashionable houses he agonized that he was too reserved to add to the pleasures of the night. Afterward he would lie sleepless, with daylight seeping through the window, and wonder why his good intentions and upright character were not evident to his fellow men. Even worse, like Kean, he had discovered that success, which he surely saw as a way to avenge himself on society, did not make the demons go away.

The world and his place in it were a wearying riddle to Macready, and when his misery and frustration brimmed over he could not restrain himself from making his views public. In 1832, a Select Committee on Dramatic Literature was appointed by the Houses of Parliament to consider the disastrous state of the national theatres—with Drury Lane running a "grand Oriental spectacle" called *Hyder Ali; or, the Lions of Mysore,* which featured belly dancers, boa constrictors, and an elephant, the patents seemed to be strangling the legitimate drama, Shakespeare included—and Macready, as one of the leaders of his profession, was called to give evidence. As a public relations exercise, his testimony was sublimely ill judged: an actor's life, he declared, was so "unrequiting, that no person who had the power of doing anything better would, unless deluded into it, take it up."[12]

The press, which had already scented easy pickings, leapt on his back and bit down.

"He is one of the proudest men perhaps existing," one feast of abuse began. "His arrogance and insolence to the members of provincial theatres is annoying in the extreme."[13] Macready could try to shrug off the personal onslaughts, but attacks on his professional abilities made him fearful for his livelihood and haunted him. For years his opponents claimed he was incapable of doing justice to Shakespeare. "In certain melo-dramatic parts . . . Macready is, unquestionably, clever; yet at *all* times his manner is lamentably offensive," one critic flamed. "As a representative of Shakespeare's characters we . . . fearlessly assert his utter incompetence. He does not understand Shakespeare—he cannot read him—he has no more ear than a pig for the exquisite beauty and harmony of his verse."[14] Many of Macready's detractors were satellites of the Kean and Kemble schools, and they had scant sympathy with his new style. Some—the Keanites—thought his performances were too cold and reasoned to involve the audience in their emotions. Others—

the Kembleites—ridiculed his touches of familiar life and derided the strange verbal tics, the staccato delivery and slurs, the catches in his throat and pauses with which he interjected his speeches in an attempt to give a sense of extemporaneous thought, as a travesty of Shakespeare's punctuation.*

Macready was his own fiercest critic when he knew he had failed to do himself justice, but when he felt undeservedly maligned he flared up with indignation. Journalists, he variously scrawled, were filth, vermin, scavengers, and a bunch of devils, and he became convinced that his enemies were trying to destroy him. Some of the worst offenders, the allies of spurned playwrights and slighted rivals, undoubtedly did nurse a personal animus against him, but as usual he was protesting too much. The truth was that the new breed of stars, with their inflated salaries and inflated egos, had become objects of fascination for the papers. The relationship was symbiotic and fraught. In the wake of the Industrial Revolution and the great migration to the cities, the press had exploded: by the start of the nineteenth century London alone boasted more than fifty papers. Competition brought factionalism, factionalism brought puffery, and celebrities were built up by one paper only to be torn down by another. Sometimes the daily vilification descended to astonishingly personal levels, and for those trapped in that hall of distorting mirrors, it was hard to reason that the vitriol was produced mostly to drum up business, and that other public figures suffered as well. "I wish I were anything rather than an actor—except a critic; let me be unhappy rather than vile!" Macready scribbled after reading one unfriendly piece.[15]

Worst of all, he was half convinced that the stigma still attached to his pariah profession was justified. Maybe by its very nature—"a sort of opium-sleep of fantasies, air-built castles, flatteries and frettings, sensual dreams, and ill-kept resolutions"—acting really was bad for the soul.[16] How was it possible to work himself up into a state of nervous excitement every night, crave the charivari of acclaim, and still keep his head? Macready had an overactive and sometimes suffocating sense of his own

---

* The "Macready pause" was his greatest innovation, and the technique was still named after him well into the next century.

inner drama, and he constantly fretted that playacting had cut him adrift from his proper self. Perhaps it was that very sense of shapelessness that made him anatomize his characters so acutely—that helped make him a great actor—but he felt both torn and empty inside. "How much I wish I could see and know myself!" he fretted.[17]

Then there was the constant temptation of being thrown into professional clinches with the opposite sex. Perhaps, he reflected, the surprising thing was not how many had succumbed, but how many had escaped the ordeal unscathed. "I should almost say, *virtue is impossible in a theatre—the mind cannot remain pure,* unless some strong attachment absorbs the heart on the first lighting up of passionate emotion . . . and THEREFORE it should be shunned as infection or as death—*for purity cannot live there,*" he heavily underscored after one actress propositioned him.[18] Some nights he would sit in the auditorium, thinking how much vice, frivolity, idleness, and folly were contained in its walls, and feel sick at the delicate sentiments and solemn protestations of purity coming from a wanton's lips.[19]*

Time, or fame, had made Macready's face less plain. Admirers begged him for locks of his hair, perfumed flowers turned up on his doorstep, and billets-doux fluttered into his scented dressing room. He knew he should burn them unopened, but he could never resist satisfying his curiosity (and, he admitted, his vanity), and sometimes, in a moonlit square after the theatre had closed, he agreed to an assignation. One young girl wrote threatening to kill herself over him; she turned out to be both pretty and virtuous, which for Macready was a killer combination, and she was inconsolable when he told her he was married. Another letter brought a meeting with a stunning beauty in a public garden. She had been seduced with promises of marriage, she explained, and then abandoned, and now she was the *grande cocotte* of a peer—though not, she hastened to add, on an exclusive basis. "*Addio, mia bella!*" Macready confided to his diary, though he could not resist seeing her one more time.[20]

---

* Macready's father was not immune to the charge of loose morals. During their last months together, his philandering had become increasingly public, and when he died he left his son to look after an assortment of natural siblings. Macready swallowed his pride and helped them out: he rescued one half brother from the iniquity of a minor actor's life and set him up as an army surgeon, though he quickly died of acute hepatitis in India.

Less easy to dismiss were the young actresses who fell under his spell—for, whatever his faults, he had a magnetic way about him—and most dangerous of all was his brilliant and delicately beautiful protégée Helen Faucit, who would become the leading mid-century actress, an intimate friend of Queen Victoria's, and the embodiment of Victorian virtue. Helen fell desperately in love with her mentor when she was twenty: he came to care deeply for her, especially when the greenroom gossips spread the rumor that she was pregnant, and he was reduced to flusters of agonies by her affectionate letters, bouquets, and dressing room visits. "God bless her! dear girl! I go to bed in very low spirits—I feel great apprehension for her. God bless and assist her! Amen!" he exclaimed, or something like it, night after night.[21] For all his scrupulousness, Macready was both gifted and cursed with painfully quick emotions and a strong streak of sensuality, and agreeable, handsome women were never far from his mind. Catherine, who knew perfectly well how the theatre world revolved, was not above the occasional fit of jealousy, but though he sometimes had to count his blessings to steady himself, Macready never succumbed to the temptations of the trade, and even many of his enemies admitted that, in that respect at least, his reputation was unblemished.

To his friends as well as his family, Macready was an altogether different figure: an upright, moral man, sometimes difficult but invariably well-meaning. He was stayed by a deep and abiding personal faith, a belief in a just and good God to whom he prayed without fail, though he was fiercely scornful of the church: sermonizing ministers, he thought, were no better than actors. The flip side of his misanthropy was a burning idealism and a lofty moral vision, and though his delicate ego made him temperamentally unable to live up to those ideals in his public life, in private he attracted a select but loyal group of friends who saw the decent, thoughtful man beneath the prickly shell: men like Charles Babbage, the inventor of the prototype computer, and Thomas Carlyle, the hero-worshipping historian, men who would have been astonished to hear him swearing his head off in a provincial playhouse.

Yet for all his distaste for his art, or at least for its means of production, it was his skill as an actor that brought Macready many of his most passionate admirers. None of his inner circle, not surprisingly, were fellow actors, though several were playwrights. Macready had sought out writers early in his career, and almost all the substantial new English plays that appeared between 1820 and 1850—plays like *Virginius* and *Ion, Richelieu* and *The Lady of Lyons,* now more or less justly forgotten but spectacular hits in their time—were written for him. Sometimes he suggested the subject; often he had nearly as much of a hand in the final result as the purported author. Since a successful original role could draw huge crowds, the impulse was hardly selfless, but he became a combination literary agent, editor, and director, and he inspired, among many, Edward Bulwer Lytton and Robert Browning to try their hand at drama.[22]* For these men, Macready was the great hope, the subtle, scholarly face of the theatre, the only one who could make the painted profession a respectable pursuit for artists and intellectuals. They were right to prize him: more often than not, his advice and acting papered over gaping deficiencies in their plays.

His most devoted friends were two writers who stood outside the profession but had an abiding passion for the theatre. John Forster, the young literary editor of the *Examiner,* a radical weekly magazine, and later Charles Dickens's first biographer, became Macready's unofficial agent and closest confidant; Dickens himself, who had watched Macready breathlessly from the pit as a boy, came to love the actor best of all his many friends, while to Macready he was "wonderful Dickens." Macready's dressing room was filled every night with their little coterie, and his dinner parties became a literary fantasist's dream. Thackeray might be there, or Tennyson, his whiskers and monocle drooping into the soup; Browning would take offense at something Forster said and aim a cut-glass decanter at him, and Dickens, genial as always, would roll his eyes and try to patch things up. Macready would sit quietly, watching it all fall apart, a mask of imperturbability badly hiding his alarm.

BY THE MID-1830s, Macready had few real challengers left. Edmund Kean, whose acting relied so much on his spirits—natural and distilled—

---

* Macready first met Bulwer Lytton in his handsome rooms at Albany, the gentleman's lodgings off Piccadilly, "dressed, or rather *déshabillé,* in the most lamentable style of foppery—a hookah in his mouth, his hair, whiskers, tuft, etc., all grievously cared for" (*Diaries,* I. 278). At first he thought the dandyish writer was being sarcastic when he told him how eager he was to improve his acquaintance, but the two forged an extraordinarily successful partnership, and Macready, never far from tears, cried when Bulwer Lytton dedicated his first play to him.

had become a dull ghost of his former self. For ten months he hobbled on stage with an ulcerated leg so painful that he stopped changing his trousers; he would have to have it amputated, he was warned, if he kept up his habitual course of life, and one night he told James Winston that he had decided to have it chopped off. The leg stayed, but Kean's memory had gone: when he tried new plays, he skipped whole pages without noticing and the audience was unsure whether to complain or cry. He sat in his hotel bed, his puffy, blotched face painted red and white so that he resembled a down-at-the-heels clown, a glass of hot wine in his hand, surrounded by scroungers and whores; then he staggered to the theatre and sat in the wings, his head nodding in his lap, sipping brandy and hot water, beads of perspiration running down his cheeks. His greatest wish, he told anyone who listened, was to build himself a remote hut in America, and drink and die forgotten. Then, in 1833—a few months after he finally performed with Macready, though his health was so ruined that he resorted to cheap tricks to upstage him—Kean walked onto the stage of Drury Lane with, for the first time, his son beside him.

Charles Kean had been educated as a gentleman, but had taken to the stage, in part to spite his philandering father, and like every other actor the elder Kean found the idea unbearable. The news that his only child had taken up acting hit him so hard that he collapsed in his dressing room with tears rolling down his cheeks; it took six years and his weakening health before he accepted the inevitable. That night the great star led his son forward and presented him to the audience, then stepped back and became, for one last time, the old Edmund Kean. He seemed to rear up from his small, sickly frame to heroic proportions; he fixed his watery but still brilliant eyes on Charles, a pale, pompous copy of his father, and electrified him into action; but in the third act his voice broke into a falsetto whimper and his head fell onto his son's shoulder.

"Speak to them; I am dying," he murmured. And within two months, at forty-six, he was dead. Macready walked behind the coffin, though he was disgusted when he heard that Kean had left his widow and son penniless and had willed the last scraps of his fortune to his mistress.

Macready's time should have arrived. England was changing, and it was changing in his favor. One writer has described the shift in the national character as a moral revolution: "Between 1780 and 1850 the

English ceased to be one of the most aggressive, brutal, rowdy, outspoken, riotous, cruel and bloodthirsty nations in the world and became one of the most inhibited, polite, orderly, tender-minded, prudish and hypocritical."²³ Middle-class Puritanism, the legacy of Hannah More and her fellow travelers, finally hooked the country to its engine, and Victorianism, that holier-than-thou creed of thrift, temperance, industry, cleanliness, and godliness, was about to come thundering into town.

Yet for more long months, Macready was exiled from London by the rage for sensational escapism, and when he was finally taken on again at Drury Lane it proved to be the lowest point of all.

AFTER THE HAPLESS Elliston had quit Drury Lane and his successors had propped it up with more squandered fortunes, Elliston's former stage manager Alfred Bunn took charge of the national theatre. Macready outdid himself in indignation. Bunn, who owed him a large sum of money from a previous engagement, rode around in a carriage attended by liveried footmen and lived in splendor amid Turkish carpets and damask curtains. He took mistresses like dinners, ran away when the affairs led to duels, and lived on the allowance of his wife's wealthy keeper; yet for all his scoundrelly ways he was accepted at court as a gentleman. On top of all this, he had proved hopeless as a stage manager, never mind as the guardian of the drama.* Bunn—"Bunny," to his friends—was, a contemporary remembered, "good-looking, boyish and light-hearted, seldom depressed, and easily elated."²⁴ He had a rough good humor, a vulgar turn of phrase, and thoroughly middle-brow tastes. He loved to spend other people's money on lavish extravaganzas; he wrote breezy librettos and bad poetry, and he was convinced that the future lay with light operas and pantomimes, broad farces and sentimental melodramas. He was therefore determined to sideline the tiresome tragedy drones like Macready as often as he could get away

---

* Bunn was the model for Mr. Dolphin, the theatre manager in *Pendennis,* Thackeray's novel of Regency bohemia: a "portly gentleman with a hooked nose and a profusion of curling brown hair and whiskers; his coat was covered with the richest frogs, braidings and velvet. He had under-waistcoats, many splendid rings, jewelled pins, and neck-chains. When he took out his yellow pocket-handkerchief with his hand that was cased in white kids, a delightful odour of musk and bergamot was shaken through the house." Thackeray goes on to give a thinly veiled account of Bunn's disastrous regime, in which Macready appears as "the great Hubbard" (Chapter 14).

with it.[25] To make matters worse, Bunn shortly became the manager of Covent Garden as well as of Drury Lane—the first and last time anyone was foolhardy enough to try this experiment—and thus master of the whole realm of the legitimate drama in London.

His first act was to slash his performers' salaries. Not uniquely among managers, Bunn hated actors with a passion, but there was reason as well as vindictiveness behind his move, because the payroll at the two great theatres had soared out of control. During one week, six hundred and eighty-four employees were counted at Covent Garden alone.[26] Aside from the actors there was an acting manager, a stage manager, a pantomime director, a property man, and a callboy, an assortment of prompters and copyists, a corps de ballet, a chorus, and a full orchestra. Up in the scenery rooms in the eaves there were various chief scene painters, assistant scene painters, and color grinders; down in the workshop, a property maker, a machinist, and a master carpenter, together with half a dozen assistant carpenters and two dozen scenery men and stagehands. Backstage were the master and mistress of the wardrobe, with their army of dressers; front of house, a treasurer and an under treasurer, a housekeeper, an assistant, ten money takers, ten check takers, and a box keeper; and, stationed all around, dozens of attendants, lamplighters, firemen, porters, and watchmen.[27] The official theatres had become monsters that chewed through fortunes and spat out bankruptcy, and something had to give.

Predictably, though, Bunn's experiment was an unmitigated disaster. Audiences were kept waiting while actors finished their scene in one theatre and skidded in the snow and rain to the other; sometimes they ran back again before they were finished, leaving someone else to complete their lines, and more than once the whole corps de ballet was withdrawn from the last act at one theatre to open the second play at the other.[28] The connecting streets were full of strange spectacles:

Actors half attired, with enameled faces, and loaded with the paraphernalia of their art, were passing and re-passing as busy as pismires, whilst the hurried interchange of quaint words—"Stage waits,"—"Music on,"—"Rung up," &c.,—would have perplexed the stranger with a thousand surmises. . . . At the season of Christ-

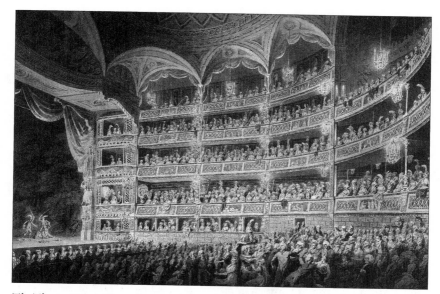

The Theatre Royal, Drury Lane, at its most monumental in a watercolor by Edward Dayes. A brawl in the pit is drawing attention away from the actors, but otherwise the scene is unusually sedate. The huge upper gallery, though, is barely shown: its edge, far away from the stage, is just visible in the top right-hand corner. The auditorium had been slightly reduced in size by Macready's time. The Huntington Library and Art Collections.

mas, when this state of alternation was at its height, the female figure-dancers pattered from one house to another six times during the evening, and underwent the operation of dressing and undressing no less than eight.[29]

After the audience revolted, Bunn relinquished Covent Garden, but at Drury Lane he ditched the legitimate drama altogether and imported an equestrian extravaganza masterminded by another of Macready's nemeses. Andrew Ducrow was the greatest showman of the age, and his specialty was a dazzlingly acrobatic brand of bare-horse drama: in 1833, the year in which the future Queen Victoria scandalized everyone by crossing the river Thames to visit Ducrow's ring, Prince Pückler-Muskau watched him "ride eight horses at once while dressed as a Chinese sorcerer, drive twelve at once while costumed as a Russian and then get into bed with a pony dressed as an old woman."[30] Macready blamed Ducrow for fostering a spate of appearances by prodigal animals on the national stage: once his *Julius Caesar* was interrupted by a chorus from the bulls, camels, and elephants cooped up backstage, which left him feeling like the curtain-raiser to a menagerie. Bunn, though, loved Ducrow, and he loved him even more when his *St. George and the Dragon* show ran from Christmas to Easter and saved the theatre. Macready disappeared in a paroxysm of disdain.

By now Bunn had come to loathe his principal tragedian: not only was Macready failing to pull in the crowds with his Shakespearean turns, but even after weeks of study and rehearsals, he fretted incessantly over whether he was sufficiently prepared in new parts to go on at all. Sometimes he would change his mind at the last minute, after the playbills had been printed, and the manager would end up chasing him around London, trying to cajole and threaten him into returning. Macready, though, had drawn up an iron-clad contract—he was absolved from fines and could refuse to play any characters "such as he, W. C. Macready, may deem as partaking of a melo-dramatic character"—and Bunn, not wishing to be sued for breach, took care not to push his irascible star too far to his face.[31] Instead he had his henchmen insult him, and taunted him from the press.[32] An automaton could play Othello as well as Macready, gibed one piece in the *Age,* a scandal sheet run by Bunn's friend Westmacott, and in the greenroom, after he had drunk too much, Macready growled his favorite insult—"Beast!"—to the editor's back. Behind closed doors, Macready met with three fellow actors and tried to engineer a coup against Bunn, but the meeting collapsed in a flurry of petty recriminations.

Eventually matters came to a head. Macready's performances were pulled to make way for a new operetta, which left him fuming that Bunn "was, is, and will be a beast to the last days of his disgusting existence."[33] Macready was relegated to appearing in the afterpiece: he refused, then, in dread of offending the public, relented, but consoled himself by firing off letters to Bunn's deputies, full of outrage at the manager's atrocious villainy. If Macready balked again, Bunn threatened, he would play him through his whole range of characters on the off nights of the opera and dump the tickets at cut price. The last straw came when the manager plastered up notices announcing his star in a truncated version of *Richard III,* followed by Bunn's own hit operetta

The Jewess and the first act of a piece of chivalric nonsense called *Chevy Chase*. It was a calculated insult. "Here," seethed Macready, "was the climax of this dirty reptile's spite; I laughed out in the street at it."[34] He tried to reason with himself and went on, sleep-deprived, ashamed, and bursting with pent-up anger—angry "to a degree of savageness and desperation," he post-mortemed later that night.[35] At the end of the third act he stalked up to Bunn's door and, almost without thinking, threw it open.[36]

Bunn was sitting at his desk looking over some bills by lamplight.

"You damned scoundrel! How dare you use me in this manner?" the Eminent shouted as he lunged toward the desk.

Bunn, who later claimed that the lamp was shaded and the rest of the room in shadow—otherwise he would certainly have been prepared to take on his adversary—tried to stand up, but Macready gave him a backhanded slap across the face, then thrust his fist at him and knocked him to the floor.

"There, you villain—take that!" he growled.

Bunn got Macready's little finger into his mouth and tried to chew it off.

"You rascal! Would you bite?" Macready screamed.

"Murder! Murder!" Bunn cried.

The desk tipped over. Bunn threw Macready off, got up on one leg, grabbed his assailant by the collar and wrestled him onto the sofa. At that point the prompter burst in with several backups.

"Sir, you had better go to your room," he told Macready repeatedly, and the actor limped off and was nursed back home by his friends. He was aghast at what he had done. The passionate, intemperate rashness that was always bubbling under his cloak of rectitude had finally gotten the better of him. "No one can more severely condemn my precipitation than myself," he chastised himself in his diary:

My character will suffer for descending so low, and the newspapers will make themselves profit of my folly. Words cannot express the contrition I feel, the shame I endure. In my own village I shall not know what I am thought of. . . . My thoughts have been scorpions to me; the estimation I have lost in society, the uncertainty and shame with which, if I am again invited by those who respected me, I shall meet in their looks, is a punishment which has anguish in it. All I can do, as I have reduced myself to a level with this reptile, is to allow him the whole advantage of it, and accept any message for a meeting that he may choose to send me.[37]

Bunn, of course, never threw down the gauntlet. Instead, he sent straightaway for a physician, a surgeon, and a lawyer and took to his bed. He had received, or so he claimed, a black eye and a sprained ankle; his person was "plentifully soiled with blood, lamp oil, and ink." If Macready had struck him two inches nearer the temporal artery, he told anyone within earshot, it would have been murder—though, he quickly added, had he not been caught off guard he would have left his mark on the actor for sure. After three weeks he got up, hobbled around on crutches, and sued Macready for assault: when the case came to trial, the spectators— half the theatre world among them—spilled out of the courtroom and down the landing. Bunn's counsel went to town: Macready, he alleged, had attempted to pull out his client's tongue.

"The wolf was tearing at my heart," Macready screeched. "I was suffering from an inward torture, which only persons of acute sensibility can conceive or sympathize with." He lost the case, though the damages were lower than he had feared. Meanwhile he took coaches everywhere to avoid seeing people and wept bitterly over the grave of the reputation he had nurtured for so long.

"Great Fight. B———nn and M———y," the *Age* splashed on its placards.

"My God! My God! can I ever be forgiven? Can I ever think without *sickening shame* of my *insane conduct*? Forgive me, oh my God!" Macready beseeched:

And you, my blessed and beloved children, pity while you condemn this intemperate ebullition of your unhappy parent, who has so deeply sunk his own reputation and thereby prejudiced your interests. Had I learned, what I have tried to teach myself, that first and best lesson of *self-control*, I should never have tarnished my character and have poisoned with the remembrance of this shocking folly every feeling of my future life. There have been moments when I have felt it not worth retaining, and when, I fear—but I must not look back upon my madness. . . . I know what misery is, that misery which cannot be escaped; it is "myself" that am the "Hell" that is consuming me. . . . If I were alone, I could bear my disgust with the world to solitude, and die and rot in peace in some lonely corner—but I am chained to bear the consciousness of the *curse* that is upon me. . . . *What will become of me* if I permit the continuance of this *odious*—this *degrading*—this *spiteful* and *little* conduct? I am really *ashamed*—deeply ashamed of my phrenetic temper. It is no excuse to say I am provoked. I am angry when the effect of the provocation is past and determined. *I am worse than ever I was!* Oh, God!—oh! God! who hearest the anguish and shame of heart it costs me, let me implore Thy Divine Grace and assistance to aid me in over-mastering and expelling from my nature this detestable and disgusting vice! Amen![38]

Unexpectedly, though, just as Macready reached the extreme verge of hysterical self-pity, he found that taking a pop at Bunn—Hot Cross Bunn, as he was now known—had been one of his better career moves. The austere Macready had turned out to be human after all: Boxing Mac was his new name. He was immediately offered an engagement at Covent Garden: he went on, in a terrible panic, as Macbeth, and the whole audience sprang to its feet and cheered. At the end, he could not resist giving a speech. He would only make two observations, he said:

first, that I was subjected in cold blood, from motives which I will not characterize, to a series of studied and annoying and mortifying provocations, personal and professional. The second, that, suffering under these accumulated provocations, I was betrayed, in a moment of unguarded passion, into an intemperate and imprudent act, for which I feel, and shall never cease to feel, the deepest and most poignant self-reproach and regret. It is to you, ladies and gentlemen, and to myself, that I owe this declaration, and I make it with unaf-

fected sincerity. To liberal and generous minds, I think, I need say
no more. I cannot resist thanking you.

"My prayers have been heard!" he sang to his diary that night. "Amen!
Amen! Amen!"[39]

It was at this strangely propitious moment that Edwin Forrest arrived in town.

CHAPTER 5

An American in London

AS THE NEWS spread that the first American star was about to challenge the English on their home ground, Forrest's debut took on the status of an international event.[1] On both sides of the Atlantic, the papers devoted pages to the great match. Was the New World about to prove that it could equal the artistry of the Old, or would the fiercely factional London audiences dare to send him home in disgrace?

It was a risky move for the thirty-year-old Forrest. For almost a decade he had reigned as the undisputed king of American popular culture. Racehorses, fire engines, locomotives, and ships had been named for him. Men modeled their beards, haircuts, and mannerisms after his. Public banquets were thrown and gold medals struck in his honor. When he sailed out of New York City, his fans hired yachts, accompanied him down the harbor, and filled his sails with rounds of cheers. His every movement was trailed in the press, and his approach was the signal for surges of national pride. "Let us support this tender sapling and prove to the pedants of Europe that our soil is fertile in genius and that her children know how to cherish and reward it," a New Orleans paper prompted when Forrest rode back into his old town in triumph.[2] He was the wealthiest actor in the world and nothing less than a national hero; surely, his friends argued, he had no need of European polish to add luster to his name.

Privately, they were not so much worried that Forrest might turn into a raging Anglophile as anxious that America's first star might be sneered off the stage. Since Macready had watched him perform, Forrest had become the cynosure of the Bowery Theatre and its b'hoys, and the b'hoys had become more rambunctious than ever. In the 1830s, as Walt Whitman, a regular visitor, recalled, the Bowery was "no dainty kid-glove business, but electric force and muscle from perhaps 2,000 full-sinew'd men."[3] The pit would surge with excitement at the sight of Forrest foaming at the mouth, his veins bulging, his voice roaring "like the angry sea, lashed into fury by a storm; till, as it reached its boiling, seething climax . . . it was like the falls of Niagara, in its tremendous down-sweeping cadence: it was a whirlwind, a tornado, a cataract of illimitable rage!"[4] His performances were as big as his biceps, and since he had taken up boxing those were beefier than ever. Women, it was said, fainted at his sheer power, and he made tough men cry. His fans wanted a larger-than-life hero who gave them electrifying emotions and stirring sentiment, and Forrest was the genuine article, the fearless, self-reliant republican, the Jacksonian giant from the woods. How he would go down in London's West End was another matter entirely.

Forrest was determined to find out. He might have been known as the Bowery B'hoy's Delight, but ten years of unbroken ascendancy had convinced him that he was a match for any actor in the world. Yet only in London could he put the final seal on his reputation. The city was not just the home of English drama: it was also the greatest metropolis of the English-speaking world. By 1836, its population was nudging two million: seven times that of New York, and hardly less than a seventh that of the entire United States.

Before he left, though, Forrest was careful to reassure his patriotic friends—and preempt any possible failure—by cloaking himself in the stars and stripes. He had accepted the engagement, he insisted at a lavish farewell banquet, for one reason alone: "to solve a doubt which is entertained by many of our citizens, whether Englishmen would receive an American actor with the same favor which is here extended to them." Reports of his speech preceded him to London, where the newspapers rebuked him for doubting that he would be judged fairly. "There are no national prejudices between an audience and an actor," the *Times* optimistically declared, "which could make it for a moment questionable that a deserving artist would be well received."[5]

ON OCTOBER 17, 1836, Forrest thudded onto the stage of the Theatre Royal, Drury Lane, as Spartacus, the slave who took on Rome.* The
U.S. minister attended, along with nearly every American in London,
and the great arena was packed to the roof.

Forrest's oiled calves rippled beneath his short gladiator's skirt. His
oiled chest, polished by twice-daily chafings with rough towels,
gleamed with a marmoreal smoothness. He sprang into action, wielding his sword with freedom's fervor and blasting his captors with defiant scorn. Jaded old London was astonished. It had never seen such
powerful physicality, seldom such sustained intensity or transparent
sincerity, and after a long, shocked silence loud plaudits began to fill
the theatre. Then, halfway through, the mood changed. As the action
mounted and Forrest lashed himself into a positive frenzy of revenge,
murmurs of dissent began to break out, and they grew louder toward
the brutal end when, bathed in blood, groaning his despair to the gods,
he went down writhing and—literally—bit the dust.[6]

This was just the thing to make the Bowery b'hoys roar, but it was
too much for the Theatre Royal, Drury Lane. An uncomfortable silence
descended. As Forrest returned for his curtain call, though, the cheers
burst out again.

"Welcome to England!" the gallery cried.

"I am sure," Forrest beamed, "that you would wish to include the author of the play in the approving verdict which you have given myself."

The cheers turned to boos. "Give us Shakespeare!" the audience
shouted. Forrest was billed as America's leading actor, and Shakespeare
was still the great test.

Within days Forrest obliged, and he was rewarded with a flood of ex-
cited reviews. They were not just the fruits of novelty. There was a lap-

---

* *The Gladiator* was one of the winners of an annual competition Forrest had launched, at twenty-
one, to nurture American playwrights: it earned him more patriotic kudos and furnished him with
some lucrative blood-and-thunder roles. The other notable winner was *Metamora, or The Last of the
Wampanoags*, a highly colored dramatization of the bloodiest war between Native Americans and the
early English colonists, and a play that pulled off a striking double standard. Its hero was a noble
savage: noble enough to pass as a patriotic, freedom-loving American hero, but savage enough to
validate Andrew Jackson's policy of Indian removal. Forrest performed it for forty years, with all his
feeling for his old friend Chief Push-ma-ta-ha and all his loyalty to his political role model.

idary precision to his actions, an iron repose about his stage presence, that attested to a natural gift honed by hard practice, and an occasional novel and arresting reading that hinted at the years of study he had put in to make up for his patchy education. But it was his hearty humor, his startling way of plunging from savage fury to dewy-eyed tenderness, and above all his sheer brawn that proved just what melodrama-mad Londoners had been looking for. "His figure is cast in the proportions of the Farnese Hercules," the *Atlas* sighed. He was almost too muscular, it added, but "his head and neck are perfect models of grandeur in the order to which they belong." The *Globe* took him more seriously: he was a scholar and master, and his performance as Othello was "far, far superior to the manner in which any other of our living performers could attempt it." The *Sun*'s review, though, was the most revealing of mainstream London's tastes. Forrest, it acknowledged, was not, strictly speaking, a classical actor: he was not "burdened with refined sensibility, which none but the select few can understand; far otherwise; he gives free play to those rough natural passions which are intelligible all the world over." Yet he had made the greatest hit since Kean, and proved himself "the first tragedian of the age. . . . If any one can revive the half-extinct taste for the drama, he is the man."[7]

Not every critic was equally fulsome. A few insinuated that the American was not first-rate in Shakespeare, and one or two snidely detected a twang of the backwoods in his accent; his voice, one particularized, was "replete with a rough music befitting one who in his youth has dwelt, a free barbarian, among the mountains." Several noted that he could only play the hero: guilt and weakness were not in his makeup, and he looked ridiculously healthy as Richard III, "curtail'd of this fair proportion, / Cheated of feature by dissembling nature, / Deform'd, unfinish'd . . ."[8]

But only one voice spoke out repeatedly against him, and that voice belonged to Macready's devoted ally, John Forster.

MACREADY HAD BEEN following Forrest's progress with close attention. Even before he made his debut, the Englishman asked around town for the visitor's address, and at his fourth attempt he ran into him. This, their first meeting, went unexpectedly well.

Pictured at thirty on the eve of his London debut, Forrest is at his most romantic in this painting by Thomas Sully. The Art Archive/Garrick Club.

"Liked him much," Macready told his diary that night—"a noble appearance, and a manly, mild, and interesting demeanor. I welcomed him—wished him much success, and invited him to my house." Later in the day he heard that Forrest was likely to be a hit: "This I could *sincerely wish,*" he added, "while it did no injury to myself."[9]

Macready's outbreak of goodwill was all the more remarkable since Alfred Bunn had blatantly orchestrated the American's appearance as a personal showdown with Bunn's erstwhile assailant. For days before Forrest's debut, Bunn had planted puff pieces in his pet journals, speciously boasting that he had spared no expense to make Drury Lane fit for the American tragedian, reminding London of Forrest's precocious fame, denouncing "the melodramatic jerks and pumpings of Mr. Macready" as the marks of a "bitter bad" actor, and daring the Eminent's "phrensied partisans" to show their teeth.[10] One piece declared that Macready's friends would rather see Forrest hang than act. When Forrest, to Bunn's surprise, turned out to be a hit, he plastered the town with playbills that took jabs at Macready by announcing the visitor as "The Eminent *American* Tragedian," adding that his enthusiastic reception had stamped him as "one of the Greatest Actors that ever graced an English Theatre" and "the most extraordinary actor of the day."[11] Macready's bile rose, but for once he had the sense to bear his cross with rueful grace. Despite the warnings, his inner circle had turned out in force to size up the opposition, and when one of them called with the verdict—Forrest was a very good actor, he reported, but not a great one—Macready was surprised. "I cannot of course have, as yet, any opinion," he responded, "but this I know, that when I saw him nine years ago, he had everything within him to make a very great actor."[12]

Macready was undoubtedly feeling more charitable than usual in the wake of the Bunn debacle, but he had a better reason to be hospitable to the American. Ever since his first trip across the Atlantic, Macready had been an outspoken admirer of the United States, and he was glad of the chance to demonstrate his fraternal feelings toward the New World. It was a sharp irony, given his later role as the symbol of an oppressive aristocracy, that the Englishman was in truth a radical democrat and a diehard republican. England, he repeatedly pronounced, was long overdue its own revolution. He shuddered at the absurdity of worshipping geriatric men and teenage girls who paraded around town like gilded puppets tricked out in tinsel and feathers: the royals, he groaned, were no better than actors. He bristled with indignation at paying taxes to support stupid aristocrats who thought only of their position and ignored the welfare of the oppressed, defrauded, and brutalized people— "such disgusting blots on humanity as these things called *Lords* generally are," he grimaced when Lord Hertford, the model for Lord Steyne in *Vanity Fair,* tried to foist a prostitute on the salary list at Drury Lane.[13] "Oh, when will Humanity *rise up* and assert itself? When will the holy vengeance of a world mash its canting and gripping oppressors?" he implored in his diary. "When shall retribution pour down upon the heads of these accursed aristocrats? Be it soon!!!"[14] His wrath was strengthened, though his case weakened, by the fact that this last outburst was occasioned by the lord chamberlain's decision to grant a rival manager an extension on his license; but for all his soreness at his own supplicant status, Macready's principles were deeply held. England, he was certain, would decline because it was governed by a self-interested class, while America would rise up the champion of freedom. He even took care to commemorate the anniversaries of the Declaration of Independence: "I, as one of the great family of mankind that have profited by that event, thank God for it," he wrote one year: "How much has the great cause of liberty and improvement been advanced by it!"[15] He was so firm in his convictions that he had seriously begun to think of disentangling his family from the English class system and emigrating across the Atlantic.

Within days of his first meeting with Forrest, Macready followed up with a formal note of invitation. The next morning he called on him again: finding him away he left another note. "My dear Sir," he wrote,

I was disappointed in not finding you at home this morning, when I called to offer you my congratulations on the fervent welcome you received last night, and on the universal testimony that is paid to your distinguished talent. My visit had the double object of pressing on you the contents of my note from Elstree, and hoping for the occasion of improving my acquaintance with you during your sojourn in the old country.—May I hope for the pleasure of seeing you on Saturday & Sunday—Pray, if not better engaged, consent to spend two dull days with us.[16]

When the reviews began trumpeting Forrest's peerless talent, Macready's magnanimity started to slip: his heart, he flapped, was chafed, bruised, and almost crushed, and the only surprise was that he had not ended it all long ago. "It would be stupid and shallow hypocrisy to say that I was indifferent to the result—careless whether he is likely to be esteemed more or less than myself," he admitted a few days later. "It is of great importance to me to retain my superiority, and my wishes for his success follow the desire I have to be considered above him! Is this illiberal? I hope not."[17] Illiberal it may have been, but it was hardly uncommon in the top ranks of his precarious profession, and despite his anxiety he wrote to Forster urging him to deal liberally and kindly by Forrest in the *Examiner.*

Forster was having none of it. He was convinced that a group hostile to Macready was maneuvering to chastise his friend by elevating the American, and he told him so. "This is ungenerous," Macready recorded, "but as I did not wish to be an ungenerous rival to [Forrest], I again re-

quested Forster not to write in harshness or hostility upon his performance. He was very peremptory and distinct in his expressed resolution to
keep his own course."[18]

The twenty-four-year old Forster, as always, did just that. He was a
burly young man with an awkward, brusque, self-inflated way about
him: his enemies sneered that he had never gotten over being the son of
a butcher. He was extraordinarily loyal to Macready, but he could also
be a pigheaded and indiscreet ally.[19] Two days later, Macready read an
advance copy of his piece. "It gave me great pain," he wrote. "I thought
it ill-natured and not just—omitting all mention of his merit, with the
enumeration of his faults. I would have done much to have prevented it.
Forster came, and I expressed candidly my dissatisfaction to him."[20]
Macready was genuinely distressed by Forster's determination to be
outspoken: their intimacy was well known, and it put him in a deeply
awkward position.

The next day Macready nervously went ahead with his Sunday lunch
party for the American actor. Forrest arrived while he was dressing:
Macready called him in, introduced him to his friends—Robert Browning was among them—and asked him to take Catherine down to dinner.
With his tousled hair and frank grin, Forrest still looked disarmingly
youthful, but he proved an unexpectedly courteous and charming guest.
Prior to his London engagement, he had put his career on hold for two
years and sent himself on a grand tour of Europe, the old privilege of the
English aristocracy; typically, he had gone further than most tourists—
to Odessa, where he fell in love with a married Polish countess, before
working his way through the Crimea to Constantinople and Greece, taking in palaces, paintings, and monuments and, as his diary records, a
generous sample of the continent's whores.[21] Though he refrained from
mentioning his three-a-night trysts over dinner, he turned out to be an
engaging raconteur, and it was, Macready thought, an agreeable and
cheerful afternoon.

Forster, meanwhile, carried on with his increasingly sarcastic slasher
jobs. Forrest's performances, he sneered, were murderous attacks on
Shakespeare. The American, he averred, had no intellectual comprehension of what he was about: he merely copied Kean's more vulgar points,
his alternate ranting and whining, rather than trying to understand his

characters or represent true passion. Forrest would start a line—"Yield up, O Love, thy crown and hearted throne"—in a syrupy sentimental tone, pause for effect, then howl out the end—"to tyrannous hate!"— until the words rang off the walls. His Richard III was all "hideous looks and furious gestures, ear-splitting shouts and stage-devouring strides," and at the end, when his wig tumbled down during the fight with Richmond so he could shake the locks, he looked like "a savage newly caught from out of the American backwoods." Worst of all was his "very bad and very ignorant" Macbeth: it was a series of cheap tricks, which simplistically illustrated Shakespeare's words but never came near connecting into a plausible character. He started and gasped nervously at peals of thunder; he triumphantly thumped his truncheon on his chest. He backed stealthily across the stage, his dagger dripping, after murdering Duncan, until he brushed Lady Macbeth's hand and leaped away with a tremendous shudder, and when the messenger delivered the news that Birnam Wood was moving "he exhibited a most lusty despair, for . . . he lifted the unfortunate officer bodily from the ground and fairly flung him off the stage!" His Thane, Forster concluded, was his Richard III in a kilt: "Not a single ray of the genius of Shakespeare's wonderful Macbeth flickered upon Mr Forrest from the commencement to the close."[22]

Perhaps, a fretting Macready tried, Forster could disclaim any personal animosity and pay tribute to the American's private character. Forster demurred. He was convinced that the Forrest craze was a dangerous trend, and he was determined to stamp it out. "There is a vicious style in art," he expounded in his paper, "which the public taste should be carefully guarded against, and Mr Forrest is one of its professors." National politeness, he added as a non-apology apology, had nothing to do with objective criticism.[23]

Macready was alarmed. He asked Willis Jones, Forrest's agent, to come to his dressing room, and inquired when the American's engagement was likely to close. He should like, he said, to pay some professional compliment to him: "I wish him to be pleased with his visit," he explained. And, he added, getting more and more trapped in grammatical involutions, while they were speaking on the subject—in strict confidence—he wished to observe that the articles which were so severe in the *Examiner*—having been written by Mr. Forster, a particular friend of his—he begged to assure him that, knowing Mr. Forster's opinion of Mr. Forrest to be less flattering than that of other persons and other newspapers, he had used all his influence with him—by word of mouth, by writing, and by the mediation of friends—to induce him to abandon his intention of expressing an unfavorable opinion; he had yielded partially in his first review, but had peremptorily and repeatedly refused to suppress or qualify his opinions on the subsequent performances.

Jones admitted that the greenroom gossip said the reviews came through Macready. But, he added, Forrest had never paid any attention to the insinuations: he had been more gratified by Macready's kind attentions than by anything else he had met with in London.

Forrest's gratitude was not misreported by his agent: he was genuinely moved by the older actor's eagerness to welcome him. Among all his new English friends, he wrote home to his mother, Macready had "behaved in the handsomest manner to me. Before I arrived in England, he had spoken of me in the most flattering terms, and on my arrival he embraced the earliest opportunity to call upon me, since which time he has extended to me many delicate courtesies and attentions, all showing the native kindness of his heart, and great refinement and good breeding."[24] Despite Forster's worst efforts, their acquaintance had started off on an auspicious footing.

Forrest stayed in England for several more months, alternating tours of the provinces with weeks at Drury Lane. His one setback came when he fell foul of the dreaded Bunn, which endeared him to Macready even more. Bunn reduced his new star to two performances a week, then to one, and twice Forrest turned up to find that the program had been changed and he was not wanted at all. He raised his fist at the dastardly manager, but held back the blow and instead withdrew from the theatre, "in consequence," he wrote home, "of a want of etiquette on the part of the Manager who by the way cannot behave well to any body."[25] On reflection Bunn decided he was glad he had had to fight the Englishman and not the American.

Forrest's American friends would later claim that his London debut had been an unqualified triumph. It was not quite that. But he had passed the test: he had played before audiences and critics who, he admitted in another letter to his mother, were more knowledgeable than their peers back home, and though the reaction had been divided, as a good republican he was sure he ought to be satisfied that the overwhelming majority was on his side. "I never have been more successful, even in my own dear land," he concluded. "In the characters of Shakespeare alone would they hear me; and night after night in overwhelming crowds they came, and showered their hearty applause on my efforts."[26]

By now, except for a brief trip home at the end of his grand tour, Forrest had been away from his beloved America for the best part of three years, and he was feeling homesick. There was only one thing to hold him back. He had fallen in love with the eldest daughter of the genial, handsome John Sinclair, a popular ballad singer whom Macready knew well. Catharine—Kate—Sinclair was nineteen, strikingly good-looking and accomplished, with advanced musical and theatrical tastes. Her eyes flashed with intelligence, and despite her ingenuous expression she was coquettishly forward—a charming trait, Forrest thought at the time. She was the only woman he had ever thought of marrying.

"O, if she were only an American!" Forrest sighed to Henry Wikoff, his companion on his grand tour, soon after meeting Kate for the first time. "I would marry her tomorrow, if she were of the same mind."

He was talking nonsense, Wikoff declared: it was not Kate's fault that she was born on the wrong side of the Atlantic.

"True, most veritable," Forrest moped, "but I am resolved. None but an American for me."[27]

Love conquered nationalism, and the most American of men proposed to an Englishwoman. Kate was equally smitten with her dashing foreign suitor. The first time she saw him a thrill ran through her: "This is the handsomest man on whom my eyes have ever fallen," she whispered to herself.[28] On June 21, 1837, under a burning sun, the streets, windows, and rooftops of London were choked with crowds cheering the eighteen-year-old Princess Victoria as she progressed through the city to be proclaimed queen. Two days later, Edwin and Kate were married at St. Paul's, Covent Garden, the actors' church. The brief announcement of the wedding appeared in the papers between heavy black borders, for Britain was still mourning its dead king. Yet death had filled the air with youth, and all the guests said they had never seen such a beautiful and promising young couple. No one predicted that before long this seemingly happy event would prove a cause for scandal and grief.

JUNE 1837 WAS an equally memorable month for Macready. He had only been back at Covent Garden for a year when the managers once again ran out of money and resigned, and as the old king and the old era lay dying Macready opened negotiations to take over the theatre. It was a huge risk, but it was matched by a grand ambition: nothing less than to elevate the dignity and standing of the English stage. If all went well, he would leave the theatre newly respectable, with the educated classes returned and Shakespeare restored to his rightful realm—and by the same stroke his own reputation gilded, his conscience salved, and the Poet Bunn outplayed. The day after Victoria rode into London, the management committee accepted his plan, and Macready became lessee of the Theatre Royal, Covent Garden.

Battle commenced. Macready issued a notice of his managership in which he spelled out his high principles: it was a matter of notoriety, he declared, that the National Drama was in a distressed state, and he promised his "strenuous efforts *to advance the drama as a branch of national literature and art.*" Bunn replied with his own address: it was a matter of notoriety, he echoed, that the distressed state of the theatres was entirely the fault of greedy actors, and he would continue his humble exertions "to sustain the character Drury Lane has long enjoyed of being the FIRST THEATRE OF THE EMPIRE."[29]

On the morning of September 30, Macready set out from Elstree, leaving behind an anxious Catherine—anxious about the toll the enterprise would take on her husband's querulous temper—and took the coach to his theatre. On stage, the new company was gathering for its first rehearsal. The familiar dirty daylight seeped in through the ventilators and cobwebbed windows, the throat-tickling scent of seeping gas thickened the air, but as the actors paced around in their day clothes, looking for a ray of light in which to make out their lines, there was real anticipation in their faces. Love him or hate him, everyone agreed that Macready was the only one among them who could bring acting into repute.

By opening night Kemble's old theatre had been splendidly spruced up. The seats were newly upholstered and the boxes newly lined, the chandelier was freshly sparkling, the walls freshly painted in vermilion, white, and gold, and the ceiling an airy azure blue. A tidal wave of cheers hit Macready as he came forward to give his opening address; he was so overcome that he ground to a halt and stood flustered and confused. Yet within days the receipts fell off steeply and he started to panic. To his fury, Bunn was drawing huge crowds with the Kentucky-born animal trainer Isaac Van Amburgh, a glamorous daredevil who wrestled with lions, leopards, and tigers and so delighted the young queen that she saw his show seven times in six weeks.[30]*

Macready toiled nervously away. He planned out elaborate sets, full-sized mechanical shipwrecks and sieges involving giant assault towers, and he pored over every detail with the artists, carpenters, and painters.[31] He read hundreds of new plays, most of them complete nonsense, and adapted several new pieces himself. Like every star he continued to arrange his fellow actors around him like furniture, but he jettisoned the old lines of casting in favor of deploying the strength of the whole company; even more radically, he orchestrated the action down to the last face in a crowd—and with two or three hundred extras in the great set-piece scenes, the price was hours of foot-numbing rehearsals every day. For a while nothing seemed to work, and when even his much-touted Shakespearean revivals aroused little excitement he began to think he had thrown away all his time, toil, and money on a hopeless cause.

Then came *King Lear*—not the *Lear* that everyone knew, but the *Lear* that Shakespeare wrote.

---

* When the queen requested a private audience with the lions the rumor spread that she was sleeping with the trainer. Victoria was quintessentially Victorian in her escapist tastes: she was particularly fond of French drama and Italian opera, though she also loved a trashy farce, a spectacular pantomime or circus act, a historical romance or a gory melodrama. Her absolute favorites were gory French romantic historical melodramas. She took equal delight in lowbrow sensations like the six-year-old General Tom Thumb, whom P. T. Barnum brought to Buckingham Palace three times in 1844. Altogether, Victoria was not helpful to Macready's mission to restore dignity to the English stage. In one year the queen attended the theatre forty-nine times: she saw thirty-two operas and fourteen French plays, and the nearest she came to English drama was the last act of a piece by an Irish-born writer. For six years she managed to avoid seeing a single Shakespeare play. Macready was not alone in complaining that her tastes were too lowbrow and foreign: the newspapers regularly attacked her for neglecting the native drama.

FOR ALL ITS surges of Bardolatry, England had long had a divided attitude toward its greatest writer.*

In 1840 Thomas Carlyle delivered a lecture entitled "The Hero as Poet." "Consider," he proposed, "what this Shakespeare has actually become among us. Which Englishman we ever made, in this land of ours, which million of Englishmen, would we not give up rather than the Stratford Peasant? There is no regiment of highest Dignitaries that we would sell him for. He is the grandest thing we have yet done." England, he vowed, would surrender its Indian empire before it would relinquish Shakespeare.[32] Yet Carlyle was never a fan of the stage, and he had no truck with the concept of Shakespeare as a man of the theatre. In the same speech he witheringly dismissed theatre managers as the most insignificant of human beings, no doubt forgetting that his friend Macready was sitting blushing in the audience. Like many of his Romantic generation, Carlyle saw Shakespeare as a poet to be read, not a playwright to be performed: the Bard, he was convinced, was simply too good for the stage.

The theatre itself was his evidence, because what it peddled as Shakespeare was often a far cry from the real thing. Ever since the Restoration, playwrights had been "improving" Shakespeare's plays with such enthusiasm that large stretches of the originals had vanished from the stage without a trace. *Romeo and Juliet* was a case in point. Sir William Davenant, who purported to be Shakespeare's illegitimate son, was the first to attack it, in 1662; in 1679, Thomas Otway remade it into a toga piece about Roman politics which was about a quarter Shakespeare and held the stage for seventy years; and in 1744 Colley Cibber, the "hero" of the final version of the *Dunciad,* Pope's bitter satire on literary dullness, mashed together the original, Otway's version, and a chunk of *The Two Gentlemen of Verona.* Even David Garrick, the great Bardolater, cut the "jingle and quibble," the

---

* The official neglect of England's national poet was crystallized in 1847 when the government refused to purchase Shakespeare's birthplace for the nation. By then the cottage was nearly derelict: a butcher's shop was operating out of the front room. At one point P. T. Barnum attempted to buy it and ship it to his museum in New York City, though eventually a committee was set up to fend him off; Macready performed a benefit for the cause.

unfashionable rhymes and puns, added an elaborate masque and a stately funeral procession, made Juliet a respectable young woman of eighteen rather than Shakespeare's girl of fourteen, excised Rosaline, Romeo's earlier love, cut most of Mercutio's sublimely ribald lines, and rewrote the ending to give himself a star's death. In Garrick's version, which was performed in place of the original for almost a century, Juliet wakes up in the charnel house before Romeo dies and the lovers pour out seventy long lines penned by the great actor. "Bless me! how cold it is! who's there?" Juliet begins, and Romeo, at first so transported with joy that he forgets he has just swallowed a bottle of poison, drags her out of the tomb and collapses from the effort. "Death's in thy face!" recoils Juliet. "It is indeed—I struggle with him now," her lover replies:

> My powers are blasted,
> 'Twixt death and love I'm torn—I am distracted!
> But death's strongest—and must I leave thee, Juliet![33]

And after all the self-explication, the lesson was left in the wings, for there was no time for a reconciliation between the warring families.* Garrick was a showman as well as a Shakespearean—as Hamlet, he famously wore a hydraulically assisted wig whose hairs stood on end when the Ghost appeared—and when the star expired the play was done.

For all his temptation to tinker with the Bard—late in his career he rewrote the entire ending of *Hamlet,* which until then had largely survived the slaughter—Garrick also restored large stretches of the plays, and it would be unfair to label him a Shakespearean sacrilegist. But in Macready's time, many of the old stage adaptations still clung on, and among them was the most notorious "improved" version of all, Nahum Tate's 1681 *King Lear:* the *Lear* with the happy ending.

Like his fellow revisionists, Tate was convinced he was performing a

---

* Garrick added a shorter but similarly self-dramatizing speech to the end of *Macbeth.* Hell, Macbeth howls,

> drags me down. I sink,
> I sink—Oh!—my soul is lost forever!
> Oh! [He dies.]

service by refashioning the plays of a primitive genius for a more refined age, and he dedicated his new *Lear* to one Thomas Boteler, who first came up with the idea. "I found the whole," he explained in his preface, "to answer your Account of it, a Heap of Jewels, unstrung and unpolisht; yet so dazling in their Disorder, that I soon perceiv'd I had seiz'd a Treasure."[34] Seize it he did, and he polished so hard that there was precious little left.

Like all of Shakespeare's greatest tragedies, *Lear* refuses to offer neat explanations for its characters' actions and so raises all sorts of teasing questions. Why does Cordelia, Lear's favorite daughter, refuse to speak up about how much she loves her father in order to inherit her third of the kingdom? Why does Lear disown her so peremptorily? Why is Edmund, the Duke of Gloucester's bastard son, so sadistically vindictive that he frames his half-brother Edgar for planning parricide? Why does the fugitive Edgar elaborately disguise himself as a mad beggar and hide out on the heath? The result, as we try to find answers, is that the characters take on a life outside of the play.* Tate's *Lear,* on the other hand, solves problems, and so replaces the complexities of character with the simplicities of plot. In Tate's version, Edgar and Cordelia start off the play as lovers: Cordelia refuses to express her feelings for her father because she would rather risk disinheritance than submit to an arranged marriage with the Duke of Burgundy. Lear is therefore politically as well as personally disappointed in her. Edmund is renamed "Bastard," which tells us all we need to know about why he turned out bad. Edgar dons his disguise so he can stay close at hand and watch over Cordelia. He gets his chance when Edmund sets his murderous brigands on her; Edgar beats them off and the two lovers tryst wordily in a dry shed, on a bed of straw, in front of a fire, at the end of which, Cordelia announces grandly,

> Bold in my Virgin Innocence, I'll fly
> My Royal Father to Relieve, or Die,

---

* Cordelia's love, we might hypothesize, is genuine: to enter a hyperbolic contest would be to defile it. Lear's long reign has left him susceptible to flattery and unable to brook the truth. Edmund's malice has been fostered by the stigma of illegitimacy and his father's belittling behavior. Edgar, secure in his feudal identity, would rather be nothing than something other than himself.

though in fact Lear has been wandering around the heath throughout their love-in, baring his houseless head to the pitiless storm. At the end, in place of Shakespeare's depleted and exhausted kingdom, Lear is restored to sense and the throne; he crowns Cordelia queen, gives her hand to Edgar, and retires to a carefree dotage. Peace spreads her balmy wings, plenty blooms, and the last line proclaims the moral of the whole exercise: that "Truth and Vertue shall at last succeed." As well as tipping his cap to Restoration politics, Tate ironed out almost every pregnant phrase; the whole thing was lumpy, meretricious, and inert, and yet it kept Shakespeare's original off the stage for more than a hundred and fifty years.[35]*

Macready's *Lear* was all Shakespeare and no Tate. He worked painstakingly on the text, planned the production down to the last detail of the costumes worn by each of the dozens of retainers, spear-carriers, and knights, and rehearsed for weeks. At first the audience watched in rapt silence; then, after Lear had borne his daughter's body on stage and his last, despairing struggle had ended with a quiet sigh, slowly the cheers built into a rapturous roar. Macready had triumphantly proved that Shakespeare's most challenging play could be successfully put on stage: John Forster was not alone in predicting that his friend's daring return to Shakespeare would resound "to his lasting honour."[36] Most famously of all, Macready had even restored the Fool—the sweet and bitter Fool, the voice of reason in a topsy-turvy world, whose merry sarcasm shivers away to silence in the storm—a character who had long been deemed unplayable and inappropriate to tragedy and plucked out. It was the defining moment in the long process of restoring authentic Shakespeare to the stage, and from that day forward "Tatification" became a Victorian term of abuse.

Over his four years as a manager—two at Covent Garden and two, satisfyingly, at Drury Lane, the old lion's den, from which a bankrupt Bunn had finally been ejected—Macready rescued nearly all of Shakespeare's plays.† After *Lear*, the greatest revelation was *The Tempest*,

---

* For instance, Cordelia's "Unhappy that I am, I cannot heave / My heart into my mouth" came from Tate's pen as "Unhappy am I that I can't dissemble."

† One of the exceptions was the *Richard III* cobbled together by Colley Cibber from bits of *Henry IV Part 2*, *Henry V*, *Henry VI*, and *Richard II*. Together with Cibber's own interpolations it was about one-third authentic, and yet its melodramatic appeal was so strong that it held the stage throughout the nineteenth century.

which Davenant and John Dryden had buried under *The Enchanted Isle,* a "corrected" musical adaptation that retained barely a third of Shakespeare's lines and added a host of new characters, including a pair of comedy sailors. "After Dryden had poured a tide of filth into the pure waters of the Tempest, after the pedantic doctoring of Garrick, and the unscrupulous 'snipping' and transposing of Cibber, the drama after having been nearly entombed by the detritus piled upon it, rose like a Phoenix from its ashes, and soared in the purified heaven, its pinions free, and its flight right sunward," one critic panegyrized. "The expense was enormous, the risk was great, and the undertaking was altogether unequalled."[37]

Macready had become a Great Victorian. He was the savior of the stage, the restorer of Shakespeare, and he became equally renowned as the defender of middle-class morals. At Covent Garden he had set out to prove what the Puritans had so long denied, that the theatre could survive without the card-carrying women of the saloon. He had no legal right to turn paying customers away, but he had swept into the upper tiers of the house the few whores who insisted on turning up. At Drury Lane, he went further: not only the pit and lower boxes, he announced, but also the grand saloon and the upper boxes with their private anterooms were to be "strictly protected from all improper intrusion." Hookers were confined to the gallery, which "they could only reach by a separate pay-office, and by passing through a dismantled lobby, where the walls were purposely left unpainted and unpapered, in which no seat of any kind was placed, and which was constantly patrolled by a policeman."[38]* Macready was hell-bent on scouring away every vestige of Regency sleaze and every reminder of his own troubled past.

Yet for all the kudos it earned him, management was double toil and trouble to such a high-strung man. Visitors found him stretched on his couch after a performance, a gaunt apparition whose curled mop of iron-

---

* Even so, some slipped through with the assistance of the saloonkeeper, who became increasingly abusive as he realized that Macready had wrecked his sinecure, and there were unseemly quarrels as screaming harlots were dragged out of the boxes. "I was in this theatre long before you came to it, and I hope I'll be in it after you are gone!" one saloon woman spat at the stage manager (Add 52478 ff. 214–15, British Library).

gray hair poked out over a woolen robe; continually interrupted by business, attentive to everyone, but almost too tired to talk.[39] The demands were unceasing, and one theatrical paper caught the overwhelmed manager in full flow:

> Where is the tailor-man, that Head, fool, brute, beast, ass? How dare you annoy me, sir, in this manner? Have you got a soul or sense . . . Look, who wrote these calls? Gentlemen, look about you, read for yourselves: here is "Macbeth" spelt "Mackbeth" and Mr. Serle's "Afrancesado" spelt "Haffrancishardo." . . . Who is that talking at the wings? Henry! Henry! go down and tell the stage door-keeper I expect him to go away—to leave the theatre immediately. . . . Mr. Forster—oh, show Mr. Forster to my room! no, stop! My dear Dickens, how d'ye do? Talfourd! your hand; another and another! Browning! Bulwer!—a—a—walk into the green-room. Mr. Bender, get on; why do you wait? Where is Mr. Willmott? I— I—this is exceedingly bad! Will you make a beginning? Where are the—the officers? Where is that—a—Paulo man? Mr. Beckett? Mr. Smith? What cat is that? Do—do—do—a—a—a—a—damn it! are you all asleep? . . . Why do we wait, gentlemen? The band? I—I really will enforce fines without any respect of persons. . . . Where's the supernumerary-master? Sir, I desired you not to employ that person without stockings. Do—do find me decent, intelligent men. Gentlemen of the band, be kind enough to discuss your—a—a—*on dits*—outside the theatre. It is—it is—a—a—preposterous. . . . What is that horrible hubbub in the green-room? I—I—really I— Where is the gas-man? Are we rehearsing the—the—a—Black Hole of Calcutta? Do—do—do—pray lighten our darkness. Man, I have spoken several times about these pewter pots. I—I will not have the theatre turned into a—a cookshop. . . . You—you—you cannot possibly dine at ten o'clock in the morning. . . . Send in your beds, gentlemen; let us have a—a—a caravansary at once.[40]

All the time Bunn's cheerers-on in the press—from raffish penny papers like the *Satirist* all the way to the august *Sunday Times*—kept up their daily imputations of stupidity, dullness, and meanness, fawning, bribery, and insolence, particularly when the Eminent retaliated by striking them off the free list; at one point, a fierce pamphlet war broke out between his disciples and his disparagers. Worst of all, though, by the end Macready was out of pocket to the tune of thousands of pounds.*

Respect was one thing, but it was not going to send his children to school. In March 1843, Macready turned fifty, and a month later he made up his mind to quit management and set off on a second tour of America. His friends were nearly as disconsolate as Catherine, who hated the idea of losing him for another long stretch. For four years, Dickens had been at his side nearly every day: "I ought not to be sorry to hear of your abdication," he wrote to his friend, "but I am notwithstanding—most heartily and sincerely sorry, for my own sake and the sake of thousands who may now go and whistle for a Theatre—at least such a Theatre as you gave them."⁴¹ Forster had virtually lived in the theatre; he had infuriated the actors with his constant interjections during rehearsals. "Put her through it again, Mac!" he called out whenever a mistake-prone actress slipped up. Once he had even tried to correct Macready's reading of a line from Shakespeare, a piece of presumption that got short shrift.

On the Eminent's last night—*Macbeth,* of course—the whole house rose to its feet, waved, shouted, and stamped, and made such a thunderous noise that he was overcome yet again. A ceremonial banquet followed, at which he was presented with a retirement gift, a shocking piece of silver-plated statuary that depicted Shakespeare standing on a pedestal with Macready seated at the base, attended by the muses while restoring his texts. He always agonized over these public occasions: he would sit pale and quiet, turning his speech over in his mind, until he caught Catherine's eyes gleaming with pride in the gallery, and then his own eyes filled with tears, he steadied himself with a glass of sherry, and he stood up to do his duty. That night, for the first time, he recognized a genuine outpouring of love from his friends and well-wishers—and

---

* At one point his negotiations with the proprietors became so strained that he turned up in the morning and found his costumes had been impounded.

yet, as he walked out down the cheering aisle, he felt disgusted with himself and sick of it all. What, in the end, was the point?

Like the lives of so many of the new professionals in that God-fearing age that listened to Carlyle and produced Thomas Macaulay and John Stuart Mill, Macready's life was a reaction against the trashy flamboyance of the Regency. Macready, the devoted family man, the conscientious scholar, the pious prude, the self-flagellating moralist, the middle-class radical, the faintly ridiculous self-obsessive, was in wholehearted sympathy with the new spirit of commerce, growth, and reform. Yet despite his best efforts, the theatre, with its motley audience of bohemians, dandies, rowdy laborers, and stage-struck stargazers, seemed to be becoming steadily more irrelevant. In America it was a vital, fresh force; in Britain it was out of touch with the greater purposes of the nation, a sideshow at best, a freaks' gallery at worst, while behind the curtain it was all fury and tatters. Through the applause, Macready heard the sound of history, and history was silent.

Macready's almost pathological pursuit of intellectual credibility and social respectability had at long last made him the right actor for his age. Yet he had grown up in another age, when the great national theatres dominated the nation's culture as they never would again. The victims of urban sprawl and class polarization, they had tried to attract everyone and managed to please no one, and their time was over. The city's leaders finally woke up to the ludicrous anomaly that suburban audiences were barred from edifying dramas and forced to watch rope-vaulters, dancing dogs, and pigs that could spell, and the minor theatres stopped bothering to have a pianist strike a chord once every five minutes to pretend they were staging a musical. One playhouse opened in blatant defiance of the law just around the corner from Drury Lane; when the ticket sellers were barred from taking money at the doors they took it at a window instead, and though after two years the theatre was forcibly closed down and the actors were summoned to court and fined, a year and a public outcry later it reopened in full sight of the law.[42] In the year Macready resigned, the patents were finally abolished. Soon afterward, Covent Garden burned down again and was rebuilt to house opera and ballet. Bunn resurfaced at Drury Lane and clung on until

1852, after which he was bankrupted, driven into exile, and died at Boulogne. Then the circus moved in, and for long stretches the most famous theatre in the world shut its doors.

It was time to leave. Macready kissed his children and took the new railway from London to Liverpool, with Catherine and Letitia, thrown together as always, at his side to see him off. Forster was already there, waiting to ferry them to the *Caledonia,* one of the new Cunard paddle steamers that had recently inaugurated the first scheduled transatlantic service. The next day Macready said his goodbyes and watched from the rail, a thin, graying man of fifty, as the sun set and the soft moon rose and the lights of England sank into the sea.

ONLY ONE DISCORDANT note had been struck: Dickens had refused to take part in his send-off.

Dickens and Macready had become inseparable. Their natures were poles apart, but the Inimitable Boz loved and revered the Eminent Tragedian.[43] Dickens shyly presented the actor with clumsy farces and was impossibly gracious when one after another was found wanting. He dreamed of Macready's performances and stored up their images and passions, the substance, he said, which they impressed on unsubstantial thoughts, to feast on wherever he went. His letters to his friend were full of loving encouragement: "The multitude of new tokens by which I know you for a great man," he wrote, "the swelling within me of my love for you, the pride I have in you, the majestic reflection I see in you of all the passions and affectations that make up our mystery, throw me into a strange kind of transport that has no expression but in a mute sense of attachment, which, in truth and fervency, is worthy of its subject."[44] Their families had become intertwined: the actor was godfather to Kate Macready Dickens, the novelist's third child, while Dickens was godfather to Macready's son Henry, and the two clans regularly vacationed together. When Charles and Catherine Dickens had traveled to America the previous year, they had left their three children and new baby in the care of William and Catherine Macready; when Macready was away on a tour, Dickens took his wife dancing, performed conjuring acts for his children, and wrote teasing letters to the actor about what a good time they had had, always followed by ardent wishes to hug him and fold him in his arms. Their intimacy was widely known, and it was fixed in print when Dickens dedicated *Nicholas Nickleby* to his friend.*

Yet as soon as Macready announced his intention to tour America, Dickens became convinced that their friendship would spell the actor's doom. The trouble was his own recent American trip. On his return he had published an account of his travels that sent America apoplectic, and he had followed it with a novel, *Martin Chuzzlewit,* that caricatured Yankees so unsparingly that he had started receiving transatlantic hate mail.

At first Dickens decided to go to Liverpool, but stay in hiding rather than risk the pleasure of shaking his friend's hand on board his ship. The steamer, he explained, "will be crowded with Americans at this time of the year; and believe me, they are not the people you suppose them to be. So strongly have I felt that my accompanying you on board, would be, after the last *Chuzzlewit,* FATAL to your success, and certain to bring down upon you every species of insult and outrage, that I have all along determined within myself to remain in the Hotel, and charge the Landlord to keep my being there, a secret."[45] But even that, on reflection, seemed dangerous, and he decided to stay as far away as possible.

Dickens's paranoia verged on the hysterical, but relations between Britain and America had become so strained that he really believed he was right to fear for his dear friend's life.

---

* Macready was immensely moved, though it is not hard to imagine what he thought of the novel's affectionately caustic portrait of Vincent Crummles and his threadbare troupe of provincial actors.

CHAPTER 6

⊶≪≫⊷

Cross Currents

ENGLISH TRAVELERS HAD been taking an ax to America's foundations long before Charles Dickens arrived. Transatlantic travelogues had become a mini industry in Britain, and the more savage the rhetoric, the better they sold. Five years before his own trip, Dickens had poked fun at the trade in *The Pickwick Papers.* "Have a passage ready taken for 'Merriker," advises Mr. Weller, who has hatched a plot to extract Pickwick from the Fleet Prison inside a gutted grand piano, "and then let him come back and write a book about the 'Merrikins as'll pay all his expenses, and more, if he blows 'em up enough."[1] There seemed no end to Britain's appetite for knocking the New World, and the friction it generated chafed vigorously on the young country's thin cultural skin.

It all started going wrong with the crossing. There you were, tossed up and down by the Atlantic, your stomach lurching one way and the ship the other, and you hardly knew whether to brace yourself against the waves or get ready to swerve away from the jets of saliva that spattered from American mouths in the general direction of the spittoon. Chewing quids of tobacco and squirting out the noxious yellow juice, visitors complained, was the national pastime of American males. They spat before breakfast and they spat after dinner. They spat in hospitals and they spat in the Senate. In the law courts the judge spat, the crier spat, the witness and prisoner spat, and the jurymen and spectators spat as well. They spat so much that it seemed to have made their lips thin and their cheeks fat.

Things hardly improved when you arrived. Service was something for slaves, or perhaps Irishmen or Scotsmen, but certainly not for proudly independent Americans, and shopkeepers were either condescendingly familiar or insolently indifferent. "Your washer woman sits down before you, while you are *standing* speaking to her; and a shop-boy bringing things for your inspection not only sits down, but keeps his hat on in your drawing-room," complained the actress Fanny Kemble, who arrived in 1832 and published her *Journal of America* three years later.[2] Tradespeople made a point of treating ordinary customers with more respect than the rich, and they took particular pleasure in pulling the snobbish English down a peg or two.

Even the most curmudgeonly travelers had to admit that educated society could be elegant and polished—if rarely *amusant*—and that on the whole the locals were hospitable, openhearted, anxious to oblige, and better tempered than the English. But the card-carrying Yankees came across as a rude, sulky breed, and they took insufferable liberties with strangers. They picked up travelers' books on steamboats or stagecoaches and started reading them without so much as a by-your-leave. "If you have a cigar in your mouth, a man will come up—'Beg pardon, stranger,' and whips your cigar out of your mouth, lights his own, and then returns yours," gawped Frederick Marryat, an English naval captain who, like many seamen and several actors, parlayed his globetrotting into a career as a writer.[3] Americans seemed to understand civil liberties as the liberty to be uncivil.

If, like Fanny Trollope, you took a steamboat up the Mississippi in 1828, you were in for a real culture shock. The early steamboats were notorious for their raucousness, or, as one traveler put it, their practical republicanism. There were no private cabins, the washroom was a couple of feet of deck with a barrel of water, a tin basin chained to a stool, and a hunk of yellow soap, and sallow young merchants and clerks sat up all night, drinking, smoking, and playing seven-up, using one sleeper's shoulder as a table and another's collar as a scoreboard. Above these luxury quarters was steerage, bursting with Irish and German laborers, equipped with a stove for cooking and two large shelves for sleeping, and above that was the hurricane deck, spread with cabbages and fighting cocks whose crowing mixed with the squeals of children and the clanging of the bell and nearly, but not quite, drowned out the incessant clanking of the engine.[4] One thing above all, though, astonished Mrs. Trollope: the natives' "frightful manner of feeding with their knives, till the whole blade seemed to enter into the mouth; and the still more frightful manner of cleaning the teeth afterwards with a pocket knife."[5] She would rather have traveled, she vowed, with a bunch of pigs.

Bad table manners were second only to spitting in the black books of English travelers, and innkeepers, who were famed for their independent spirit, terrorized visitors' feelings most of all. If you were foolish enough to arrive after dinner, shuddered Charles William Janson, the host would bring out the leftovers and install himself next to you,

> drinking out of your glass, and of the liquor you are to pay for, belching in your face, and committing other excesses still more indelicate and disgusting. Perfectly inattentive to your accommodation, and regardless of your appetite, he will dart his fork into the best of the dish, and leave you to take the next cut. If you arrive at the dinner-hour, you are seated with "mine hostess" and her dirty children, with whom you have often to scramble for a plate, and even the servants of the inn. . . . The children, imitative of their free and polite papa, will also seize your drink, slobber in it, and often snatch a dainty bit from your plate. This is esteemed wit, and consequently provokes a laugh, at the expense of those who are paying for the board.[6]

Even in New York, the company at mealtimes was far from congenial. Basil Hall, another naval captain and well-known travel writer, visited the Plate House, a dinner room in the business district, and was bemused to find his fellow guests gobbling away as silent as monks. The only noise came from the boy waiters crying out orders and the clatter of knives and forks. The diners barely muttered the name of a dish, seconds later corned beef, potatoes, and bread were dumped piping hot on the table, and it was all over in ten minutes. Everyone was Moving On: no time for small talk.

Perplexingly, though, there was always time to quiz strangers on one subject. Americans strolled into visitors' hotel rooms, collared them without an introduction, pulled up a window and whistled to their friends to come join in the interrogation; they accosted travelers on stagecoaches, steamboats, and trains, and the subject was always the same: America.

"Well, sir, what do you think of us?" was the first question. "How do you like our country? Do you not think it very superior to England?"

The diplomatic traveler, a rare enough breed, waffled—"I have seen nothing like it in the world," more than one took to answering—because anything less than rapture met with an icy silence, and anything bordering on criticism unleashed a point-blank lecture on the splendors of America, accompanied by a strong hint that European minds were too weakened by despotism to understand the true grandeur of the new country's institutions. "The conceit and boasting of the Yankees is quite absurd and ridiculous," warned the author of *A Practical Guide for Emigrants to North America,* "and their notions of the English manners and constitution rather amusing to an Englishman: but it will be prudent, however, for the emigrant to listen to their remarks."[7]

The English had always cherished their God-given right to grumble. They griped nonstop about England, and complaining had never done anything to wound their amour propre. They were thus disconcerted to discover that Americans liked nothing better than talking up their homeland, and that to insult America was as good as insulting them personally. It was all deeply déclassé, and it was also deeply suspicious: America's covetousness of British praise seemed to hint that those noisy demonstrations of pride were not all they appeared. "Do you not think the people of America, upon the whole, particularly intelligent?" an American lady asked Basil Hall in a stagecoach. "Thus it was ever, in great things as well as in small," Hall illuminated his readers; "they were eternally on the defensive, and gave us to understand that they suspected us of a design to find fault, at times when nothing on earth was farther from our thoughts. Whenever anything favorable happened, by chance or otherwise, to be stated with respect to England, there was straightway a fidget, till the said circumstance was counterbalanced by something equally good, or better, in America."[8] Every traveler belabored the same point, and at least a few Americans agreed. "Why," asked Washington Irving, "are we so exquisitely alive to the aspersions of England?"[9]

One reason lay in the visitors' own hands. English travelers were the best and the worst in the world. They tramped chin up and pen poised around the globe, and wherever they landed, the first things most unpacked were their prejudices. What they unpacked in America was a preconceived notion that Americans were uncultured, uncouth, and ignorant of proper etiquette. Britain, in their eyes, was the sophisticated Athens to America's swaggering Rome.

Yet Europe still set the pace for fashionable society in America, and fashionable society was growing larger by the day. As industrialization and capitalism turned artisans into wage laborers and employers into the new rich, aspirational Americans became obsessed with class as never before.* Visitors were astonished at the lavish finery displayed by the middle classes: since democracy had put an end to bowing and scraping—for white folks—it seemed they had to go the extra mile to exhibit their superior status.†

That was what made Fanny Trollope the most notorious ransacker of American self-esteem. She called her book *Domestic Manners of the Americans;* the thrust was, they had none. "Their evening parties are supremely dull," she reported: there was little music, "and that little lamentably bad. . . . I scarcely ever heard a white American, male or female, go through an air without being out of tune before the end of it. . . . To eat inconceivable quantities of cake, ice, and pickled oysters—and to shew half their revenue in silks and satins, seem to be the chief object."¹⁰ That was in the best society; out in the sticks, things were much worse. Even in prosperous Cincinnati, Longfellow's Queen of the West, with its pretty villas and gardens tumbling down to the rows of steamers moored along the Ohio, Trollope decided that democracy might be a fine thing in principle, but in practice it led to her neighbor, who looked like a Covent Garden market woman, taking her by the arm to walk down the street, a liberty which led Fanny to expostulate that equality "will be found less palatable when it presents itself in the shape of a hard greasy

---

* "There are three classes in society, the high, the middle and the low," the New York *Sun*—motto: "It Shines for All"—editorialized on October 8, 1833. "The higher classes of society are composed of the educated and refined; the middle classes, of the intelligent and respectable; the lower, of the ignorant."

† In that, they were the opposite of London's Regency rakes, who advertised the security of their position by slumming with impunity.

paw and is claimed in accents that breathe less of freedom than onions and whisky."¹¹* Her conclusions left no room for doubt about her opinion of Americans: "I do not like them," she declared. "I do not like their principles, I do not like their opinions, I do not like their manners."¹² Nice country, shame about the people.

Domestic Manners was a sensation in America. Old-money elitists in the eastern cities saw much sense in what she said: they even hoped her book would serve as a corrective to the worst crimes against the gods of taste. But the vast majority burst out in indignant anger. Reviewers wondered whether Mrs. Trollope had ever heard of London's boxing and bruising and beer guzzling, its mobs, misery, and crime, never mind the vicious voluptuousness of the wilder fringes of the upper classes, however finished their style might be. Even the *Edinburgh Review,* never an uncritical friend of America, saw Trollope's obloquy as all but a casus belli for the New World.

To make matters worse, all this rancor at republican manners was really an insidious way to make a larger political point. In truth, the bad case of republican jaundice that many travelers developed in the 1830s had little to do with America at all: the real enemy was English parliamentary reform, which was busy widening the franchise at the expense of old landed interests. It was no coincidence that Trollope ascribed America's supposed failings to the lack of a proper caste system, which she was sure made everyone happier and more useful, nor that Basil Hall's book ended with a forty-four-page explanation of why the British political settlement, down to every last rotten borough, was a marvel of evolution impossible of improvement. Captain Marryat was even more upfront. "I have not written this book for the Americans," he wrote: "they have hardly entered my thoughts during the whole time that I have been employed upon it, and I am perfectly indifferent either to their censure or their praise." His great object, he explained, was "to do serious injury to the cause of democracy."¹³

Unsurprisingly, Marryat and his fellow travelers found what they

---

* Cincinnati, though, was also already known as Porkopolis after its processed pigs: fifteen hundred hogs were salted and barreled every day at the giant packing plants that smoked along the north bank of the Ohio and made the whole city smell of ham.

came looking for. The absence of rank made the dollar king. Representative government had given way to the tyranny of the majority, and democracy was slipping into ochlocracy, or at least the subversion of Congress and the accretion of executive powers in the name of the people. Jefferson's "natural aristocracy" had been hounded out of office in favor of professional baby-kissers and flesh-pressers for whom politics was about influence, not principle, and who bought elections with boosterish promises and blatant bribes. Even worse, Jacksonian stumping had taught Americans to despise other nations, and one nation above all. "The feelings towards England of the majority, or democratic party," Marryat claimed, incendiarily though not entirely wrongly, "were of *deep irreconcilable hatred.* . . . This feeling becomes stronger every day. They want to whip the whole world."[14]

Not every English traveler came armed with the same political agenda, though even confirmed democrats like Macready's friend Harriet Martineau went home despairing that Jacksonian America was not living up to its high founding ideals. Equally, some Americans agreed with the symptoms, if not the diagnosis: William Ellery Channing, the great Unitarian preacher, eloquently warned that America's institutions had encouraged the "sordid, base and groveling" race for dollars over "that elevation of character which is the most precious, and, in truth, the only substantial blessing of liberty."[15] But there was a difference between reasoned opposition and vitriol, and patriotic Americans were outraged to find themselves the whipping boys of disingenuous English conservatives. The English, they riposted, had good reason to grumble, because their system of government was a dungeon world of sewn-up elections and despotic aristocrats, while Americans had the right to be proud, because they had a stake in their government—at least, the majority of white males did—and Washington, D.C., was a city on a hill, a place of hope and enthusiasm, a beacon to humanity.[16] It was not lost on more dispassionate observers that underneath the differences in national temperament there was a family resemblance, which both sides affected not to see. Both countries were equally stubborn, both refused to let outsiders interfere in their affairs, and American pride resembled nothing so much as English *amor patriae* writ large on a great new stage.

America's divided and inconsistent attitude to Britain was nicely summed up by Edwin Forrest himself.* In 1838, he delivered the oration at the Democratic party's Fourth of July celebrations.† "We come, not to celebrate the birthday of a despot, but the birthday of a nation," he boomed off, and he ended, a cramping hour and a half later, by reassuring his audience that the Old World was "cankered with the diseases of political senility, and cramped by the long-worn fetters of tyrannous habit," while "the empire of the west is in the bloom and freshness of being." In between, though, he had something else to say about the old country. "I reverence England," he declared:

> with all her faults, I reverence the mother of my country, and the great exemplar of the world in arts, in arms, in science, literature, and song. I reverence her for the principles of civil liberty which she has scattered, "like flower seeds by the far winds sown," over the whole surface of the globe. . . . Yes! though she drove our fathers from her shores with the accursed scourge of political and religious persecution, and though, like an unnatural parent, she battled with her children when they asserted the unalienable prerogatives of humanity and nature, I reverence England.

But, he roared, "let not my eyes be turned to where she sits in the swollen pride of aristocratic grandeur!"[17]‡

ANGLOPHILE AMERICANS WATCHED the mounting ill will with deep regret. Washington Irving took up the theme in *The Sketchbook of Geoffrey Crayon,* the first American book to win an international audience, and worried that both sides had much to lose. England, he fore-

---

* Mrs. Trollope saw Forrest in Cincinnati and was unimpressed. "I was greatly amused when a gentleman, who asked my opinion of him, told me upon hearing it, that he would not advise me to state it freely in America, 'for they would not bear it,' " she wrote (*Domestic Manners,* 103).

† Forrest had long toyed with the idea of leaving one national stage for another. He had become closely linked with the Loco Focos, the radical wing of the New York Democratic Party: five years earlier the nominating committee had invited him to run for Congress, and he was even talked of as a future president. He soon found out that congressmen were paid a paltry eight dollars a day and decided his future lay with the theatre.

‡ Nathaniel Hawthorne put his views more crisply: "I hate England; though I love some Englishmen" (*Letters,* ed. Thomas Woodson et al. [Columbus, Oh., 1987], 401).

cast, would regret its misplaced trust in the xenophobes of Grub Street, the spiritual home of London's hack writers: when her empire met the end of every other empire, "she may look back with regret at her infatuation, in repulsing from her side a nation she might have grappled to her bosom, and thus destroying her only chance for real friendship beyond the boundaries of her own dominions." Meanwhile England, he maintained, with its intellectual activity and freedom of opinion, was still America's kin, however timeworn and overrun by abuses its political structure might be, and copying the rancorous animosities of the English press only poisoned the fledgling national literature by fostering a querulous and peevish temper. "Let it be the pride of our writers," Irving concluded, "discarding all feelings of irritation, and disdaining to retaliate the illiberality of British authors, to speak of the English nation without prejudice, and with determined candor."[18]

Irving's magnanimity found few takers, though James Fenimore Cooper attempted to correct Britain's misconceptions about America while showing Americans how to act more like citizens of the world and less like sensitive provincials; he ended up pleasing no one.[19] America was so fed up with being boxed on the ears by schoolteacherish travelers that uneasiness turned to outrage, outrage to defiance, and its writers began to retaliate in kind. For a while the favored weapon was parody: one spoof volume purported to come from the pen of George Fibbleton, "Ex-Barber to His Majesty the King of Great Britain," which seemed plausible enough that it fooled the New York *Sun* for a while.[20] By the 1830s, though, as droves of English travelers turned up to ambush Americans and clobber them with condescending books, the tone turned to direct abuse. The Baltimore *Chronicle* denounced Captain Marryat as an "*unmitigated blackguard.* His awkward, unwieldly misshapen body, was but a fair lodging for a low, depraved, licentious soul . . . he is a beast."[21] Basil Hall was "exposed" as an employee of the British Treasury, by whom he had supposedly been commissioned to check the growing admiration of the English people for the government of the United States. In Mrs. Trollope's case, the whole arsenal of revenge tactics was wheeled out. She was exhibited in a waxworks museum as a goblin, a lengthy verse satire called *The Trollopiad,* composed by "Nil Admirari,"

Fanny Trollope, seated center with her two daughters, holds court while her son's portrait is painted in a highly flattering style. In this caricature by a Cincinnati artist, the Trollopes appear as moon-faced country bumpkins who are trying to pass themselves off as chivalrous blue bloods. Courtesy of the Library of Congress.

was dedicated to her, and a quickstep was composed in her honor, with the legend "A New Tune on an Old Subject. Composed and Dedicated, to all the Trollops." Running with the possibilities of her unfortunate name, a best-selling series of prints caricatured her as a whore. "She did not succeed amongst us," the *Cincinnati Gazette* echoed. "Her whole appearance and conduct corresponded with her name."[22]

Infuriatingly, though, while Americans pored over every sarcastic comment in the latest British jeremiad, getting them to read the ripostes of their own writers was a losing battle. Like its drama, America's reading matter was almost exclusively supplied by England; despite repeated appeals, Congress had refused to recognize the copyright of foreign writers, a policy that chiefly encouraged American publishers to flood the market with cheap pirated editions of British books, to the detriment of

American authors, who had trouble getting anything published at all.*
Instead, they read English taunts that they had no talent for literature,
art, or philosophy, that sitting around drinking mint juleps and chewing
tobacco, talking up the glories of independence, and swearing that they
were very graceful and agreeable people would not make them scholars
any more than gentlemen, and nothing stung more.

By the 1830s, calls for a distinctively American art—an art, proposed
Emerson, which would unabashedly express the nation's civilized-savage
spirit—were growing steadily louder, and by the end of the decade the
great flowering of New England literature was already under way. In
1844 Emerson returned to his theme with a lecture entitled "The
Young American." "It is remarkable, that our people have their intellectual culture from one country, and their duties from another," he began.
"This false state of things is newly in a way to be corrected. America is
beginning to assert itself to the senses and to the imagination of her
children, and Europe is receding in the same degree."[23] His hopes were
shortly to be fulfilled, above all by Walt Whitman and, later, Mark
Twain.

Even so, American proselytizers for a national literature had one
great problem, and that problem was Shakespeare.

By now, Shakespeare had become the voice of America as much as of
England. Yet it was inevitable and necessary that the new nation would
define itself in opposition to the Old World: the rejection of the parent
was an indispensable first step in forging a new identity, and where politics had led, culture needed to follow. The result was that Jacksonian
America began to celebrate a sort of atavistic Anglo-Saxon heritage, at
the same time as it bitterly resented modern British hegemony. Thus
the Bard could be prized away from the political leaders of the English
nation after his time and claimed as a fellow traveler in the American
fight against tyranny. The rationale for this bit of special pleading led
only in one direction: Shakespeare was yoked to the cause of the Mani-

---

* The lack of copyright was one of the great bones of contention for English writers, including
Dickens, who made pointed references to the subject during his tour. England granted copyright to
American authors, but the United States did not follow suit until 1891, after which copyright for
books written in English was conditional upon their being printed in the United States. This remained the state of U.S. copyright law until 1986.

fest Destiny of the Anglo-Saxon race in its perfected political form: the American nation. Every year, on the Fourth of July, America bonded around fiery rhetoric about its heroic struggle against the English tyrant, and every year Shakespeare was paraded, not as an example of England's cultural dominance, but as an enlightened ally of the American dream.[24]

It was a tension that made it all the more vital to draw a thick line between American Shakespeare and English Shakespeare, and it was bound to end in trouble.

WASHINGTON IRVING'S EXPLANATION for the opprobrium America attracted from English travelers was that the travelers were not up to the job. Only broken-down tradesmen, scheming adventurers, and wandering mechanics, he reasoned, turned up in America, usually in search of easy money, and when they found they had to work for a living their high expectations turned into low revenge. It was true that incompetents like Janson, who was swept up in the Yazoo land fraud, and Trollope, whose failed speculations included an early shopping mall and several forays into show business—one involved setting her son up as a mysterious multilingual oracle called the Invisible Woman—paid scant heed to the size of America or its distance from Europe: the vastness made patriotism a necessary glue to bind together a far-flung and diverse nation, and the isolation inevitably led to introspection. A grand experiment in self-government was unfolding before their eyes, and yet all the travelers could talk about was tobacco and two-pronged forks.

Charles Dickens put an end to Irving's rationalization. Dickens was not just the most celebrated writer but the most celebrated Briton who had visited the United States, and America fell over itself to welcome him. He was banqueted, cheered, and carried on shoulders at every stop. Committees waited on him daily; deputations traveled a thousand miles to invite him to their town. Boston's Dickensian enthusiasm earned it the new name of Boz-town, and New York, determined to outdo its rival, threw a Boz Ball on Valentine's Day, 1842, at the Park Theatre. It was the most spectacular festivity America had seen. Charles and Catherine Dickens entered the shimmering auditorium along a runway built through the center box, and they were paraded twice around the three thousand cheering guests to the tune of "See, the Conquering Hero Comes." The pit had been raised to the level of the stage to create a giant dance floor; the walls were decorated with scenes from Dickens's novels, portraits of U.S. presidents, state flags, and seven thousand yards of bunting, with a massive portrait of Dickens surmounted by an American eagle as the centerpiece. During the evening more scenes were presented as tableaux vivants, thirty-eight thousand oysters slipped down throats, and the champagne flowed. It all went brilliantly—but the next day, the managers of the Park announced they would repeat the ball at half price for those who had failed to get in, an attempt to turn Dickens from an honored guest into a commercial attraction, which caused him to develop a sore throat; they compounded the insult by sending a messenger around with a request for a doctor's note as proof. New York's elite was mortified, but the rest of America thought the great novelist had been received like a king, and it was impatient to read the verdict.

Shortly after Dickens returned to London and joyfully held Macready in his arms, he gave him the first chapter of his *American Notes* to read. Macready was dismayed by its style and matter—"*I do not like it,*" he underlined in his diary—but he had already expected the worst from the many letters he had received from his friend.[25] Early in his trip, Dickens had been full of cheer: Americans, he wrote to Macready, were "as delicate, as considerate, as careful at giving the least offence, as the last Englishman I ever saw," and altogether less prejudiced, greedy, and indecorous than previous travelers had led him to expect.[26] But within weeks he had changed his mind. The problem was not just the Boz Ball fiasco, nor the atrocious spitting, nor even the infuriating familiarity of strangers who examined, discussed, and pawed him on trains and in hotel rooms as if he were a stuffed bear. It was the government. Dickens had set sail with impossible expectations—he was full of excitement, he told Forster, to see a utopia of liberty where good nature must be universal—and the human reality hit him hard. Congress, he acknowledged, had its outstanding men of high character and great ability, but the legacy of Jacksonian politics was a political class which played such a fierce and brutal game that self-respect had been hounded out of town. What was left, he proclaimed in print, was the meanest perversion of virtuous Political machinery that the worst tools ever wrought. Despicable trickery at elections; under-hand tamperings with public officers; cowardly attacks upon opponents, with scurrilous newspapers for shields, and hired pens for daggers; shameful trucklings to mercenary knaves . . . aidings and abettings of every bad inclination in the popular mind, and artful suppressions of all its good influences: such things as these, and in a word, Dishonest Faction in its most depraved and unblushing form, stared out from every corner of the crowded hall.[27]

The Declaration of Independence, he added for good measure, should have been turned to the wall in shame or taken down and burned, because the foul disgrace of slavery made a gross mockery of its noble words.

Macready, who for once found himself playing the optimist to Dickens's gloomy Gus, wrote to his friend begging him not to take rash leaps at hasty conclusions. It was too late. As Dickens made his way south, slavery cast its shadow over the second half of his journey. It seemed to infect the very scenery with an air of ruin, decay, and gloom: it was, he thought, a miserable aristocracy of a false republic that demanded to be waited on by inferiors. The men who defended the trade in human flesh, he expostulated, were brutal savages and cowards, and so were the people's representatives in Congress, where for eight years a gag rule prohibited discussion of slavery on the floor of the self-styled home of human rights and free speech. Behind it all, he was horribly convinced, lay a numbing obsession with money: America seemed like a giant countinghouse full of merchants constantly shuffling the almighty dollar with no time for the graces of life. It was a nightmare to a man for whom eccentricities were oxygen.

The views Dickens privately expressed to Macready were even blunter than those he published. He could not change his opinion of America, he told his friend in long, densely written letters. He was sure it would fail as an example to the world, and when it did it would deal the heaviest blow ever dealt to the cause of liberty. It was, he anathematized at the end of his trip, a "low, coarse and mean nation . . . led and driven by a herd of rascals, who are the human lice of God's creation. . . . Pah! I never knew what it was to feel disgust and contempt, 'till I traveled in America."[28]*

American Notes was published in Britain in October 1842, four months after Dickens's return; by the end of November, it had sold a hundred thousand copies in the United States, all of them, of course, pirated. The reaction was immediate and violent. "All Yankee-doodledom blazed up like one universal soda bottle," Thomas Carlyle remembered.[29] America took the *Notes* as a great betrayal of its hospitality: Dickens, reviewers seethed, was a flashy reporter who had dined for most of his life off the garbage of hotels and gentlemen's tables, and his book was sheer trash, a noxious stew of "egotism, coxcombery, and cockneyism."[30] He compared hate mail with his new friends Captain Marryat and Fanny Trollope, and even Washington Irving, whom Dickens greatly admired and had eagerly sought out, cut off their friendship. Undaunted and provoked, he started work on *Martin Chuzzlewit,* during the course of which Martin's servant suggests that the American eagle should be drawn "like a Bat, for its short-sightedness; like a Bantam, for its bragging; like a Magpie, for its honesty; like a Peacock, for its vanity, like an Ostrich, for its putting its head in the mud, and thinking nobody sees it."[31] Macready gave the same short shrift to *Chuzzlewit* that he had given to *American Notes:* he thought it was "as bitter as it is powerful, and against whom is this directed? 'Against the Americans,' is the answer. Against how many of them? How many answer to his description? I am grieved to read the book."[32]

America became the only bone of contention between the two friends. On his first transatlantic trip, Macready had coincided with Basil Hall, and they had gone on several excursions together. Like Captain Hall, Macready had found he was expected to admire everything without reserve, but unlike Hall, he found almost everything admirable. Americans, he thought, were unfailingly obliging; as courteous and polite, he said, as Parisians, which he evidently intended as a compliment. "The simple fact being," he noted, "that civility meets with civility."[33]

---

* Dickens did, though, have one pleasant piece of news. "Forrest breakfasted with us at Richmond last Sunday," he wrote: "he was acting there, and I invited him—and he spoke very gratefully and very like a man, of your kindness to him when he was in London" (March 22, 1842, MA 106, Pierpont Morgan Library).

But Dickens would not be moved. He was sure, he wrote to his friend, that Macready would not question the elaborate precautions he insisted on taking if he knew but "one hundredth part the malignity, the monstrous falsehood, the beastly attacks even upon Catherine, which were published all over America, even while I was there, on my mere confession that the country had disappointed me—confessions wrung from me in private society, before I had written a word upon the people." He had still more instructions: "Never claim me for your friend, or champion me in any way. I not only absolve you from any such office, but I distinctly entreat you to consider silence upon all such topics, your duty to those who are nearest and dearest to you." Macready should not write to him directly, he insisted, but enclose any letter with one addressed to someone else. And he added a postscript: "I wish to Heaven I could undedicate *Nickleby* until you come home again."[34]

MACREADY SHRUGGED OFF Dickens's anxiety: even the greatest man, he sadly observed, was but a man. Yet he only had to look to his own profession to realize that there was, indeed, good reason for him to approach America with circumspection.

The Inimitable Boz aside, it was actors who had been the public face of England for as long as America could remember. English politicians and public dignitaries rarely made the trip across the Atlantic; English actors, though, traveled more regularly and more widely around the United States than did most American politicians. It was only to be expected that the visiting stars would become the focus of anti-English feeling, and they had duly been dragged into the culture wars.

The pattern was always the same. The slightest offense against American honor was enough to bring resentment at England bubbling to the surface, resentment turned into an excuse for a show of national pride, and the show of pride became an opportunity for rowdies to let off steam. Posters went up calling on patriots to pelt the slanderer off the stage; the authorities—who were no more sure whether theatres were business premises or public gathering places than their London forebears had been during the O.P. Riots, and who anyway much preferred the trashing of private property to mayhem on the streets—refused to intervene; and at little cost to the crowd, though some to the manager, a highly visible symbol of English effrontery could be trounced in one satisfying night's work. The task was made particularly easy by the stock system. As in the British provinces, stars would move between short engagements, usually of one to three weeks' duration, in different towns, at each stop acting with a local company that was more or less able—though mostly less—to play through the standard repertoire. Usually the visitors traveled alone, or at most accompanied by one other actor, either a stage partner or a subordinate who would act as an assistant, and as they arrived in town on their own, so they could conveniently be hounded out of town on their own.

American theatre riots were not trifling affairs. It was not unusual for five thousand demonstrators to turn out, as many as for any other cause, and the agitation often ended in rampaging violence. The case of Joshua Anderson, an English tenor who visited New York in 1831, was typical. During the Atlantic crossing Anderson's wife, a dancer and singer, had taken offense at the insinuations of an American gentleman, and Anderson unwisely called the offending passenger an impudent Yankee and threatened to thrash him. The outraged New Yorker gathered his friends for revenge, and as soon as Anderson stepped on the stage of the Park Theatre he was hit by a barrage of coins, oranges, and eggs and silenced by stamping, catcalls, and shouts of "Off! Off! Go back to England! Tell them the Yankees sent you back!" Anderson struggled on in pantomime, but the evening came to a hasty end when a crowd burst in from the street, cried "Fire!," and leaped over the orchestra railings; Anderson was hustled out of the greenroom window onto the roof of a shed. The next day, he published a conciliatory letter in the papers and tried again, but again he was driven away with rotten fruit and eggs, while the rioters broke up the benches and milled around till dawn. The next night they gathered again, battered down the doors and windows and dispersed only when the façade was festooned with the Stars and Stripes and transparencies painted with patriotic scenes. A year later, Anderson ventured another appearance, and though the manager appealed for a show of hands and the audience voted to let him play, five thousand protestors stormed the theatre and he went home for good.

Some of the provocations that the rioters claimed as justification were ridiculously insignificant. In 1833 the Woods, another English husband-

and-wife act, were driven off the Park stage and out of the country by another violent riot when they declined to appear at a benefit for an actress who was a favorite of the town; another account suggests their crime was merely to choose the same play for their own benefit. The demonstration was organized by the *Courier and Enquirer,* a supposedly respectable broadsheet: Joseph Wood challenged its editor, James Watson Webb, a notorious ladies' man who went around town in a white coat, white hat, and white linen, to a duel, but he demurred. The same year Fanny Kemble took to the stage in Washington, where she was so sought after that Congress ended its business early to attend the play: even so, when she declined to ride an American gentleman's horse on an outing, sheets detailing the supposed slight were thrown into the audience, followed by an appeal to American patriots to show their feelings.

As the transatlantic rift deepened, the riots became more serious. In 1834 a butcher filed a complaint alleging that George Farren, the English stage manager of the Bowery Theatre, had insulted Americans— "Damn the Yankees; they are a damn set of jackasses, and fit to be gulled," he was said to have sworn—and then hit him when he protested. The shocking details were bruited by the papers and plastered on placards. Four days later, on a hot July night, an anti-abolitionist mob was roaming around town, at loose ends after breaking into a chapel where an abolitionist meeting had been abandoned. Perhaps connecting Farren with Britain's support for abolition, which some Americans supposed was a plot to break up the Union, the mob caught at the chance. "To the Bowery!" the cry went up, and five thousand malcontents surged up the avenue, busted open the doors, and streamed down the aisles. Edwin Forrest was in the middle of a scene from *Metamora.* He tried to talk to the insurgents, but they took over the theatre and pelted Thomas Hamblin, the English manager. Hamblin, who had already preemptively renamed the Bowery the American Theatre after the Anderson affair, defended himself with the American flag and announced that he had dismissed the hapless Farren, but the protestors refused to leave until the police marched onto the stage.[35] After the Farren trouble, one newspaper declared that if riots were going to take place in America, the outrage of foreign actors assailing the country's character while milking it for money was the one trigger everyone could understand. "This will teach English play actors a lesson they will long remember," it warned.[36]

Even the greatest actors were not immune: quite the reverse. The riots that came closest to the scale, though not the bloodshed, of the looming Astor Place disaster were directed at Edmund Kean. Kean's first visit to America started in triumph and ended in catastrophe. Having prolonged his season into the summer against strong counsel, he stormed out of a Boston theatre in a fit of pique because a mere handful of people had turned up to watch his *Richard III*. The entire nation's press took violent offense at the snub. "One-Cent reward!" a Boston newspaper offered, signing the piece "Peter Public":

> Run away, from the "literary Emporium of the new world," a stage player calling himself Kean. He may be easily recognized by his misshapen trunk, his cox-comical, cockney manners, and his bladder actions. His face is as white as his own froth. . . . As he has violated his pledged faith to me, I deem it my duty to thus put my neighbors on guard against him.[37]

To add insult to injury, Kean declared that Americans did not sufficiently honor Shakespeare. He fled the country, but four years later, having been chased out of England after the Cox affair, he had little choice but to try again. *Cox vs. Kean,* though, had scandalized American as well as English breakfast tables, and the prospect of playing host to an adulterer whom England had spurned revived the resentment at his earlier insult to America's pride. One New York paper labeled him a "lump of moral pollution" and declared that no manager should have allowed him to contaminate the stage; since they had, it added, women should stay away and men must do their duty and hiss.[38] They not only hissed but threw oranges, nuts, and apples, tore up benches, shouted out ribald comments about Mrs. Cox, seducers, and cuckolds, and made pointed references to Boston, while another four thousand gathered outside and pelted the doors and windows with rocks. After two nights of mayhem Kean issued a groveling apology in the papers. "I visit this country now," he pleaded, "under different feelings and auspices than on a former occasion. Then I was an ambitious man, and the proud representative of

Shakespeare's heroes. The spark of ambition is extinct, and I merely ask a shelter in which to close my professional and mortal career."[39] The plaintive appeal worked on New York, but Bostonians were not minded to indulge him. "Off! Off!" they shouted, and nuts, pieces of cake, and metal balls rained down and drove him away. Another actor announced that Kean wished to make a humble apology, but again he was driven off the stage, and he collapsed in tears in the greenroom before being smuggled out the back and conducted out of town. A placard went up on the stage: "Mr. Kean Declines Playing," it read, and with a triumphant roar the rowdies smashed up the seats and lamps, while the crowds that had been locked outside broke down the doors and surged in, causing the Keanites in the boxes to clamber through the windows. Even then Kean's trouble was not over. Philadelphia welcomed him with a hail of buttons and rotten eggs, and the uproar was so loud that once again a performance of Shakespeare went on in pantomime. In Baltimore another mob rushed the theatre; the place was only saved from destruction by the mayor, who planted himself in front of the doors and proclaimed it would be stormed over his dead body. Kean fled again, just in time, because the mob searched every carriage in town until daybreak.

Macready himself had had a small foretaste of American sensitivities. On his first visit he had complained about not being able to get hold of a certain type of stage arrow. The comment was taken as an insult to American timber, and anonymous letters were sent to the press. Macready assembled the actors on stage and appealed to them to speak up if he had ever deprecated the local wood. No one did speak; even so, he felt it wise to state that if he had offended anyone, he regretted it and held himself personally responsible, and he hoped they would not blacken his name by taking revenge. It was only because the penny press had not yet been invented, one actor later reflected, that Macready's American career had not ended in a matter of days.[40]

The hooey over the arrow had been a brief moment, and it was long past. Seventeen years later, Macready was returning as the Eminent Tragedian, the apostle of Shakespeare, the gentleman savior of the stage; the idea that America might turn against him never seriously crossed his mind.

CHAPTER 7

The Paper War

MACREADY ARRIVED IN New York on September 21, 1843, after a crossing twice as quick as his last, and found the Empire City changed almost beyond recognition. In 1826 Broadway had drawn to a halt at Canal Street; walking uptown from City Hall Park, you were in the countryside in under a mile. Now Manhattan was paving its way up to Forty-second Street, following the grid that had been branded on the island as severely as griddle marks on a strip steak, and the lots were filling in at the rate of three blocks a year. The old twisting alleys had been widened into broad gaslit thoroughfares, the patrician mansions on Broadway had turned into boardinghouses, offices, and shops, and whole ways of life had been wiped out as neighborhoods were recycled for new uses. With the unceasing noise of traffic and construction, the old overgrown village had become a deafening metropolis, and many locals were bewildered by the pace of change. All over town, the followers of William Miller were busy preparing for the end of the world, which he had predicted would occur within a year of March 21, 1843, with April 1 as the most likely date. Newspapers commemorated the event with a special edition, while believers donned white robes furnished by enterprising Bowery dry goods merchants and climbed trees. When nothing happened Miller changed the date to October 22, 1844, and when the apocalypse again failed to arrive everyone climbed down.

Macready checked in, unpacked, went to rehearsal, and walked back to his hotel. He was sitting in the reading room when his first visitor called. Edwin Forrest's beaming face appeared over his newspaper— jowlier now, flanked with bushy sideburns down to his collar and topped with a great swirl of hair, a streetboy look that gave him the air of an antebellum Elvis. His eyes betrayed a steelier, more knowing expression than before, and in repose his lips had developed a sensual curl, but his smile was as winning as ever. "I was very glad to see him," Macready recorded.[1] They went up to his room, where they could talk properly, and renewed their friendship; the next day Forrest came for another long visit and invited Macready to dine at his house. Forrest had installed Kate and himself in a broad double-fronted mansion on West Twenty-second Street, in the new residential enclave of Chelsea: its centerpiece was his grand library, where a First Folio of Shakespeare held pride of place on a custom-made velvet-covered stand. He had assembled such a large party to meet the Englishman—uncharacteristically, because he disliked entertaining—that Macready felt overwhelmed; "but it was most kindly intended," he acknowledged to his diary, and the day was very cheerful. "I like all I see of Forrest very much," Macready added. "He appears a clear-headed, honest, kind man; what can be better?"[2]

Forrest was equally fond of the older man. Two days after the grand dinner, he called again and asked Macready to do him the honor of accompanying him to have his daguerreotype taken. Macready sheepishly submitted to the new process, and though he grimaced at the result he was secretly much tickled.

The two actors were more than civil colleagues, they were professional friends. Anyone who knew them well would have been amused at the match, for Macready's skittish dignity and permanent air of exasperation were strange bedfellows with Forrest's rugged self-assurance. But the two stars had plenty to talk about: they were bound by a ligament of experience which few others shared. How many people could understand their lives—the petting and pelting, the feuds and lawsuits, the daily requests from strangers for gifts, loans, and trysts? A handful of performers; perhaps a few politicians.

Macready and Forrest have always been built up as polar opposites. The more interesting truth is that in many ways they were strangely similar. They were earnest men, strongly emotional, often difficult, but with a tenderness that made them loved by their friends and a magnetism that made them stars. They were both proud, hardworking, ambitious, willful, and impulsive, and they both had world-class egos, a job requirement in a violently competitive profession. As with so many mold-breaking men, there was a stubborn contumacy about their need to prevail, and the flip side for both was a susceptibility to black moods, or, occasionally, full-blown bouts of depression. Both, too, had been shaken by family tragedy. Macready's favorite child, Joan, had died three years earlier, at three years old; he was thrown into an agony of grief and he poured out threnodies of mourning to his diary for the rest of his life. Forrest had bought his roomy house two years after he and Kate returned from England; four years later, its top floors were still as silent as the grave. Kate had conceived four times; four times their children had died at birth or soon after.

Though they started out with antipodal attitudes to the theatre, as time went on even that difference narrowed. As fame brought Forrest more enemies, as he grew used to the power of his stardom, he became more imperious, more outraged by the sniping of penny-newspaper editors who were nettled by his proud independence and populist politics, and more intolerant of bungling inferior actors. "Such infernal rehearsals," he wrote home to Kate, "every one needed prompting, make the profession anything but agreeable"; touring with "EXECRABLE" companies, he underscored, was a *"hateful vagabond life."*[3] Both men were democrats in theory and rulers by fiat in practice: like Macready, Forrest had raised himself above the easy-come, easy-go intemperance of the theatre; like Macready, he saw as simple self-respect what others took as churlish impatience and insufferable arrogance; and for each man, the other was about the only actor whom he counted as a friend.

Yet as far as Forrest's fans were concerned, the two were as unlike as air and earth. To the b'hoys Macready was the very figure of epicene, snobbish England, the land of the Trollopes, and Forrest was the robust voice of democracy, the patriot who had exhibited true Americanism abroad— a man radically American, extolled the speakers at the flag-waving homecoming banquet thrown on his return from Europe; the Genius of

Democracy, moreover, who had made Shakespeare *"ours."*4* It scarcely mattered that Forrest was no more an egalitarian than his veto-wielding hero Andrew Jackson was a consensus politician: if anything, his commanding ways made him even more representative of the new land, a land of big men and big deeds. Nor would Forrest's partisans have cared much if they had known that Macready loathed English aristocrats almost as much as Forrest balked at their counterparts in America. It was enough that their backgrounds and personalities had made them the leading representatives of two opposed concepts of culture: in the end, one was American, the other English, and to Forrest's fans that was the same as saying, however mistakenly, that one was a populist, the other an elitist.

It was on stage that the contrast became clearest. For all his homely touches and flashes of white-hot emotion, Macready was the scholar attempting to inject some taste and decorum into the theatre. For all his skill and study, Forrest was the crowd pleaser who thrust his own rugged personality on the stage. People admired Macready; they loved Forrest. Macready was the greater actor, but Forrest was the greater star.

They were vital differences, because the two men's styles would become the battleground of the escalating cultural war, a war whose lines of engagement would lead to Astor Place.

MACREADY QUICKLY REALIZED that something was wrong. On his first night, a huge crowd braved the scorching weather and welcomed him with rounds of cheers and waving hats, but soon the numbers and the enthusiasm started to fall off. Wondering why, he asked around. "From what I can learn," he concluded, "the audiences of the United States have become accustomed to exaggeration in all its forms, and have applauded what has been most extravagant; it is not, therefore,

---

* Unlike his fellow American grand tourists, who had become notorious at home for falling prey to an undemocratic eagerness to see lords and ladies in the flesh, Forrest had been determined not to be corrupted by the decadent Old World. In Paris, he was presented to Louis-Philippe: for all the brilliance of the scene, he wrote home, he made his debut before the king of France "with not half the trepidation I experienced on presenting myself for the first time before a *sovereign* in New York— I mean the sovereign people." In Genoa, Columbus's birthplace, he spotted an American warship in the bay and hired a boatman to row him over. He clambered up the side, asked permission to come on deck, fell to his knees, and pressed the Stars and Stripes to his lips; breathing in the free air, he felt prouder than ever to be American (William Rounseville Alger, *Life of Edwin Forrest* [Philadelphia, 1877], 269; Montrose Jonas Moses, *The Fabulous Forrest* [Boston, 1929], 124).

Macready at fifty. This portrait by Henry Perronet Briggs was painted in 1843, shortly before the Eminent's departure for the United States. The Art Archive/Garrick Club.

surprising that they should bestow such little applause on me."[5] For now he shied away from considering just who had fostered that taste, and he struggled ahead as usual. On his last night in New York, when he played *Macbeth* for his benefit performance, he was more English than ever. "Ladies and gentlemen," he bowed, when he was dragged before the curtain:

> the custom peculiar to this country of a performer addressing the audience on his Benefit night has long been strange to me, and I really do not know how to convey the impression which my very gratifying reception here has made on me without indulging in a fervency of expression that might call my taste into question.[6]

The next day he moved his show on to Philadelphia, where he found Forrest already encamped in the rival theatre, and he took advantage of his night off to catch the American's show. It was the first time he had seen his colleague perform in seventeen years.

The play was *King Lear.* Forrest was dressed in an ankle-length velvet skirt and a full-sleeve jacket embroidered with garlands and trimmed with fur. He sported a giant wig and beard and drooping mustaches at least a foot long. It was hard to make out his face at all; but surely, Macready thought, the full breadth of his matured powers would shine through.

It did not take him long to decide not.

"I had a very high opinion of his powers of mind when I saw him exactly seventeen years ago," he told his diary.

> I said then, if he would cultivate those powers and really study . . . he would make one of the very first actors of this or any other day. But I thought he would not do so, as his countrymen were, by their extravagant applause, possessing him with the idea and with the fact, as far as remuneration was concerned, that it was unnecessary. I reluctantly, as far as my feelings towards him are interested, record my opinion that my prophetic soul foresaw the consequence. He has great physical power. But I could discern no imagination, no original thought, no poetry at all in his acting. . . . In fact, I did not think it the performance of an artist. . . . There was much to praise in Forrest's execution frequently; he seems to have his person in perfect command, but he has not enriched, refined, elevated, and enlarged his *mind;* it is very much where it was, in the matter of poetry and art, when I last saw him.

Most damningly of all, he was certain that Forrest did not properly understand Shakespeare.

"He had all the qualifications," he concluded, "all the material out of which to build up a great artist, an actor for all the world. He is now only an actor for the less intelligent of the Americans. But he is something better—an upright and well-intentioned man."[7] For all Forrest's qualities as a man, as a Shakespearean interpreter Macready was convinced he was in a different league. He would have been astonished to discover that Forrest, in private, also admitted to reservations about Macready's abilities. He had a much greater admiration for the Englishman's scholarship, he told a fellow actor, than for his skill as a delineator of Shakespearean character.[8]

America was about to get the opportunity to decide who was right. Macready began his own run, as usual, with *Macbeth;* Forrest, curiously, had elected to play the same part the following night, and the critics leaped at the chance to compare the two greatest tragedians of the age.

More than any other role, Macbeth crystallized their contrasting styles. Forrest played the Thane as a fiercely ambitious despot whose crises of conscience were scarcely more than an inconvenience: to be led into evil by an excess of willpower was one thing, but to be unmanned by an overactive imagination and his wife looked too much like lily-livered cowardice. When his fancy drew the dagger in the air, one critic likened him to a dyspeptic bear straining for a lump of meat through the bars of a cage; he would have made a great Lady Macbeth, another suggested. Macready, who was always darkly attracted to the supernatural, played Macbeth as a worthy soldier whose conscience buckled under the blandishments of fate. Nothing, said his critics, was less heroic than his conception of the great criminal: his wife's taunts made him fretful, remorse made him crumple into ignobility, and when he stole into the King's chamber he looked like a thief going to purloin a purse rather than a warrior about to snatch a crown. Both Macbeths are within the bounds of the play: its fascination partly lies in the balance between the two. But the two actors' interpretations were also the products of their natures, natures that were thrown into focus under Shakespeare's searching lens: Macready burningly insecure and guilt-ridden, Forrest recklessly determined to sweep opposition out of his way.

To the surprise of no one except Macready, the majority came down on the side of Forrest, "our great national tragedian."⁹ One critic gloated over the Englishman's "failure" at Drury Lane; another pointedly proclaimed Forrest the greatest living actor. Macready felt the old burning indignation rise up, and he began to resent Forrest's rave reviews. "*He is not an artist,*" he insisted in his diary. "Let him be an American actor—and a great American actor—but keep on this side of the Atlantic, and no-one will gainsay his comparative excellence. Much disgusted."¹⁰ This time there was no mention of Forrest's personal virtues.

By now Forrest was matching Macready's plays night for night—"not handsomely, I think," the Englishman noted.¹¹ He chose to put the contest down to theatre managers trying to drum up publicity, but vindictiveness began to creep into his thoughts toward the American actor. "They have announced him in *American* letters, as 'Mr. E. Forrest, *The National Tragedian!'*—and put him up in my parts the nights after I have played them," he wrote home to Letitia. "It would (except that he is not estimated highly by the *leading* people) do him disservice with the intelligent and better sort, but I believe it has an effect of making a sort of factious rush to the Theatre—as his houses were very *bad* before this device was practiced. —I do not grumble or concern myself at all about it. —I feel almost confident my visit must lessen his consideration as an artist, when I am gone away."[12] Fortunately, before things heated up any further, Forrest got into another of his squabbles and stalked out of town.

After an engagement in Boston, Macready returned to New York, where Forrest came calling after dinner with the news that he had received a letter from England. Catherine Macready had seen the daguerreotypes, and her letter beamed with pretty chidings:

Having this moment looked upon what The Sun is pleased to call a likeness, but, what I should declare, the most unpardonable libel any poor human being had ever to contend against, I cannot refrain from asking you, whether it was a friendly act to persuade, that disobedient husband to sit to so unkind, so untrue a limner, as the one you have chosen for him? Will not that sweet lady your wife have some sympathy with me, when she reflects, what my sensations must have been in opening that case, which contains the horror? — I pray her, as a true woman, to give you a very good scolding, and to ask her how you should like *her,* to receive such a remembrance of you, were she three thousand long miles away from you? When she has fulfilled this wish of mine, and you are justly penetrated with the crime, of which you are guilty—I shall forgive you—like a true philosopher—and tell you, nothing has given me greater pleasure from America, than that, which the relation of the hospitality, and kindness Mr. Macready has received from you, my dear sir, and Mrs. Forrest, during his sojourn in New York, has communicated. —I only wish I had any means here of testifying my gratitude to you for your recent attention to him; which has gratified him very much, and which is one of the delightful things, among the many he will have to reflect upon in remembering his visit to your great country— A country you must be aware, he has taught his whole family to reverence, and from the high tone of his letters now, one that will not disappoint—his previous high estimation of it.[13]

The mailboat carrying Catherine's letter crossed the one carrying her husband's complaints to his sister.

MACREADY SNOWBIRDED SOUTH for the winter, the first time he had ventured onto Forrest's old stamping ground. It was January and the route through vast pine barrens and paludal swamps was hard going, almost as trying as his ragged fellow travelers. From Savannah he took the new Central of Georgia railway to Macon and Griffin; in places the little engine wheezed along so slowly, between stops to chop wood for the fire and occasional bouts of pushing when it ground to a halt, that he got out and walked. Where the tracks ran out he was tumbled about by a pitching stagecoach that forded streams, bogs, and rivers and at one point overturned in heavy rain, while his baggage, which went by cart, got stuck in mud. Eventually he arrived in Montgomery and took a steamboat—one of the old models with the communal hairbrush chained to the wall that had so horrified Dickens—down the winding Alabama to Mobile. When the rains set in his impressionable temper darkened still further, and he started repeating to himself that his venture was hopeless and his children would be better off if he were dead.

After Mobile, though, his prospects brightened. Another boat, one of the palatial new steamers cocooned with carpets, skylights, and grand pianos, took him to New Orleans, where he found himself in the capable hands of Sol Smith and Noah Ludlow. The two runaways from Albany had entered into a tempestuous but profitable partnership; soon they would become the first American impresarios to control an entertainment empire that stretched halfway across the country.

The south took to Macready from the start. His appearances created an extraordinary excitement. Steamboats delayed their departure so the passengers could see him; women shrieked in the last act of his *Hamlet*. It was clear that to cultivated southerners Macready's intensely contained style of acting was more congenial than Forrest's grandstanding, which suddenly looked crude in comparison. Macready, Sol Smith recalled, was "*the* subject of conversation" among the men smoking by the stove on the steamboats leaving New Orleans. "Great man Ned is," one self-styled expert held forth, "but, after seeing Macready, one doesn't relish Ned's acting as formerly. He is all very well as Metamora and Jack Cade, but when he attempts Shakespearean characters . . ." The critic concluded the sentence by shaking his head and shuddering as if he had taken a dose of salts.[14]

America was still hungry for Shakespeare, and above all for the great tragedies: *Hamlet* made Macready more money than anything else. But as his trip progressed, the Englishman began to realize that was he was becoming one side of a deepening argument. The elite had never much cared for Forrest, and it was growing increasingly tired of his proudly worn populism and his rowdy b'hoys. It wanted the Bard done properly, not frontier style, and the highbrow papers started to come out for the English actor. Forrest's supporters countered by accusing them of Anglomania, often with good cause. One critic echoed Macready's own opinion when he declared that Forrest's "noisy, determined, radical partisans" had applauded him indiscriminately: it would be "unjust, if not unkind to Mr. Forrest," he added, "to place him in rivalry or competition with a veteran, who has passed through the fiery ordeal unscathed, of the most able, intelligent, if not illustrious critics that England has produced; who, as a scholar, an actor, and a man of genius—a hard student, a severe disciplinarian, has maintained possession of the British stage, almost without a rival, for the last twenty years."[15]

Macready began to unwind. Despite the bumbling incompetence of the local stock companies, the rough-and-ready conditions, and the vulgar rural audiences who were oblivious to his finer points, there was plenty about his southern adventure to delight him: the woods and wild gorges, the dazzling views across the bay from the low cliffs at Mobile, the fresh warm air and the neat white houses with their green verandas and peach trees in full winter bloom. New Orleans enchanted him—though he was taken aback when a professor of elocution called and asked him to speak more clearly on stage—and there was one striking difference from the north: "The people seem so happy!"[16] His enjoyment, though, was sliced through with the scourge of slavery. At one stop he drew up in front of an auction, and when his face filled with horror a bystander assured him that Negroes had no feelings and no more minded being parted from their families than cats nursed a grudge when their kittens were drowned. Macready thought the slaves would be perfectly justified in plunging knives into their owners' brutal hearts. Surely, he thought, America must be a great country one day, in the arts, in literature, and in moral elevation, but it was clearly not there yet: southern generals who were lionized for shooting young beaus who seduced their daughters were not his idea of ethical men. Yet Macready was far more sanguine than most English visitors: unlike them he saw improvements everywhere. "Dickens's misjudgment is as clear to me as the noon-day sun," he declared to his diary.[17] The fraught subject of his friend had first come up three days into his trip: Macready immediately broke Dickens's edict and did his best, considering how strongly he disagreed with him, to explain and defend his views.

The day before Macready's closing performance in New Orleans, Edwin Forrest walked on the stage during a rehearsal of *Othello* and greeted his English friend. Forrest had realized what good business their playoff had been: he had decided to give it another go, and for the next three months the two played musical chairs around the south. Macready retrod his steps to Mobile and opened on March 4; the same night Forrest began a run in New Orleans. After two weeks, Macready returned to New Orleans, and Forrest took his place in Mobile. Two weeks later, as Forrest arrived back in New Orleans, Macready moved on to St. Louis and Cincinnati, marveling at the beauty of the same Mississippi that had so depressed Dickens and Trollope—a slimy monster, his friend had shuddered. After another round, Forrest left New Orleans for Cincinnati, turning down a proposed banquet in his honor—to match one thrown for Macready a week earlier—in order to arrive while the Englishman's chair was still warm, and then doubled back to St. Louis.

In dollar terms Macready came out ahead, partly because he was first on the ground. But Forrest was winning the headline wars by a wide margin. "Those who see a superiority in Macready over our own great actor, must be blinded by prejudice," scoffed the St. Louis *Republican:* "for not only have foreign critics pronounced him great, but the applause forced from the coldest spectators of his efforts, manifests that skill as an actor, which Macready fails in."[18]

Forrest's supporters had the edge over Macready's: they were noisier and more ardent. They became noisier still when, halfway through Macready's tour, the verbal skirmishing between Britain and America escalated to its worst pitch since the War of 1812.

WAR, IN FACT, was in the air again.

In 1842, Lord Ashburton, the British foreign secretary, led a special delegation to Washington and sat down with Daniel Webster, the secretary of state, to resolve the long-standing matters that had bedeviled Anglo-American relations. The resulting Webster-Ashburton Treaty did lay several thorny problems to rest. It called for a final end to the slave trade on the high seas; Webster denied Britain the right to inspect suspected slavers flying the American flag, but he agreed, in principle at least, that the U.S. Navy would patrol the African coast itself. It also settled the border dispute between Canada and Maine which had precipitated the Pork and Beans War of 1838–39, and the crazy squabble over the Republic of Indian Stream, a disputed border territory that had declared independence and provoked an international incident when several of its three hundred and fifteen citizens invaded Canada and shot up the house of a British judge to free a comrade who had been arrested over a debt of a few dollars he owed to a hardware store. Ashburton and Webster also drew a line under the *Caroline* Affair, a messy business that began in 1837 when a band of fugitives from the failed Upper Canada Rebellion dug in on an island in the Niagara River, where they were supplied with money, arms, and freedom fighters by the S.S. *Caroline,* an American-owned steamer. The Canadian militia slipped out at night, seized the steamer in U.S. waters, set it on fire, and cut it loose to drift over Niagara Falls. Outraged Americans pressed for an invasion of Canada; for months, there were skirmishes along the border, and the British steamer *Sir Robert Peel* was retributively boarded, plundered, and burned. The State of New York put a man on trial who boasted in a bar of being one of the *Caroline* incendiaries; Britain loudly hinted that his execution would bring reprisals, and though in the end he was acquitted the affair gave rise to the first definition, by Webster, of the principle of preemptive self-defense.

Webster and Ashburton also settled the old issue of the impressment of American sailors and a dispute over the *Creole,* an American slaver whose cargo overpowered their captors and sailed to the British-controlled Bahamas, where most were freed. But the two biggest diplomatic headaches of all were left untouched. In 1818 John Quincy Adams had agreed to the joint management with Britain of the vast Oregon Territory—the land, north of California and west of the Rockies, that included the modern states of Oregon, Washington, and Idaho, and parts of Montana, Wyoming, and British Columbia—while its disputed status was resolved. Britain argued for the Columbia River as the border; America proposed to extend the U.S. border west from the Rockies along the Forty-ninth Parallel. The decision had twice been postponed, the second time indefinitely, but the galloping belief in Manifest Destiny and increasing American migration along the Oregon Trail brought the issue to a head. Meanwhile, there was the problem of Texas, a self-declared independent republic since American settlers, led by Andrew Jackson's old Tennessee comrade Sam Houston, had seized it from Mexico in 1835. By the early 1840s, Britain was putting pressure on Mexico to relinquish its claim in the hope that Texas would remain independent, abolish slavery, and become a friendly trading partner. Britain pleaded principle; America suspected self-interest, since many believed that a slave-free Texas would undermine slavery in the United States, thereby raising the price of cotton and sugar and making exports from Britain's colonies, where slavery had been abolished in 1837, economically viable. Toward the end of 1843, a flurry of letters from Abel Parker Upshur, Webster's successor as secretary of state, to Edward Everett, the American ambassador to Britain, predicted all sorts of horrors if Britain got its way—epidemic smuggling of British goods into the United States, the collapse of America's agriculture, the ruin of its industry, a bankrupt government, labor unrest, an exodus of slaves, an increase in repressive violence by slaveowners, racial conflict, civil and international war, and the extermination of two and a half million African Americans—and the consequence of Britain's interference was the renewal of American calls for annexation.

In 1844, while Macready was still in the midst of his tour, the presidential race was dominated by the impassioned debate over expansionism. James Polk, the Democrats' dark-horse candidate, campaigned on a platform of annexing Texas, acquiring California, and occupying the whole Oregon Territory, from the California border to a latitude of 54′40″, the southern boundary of Russian Alaska, even if the price was war. His slogan—"The reannexation of Texas and the reoccupation of Oregon—Fifty-four Forty or Fight!"—claimed them as spiritually American anyway.

"The crisis is at last on us," the *New York Herald* warned on March 18: "the crisis involving questions of the annexation of Texas, the negotiations on the Oregon territory, and, probably, war with Mexico and England."[19] The only question was which war would be first, and in the case of England, whether it would be provoked directly, by the Oregon dispute, or indirectly, by the Texas crisis.

There was one more issue that divided the two countries, and in its repercussions on transatlantic relations it was the most destructive of all. It was summed up in one word: repudiation.

America was a debtor nation. It had borrowed abroad to pay for the Revolution and the Louisiana Purchase, and in the 1830s foreign loans and investments, mainly in the form of state bonds, had funded the great surge of railroad and canal building. In 1837, the economy went into free fall, the victim of an unholy trinity of triggers—the Bank of England's interest rate rises, a slump in the price of cotton, and the surge in inflation fueled by the lending spree that followed Andrew Jackson's attacks on the monopolist Second Bank of America—and as the depression deepened, bankruptcy stopped being a taboo word. By 1840 the state debt of Pennsylvania had mounted to more than thirty-four million dollars; that year, its legislature voted to postpone repayments. By 1842, after "repudiating" representatives—so called because they actively campaigned to stop paying state debts rather than raise taxes—had been elected in large numbers, of the twenty-eight American states another three, Illinois, Indiana, and Maryland, had defaulted on repayments, while a further four, Arkansas, Louisiana, Michigan, and Mississippi, together with the Territory of Florida, permanently repudiated part or the whole of their outstanding debt.

English banks were the largest creditors: of Pennsylvania's thirty-four-million-dollar debt, more than twenty million dollars was held in

England. Feelings grew so bitter that the Reverend Sydney Smith, the genially trenchant canon of St. Paul's, declared in the course of a series of published letters and petitions that if he met a Pennsylvanian at dinner he would strip him of his clothes and boots and distribute them among the guests, most of whom had probably suffered by his state's dishonor. Grand financial institutions were not the only casualties: English widows, orphans, and pensioners had been persuaded to invest their savings across the Atlantic. Huge numbers were affected: at the Oriental Club in London, three hundred members, retired officers of the India Service, held U.S. state bonds.[20] In March 1845 Edward Everett wrote from London to Robert Walker, a U.S. senator from Mississippi, to impress upon him "the distress which has been occasioned in the bosom of many families in this country" by the defaults:

> You would, I know, excuse me for calling your attention to the subject, if you could be aware of one tithe of the sorrow and shame which, in common with every American in Europe who has any sensibility to the estimation in which his country is held abroad, I have suffered in consequence of this default.
>
> If the sacrifice of the little which I can call my own in the world would have wiped off this blot upon our character, I feel that I could at any time have made it. —I should have felt that poverty thus entailed on those dear to me was a richer inheritance, than the entire domain of the United States under the intolerable burden of reproach which, in the estimation of the civilized world, attends such a breach of public faith.[21]

The bonds pledged the faith of the states on their face: Mississippi's reputation, Everett added, had been blackened, the rest of the country shared in her reproach, and "repudiation" had become a byword for dishonor throughout the world.

England finally had a clear-cut reason for resenting its old colony. A few years back, James Gordon Bennett editorialized in the *Herald,* an American visiting Europe was received like a kind of sovereign. No longer. As soon as repudiation struck, a very marked change indeed took place in the social intercourse of the two nations. The feeling then awakened, unfavourable to this country, has since been every year increasing; and an American traveller in the land now, instead of being received as before with respect and kindness, is regarded with undisguised suspicion, and is sure to encounter, on all hands, the most mortifying evidences of the altered tone of public feeling. In fact, the very waiters at the inns, as they show the "American gentleman" to his room, make sure, by repeated examination, that their pockets are safely buttoned, lest they might lose the sixpence or shilling lying comfortably there. We might allude to many instances of this kind, shewing that American travelers are looked on in Europe as a species of sharpers and pickpockets, and a very dangerous species too.

"The country is disgraced in Europe," he added; it had lost its "respectable position amongst the nations of the earth."[22]

Bennett was not exaggerating. The London *Times* weighed in around the same time with a blast of withering scorn which was a fair sample of the anger rife among every class in England. "Frenchmen are sometimes impertinent, Irishmen impudent, Welshmen voluble, Englishmen blustering, Scotchmen cool," it began, "but the conjoint coolness, blustering, volubility, impudence, and impertinence of a true Yankee has a height and depth and breadth about it which 'flogs' each of these nations in their most characteristic accomplishment." America, it pursued, was "a confederation of public bankrupts" who had coolly refused to pay their debts, not from necessity but because it suited them not to. They were swindlers and scoundrels, and some even had the cheek to demand that Britain, if it was really serious about abolition, unilaterally lift its import duties to help American business contemplate life without slavery, while in the next breath advocating U.S. protectionism as the proper response to British intransigence over Oregon: "This is, was, and will be, the American cry—'Give! Give! Give!' But the English counter-cry will be—'Pay! Pay! Pay!' Before you ask us to believe a single word you say—before you expect us to entertain a single argument you use—'pay your debts.' Till then, you have no right to a place among honest nations—you have no claim to ordinary credit or common courtesy."[23]

The world was becoming a smaller place. The new transatlantic steamers were shuttling passengers back and forth more quickly than ever, and thanks to relays of boats and coaches and the new telegraph wires, the newspapers they brought with them were flashed to news-hungry editors before the steamers put into port. The disputes of the 1840s were thus conducted not in the careful language of diplomacy but in the invective of columnists, with one side lobbing accusations of flagitious crimes and the other side batting back still harder. In January 1844, as Macready was plowing through the woods to New Orleans, the *New York Herald,* the most widely distributed paper in America, had reprinted an even more savage piece of Yankee-bashing from the English *Foreign Quarterly Review* across its front page.* Americans, the writer averred, were all swagger and impudence: they were pigheaded and unscrupulous, "with an incredible genius for lying, a vanity elastic beyond comprehension, the hide of a buffalo, and the shriek of a steam-engine." The all-powerful vulgus had pulled everything down to its level; all dignity, truth, consistency, and courage had evaporated from public life, lynch law had replaced state law, Bowie knives glittered in the hands of murderers on the floor of Congress, and orators peppered their speeches with expletives and lies and stuffed their supporters' pockets with bribes. The people might be independent in the aggregate, but no individual dared stand up to the wishes of the mob, and the consequence was a deadening conformism and a "tangled and hideous democracy." As for American literature, its two great subjects were the joys of liberty and the picturesque heads and flowing limbs of Indians; while slaveowners increased their stock by breeding and trafficking their own children, and the servants of Congress liquored up Indian chiefs to entrap them into signing away their hunting grounds, it was impossible to account for the incredible folly that tempted them to indulge such themes, "unless we refer it to the same infatuation which makes them

---

* Macready was aghast lest it turn out to be one of Forster's productions, but his friend wrote to reassure him that he would never have done such a thing while Macready was in the United States.

boast of their morality in the face of their filthy newspaper press, and of their honesty in the teeth of pocket-picking Pennsylvania." Altogether, the philippic concluded, America was no better than a "vast deposit of human dregs."[24]

The *Review*'s piece was the last word in English mudslinging, the culmination of a verbal battle which became so fierce that it has been called the Third War with England. Here was the full-fledged stereotype of the obnoxious American: vain, grasping, crude, sanctimonious, and hypocritical. In retrospect, it is surprising that Macready lasted so long.

THE COMPETITION LULLED over the summer. Between engagements, Macready went camping and deer hunting in the Adirondacks (he came back awestruck by the scenery but empty-handed) and paid the obligatory trip to Niagara Falls, the Victorian traveler's Alps. "I suppose you actually intend to die without seeing Niagara! Well— chacun à son gout," he wrote home to a friend.[25]

Toward the end of August, Forrest was back on stage in Philadelphia, and when he heard that Macready was en route he took a week off in order to go head to head with him. The Englishman arrived at his hotel and found a note waiting from the American tragedian, inviting him on his free night to *Damon and Pythias,* a popular play based on the Greek legend of two devoted friends who save each other from death. Macready went along, but he did not catch the spirit of brotherly love. Forrest's performance, he noted, was "very dull, heavy-mannered, unpleasant. . . . He is not a good actor—*not at all an artist.*"

Macready's mood had been soured by his discovery that Forrest, this time on his own initiative, had contrived to act in competition with him—"in *opposition* to me," he spluttered, "and, I hear, made this engagement to oppose me! This is not the English generosity of rivalry." He relented only slightly when his Hamlet won the first round. The gentle prince was never Forrest's forte: half of him could have played the part, the critics quipped, and it would have made more sense if he had stormed off after seeing the Ghost, stuck his sword into Claudius, and finished things off in the first act. Two days later, Macready heard that the American Tragedian's performance had been thinly attended. "If it be so," he self-righteously concluded, "he is justly punished for his un-gentlemanly conduct."[26]

On the surface, the two were still friendly. The next Sunday they met and chatted amiably enough; Forrest invited Macready back to see Kate, and the three passed a pleasant day together. Forrest undoubtedly in-tended the contest as a cheerful rivalry between equals, even if he was sure he was more equal than Macready. But, like the rubble before an av-alanche, the warnings were becoming louder, and Forrest's tactics were not exactly diplomatic. In the course of the paper war, his supporters had turned overtly nationalist in tone. "Native Americanism vs. Foreignism. Which of the two to choose? Why, Forrest of course," advised the *American Advocate,* of Philadelphia.[27] Macready responded with an equally undiplomatic curtain speech in which he adverted to "some unworthy attempts, that have been made to excite a prejudice against me and my countrymen engaged in this profession on the plea of being foreigners." That brought uneasy noises from the audience, and he quickly added that he knew such influences could not reach their liberal minds.[28] It was Macready's first politically charged pronouncement before an American public, though it would not be his last.

As his tour came full circle and he returned to New York, Macready's supporters were in the ascendant. This time he was treated to cheering, handkerchief-waving standing ovations every night, and in Boston, his last stop, a theatre fire prompted a committee of leading families to subscribe to convert a music hall into a venue fit to host him. Macready felt thoroughly at home in solid, respectable East Coast society, among New York Knickerbockers and Beacon Hill Brahmins who treated him as a gentleman by virtue of his character rather than as an outcast be-cause of his profession. He was invited to sherry parties and picnics, where his genteel behavior was held in high favor. He dined frequently with businessmen like Philip Hone, the former mayor of New York, and Samuel Ruggles, the developer of Gramercy Park and Union Square, and he became close friends with statesmen and writers, above all Charles Sumner, the reformist future senator, and Henry Wadsworth Longfellow, already an admired poet though *Hiawatha* was still a decade away.

As he sailed home, he reflected that all in all it had been a rewarding trip, and not just financially. "I have passed a very delightful year on this continent," he wrote to a friend, "and I wish more Englishmen would travel here, would leave their prejudices at home, and put only their better and happier feelings into their travelling-bags."[29]

Two months later, Edwin Forrest set out on his trail.

CHAPTER 8

The Man in the Box

EDWIN FORREST, BIG and beaming as always, arrived in Liverpool on January 12, 1845, with Kate at his side. Two days later, while his wife was reunited with her family, he had already traveled on to Paris, and that was where the real trouble began.

William and Catherine Macready were already there. With Covent Garden barely alive and Bunn back in charge at Drury Lane, London's doors were shut to the Eminent. Paris, though, welcomed him with open arms. On his first visit to the French capital, in 1828, Macready had made such a deep impression that audiences wept and fainted and carried him on their shoulders, and the city had not forgotten him. He was enthusiastically welcomed by the literati, and though his audiences now were better prepared for his once revolutionary fusion of nature and artistry—it was Macready, more than anyone, who had ignited the spark of French Romanticism from the classical ashes of the Comédie Française—he still awoke a flurry of excitement, and when he played Hamlet at the king's theatre in the Tuileries Palace he was presented by Louis-Philippe with a jeweled poniard.[*]

There is no record of the two stars meeting in Paris, but Macready certainly knew of the other man's presence. For several days, Forrest tried to make an appointment to see John Mitchell, the impresario of

---

[*] He should have been suspicious when one of the emeralds dropped off; back home he had the knife examined and found the metal was silver gilt and the jewels paste, which just about summed up his view of royalty. "That *shabby dog*," he called the Citizen King (*Diaries*, II. 291).

the English theatre in the city. Mitchell, Macready noted without comment, avoided the American, and Forrest retreated to London, half suspecting that someone was trying to sabotage his tour.

Instead, on February 17, 1845, Forrest opened at the Princess's Theatre in Oxford Street, one of the shabby minor theatres where the legitimate drama had taken refuge, as half of a novel double act with Charlotte Cushman, an American who had just made her London debut. Yet within seconds of striding on stage as Othello he realized something was amiss. The unwonted sound of hissing assailed him from three distinct areas of the auditorium: clearly, he thought, there was an organized opposition afoot. Or so he later claimed: the newspapers reported no hisses, only sustained applause. When he played Macbeth four days later, though, the dissent was unmistakable. "Forrest has failed most dreadfully," his costar wrote home. "In Macbeth they shouted with laughter and hissed him to death."[2]

Even more unexpected was the reaction of the press. The *Spectator* called his Othello a burlesque of Kean "varied by the Yankee nasal twang. . . . His passion is a violent effort of physical vehemence . . . his tenderness is affected, and his smile is like the grin of a wolf showing his fangs."[3] His Lear, the newspaper followed up, was even more of a caricature: "a roaring pantaloon, with a vigorous totter, a head waving as indefatigably as a china image, and lungs of prodigious power. There only wanted the candlewick moustaches to complete the stage idea of a choleric despot in pantomime."[4] The *News*'s critic simply said he found himself yawning.[5]

The reaction was not all bad. In the theatre, Forrest's Lear was cheered at the end of every act: the *Times* called it masterly, intelligent, and powerful, the *Sun* a triumph.[6] But it was clear that a large portion of the press had turned against the American Tragedian. *Punch* captured the flavor in an open letter to Forrest. "Dear Sir," it addressed him,

> Allow me, as an old critic, to very sincerely thank you for the handsome palsy which you have put upon King Lear. Had Shakespeare really known any thing of his art, he would—by two or three lines—have strongly marked the necessity of King Lear's shaking his head to show the age of the man. The poet, however, only half knew his business. You have been his best, his most practical anno-

tator; and in your hands there can be no doubt of the senility of King Lear, seeing that he continually niddle-noddles his head like a toy mandarin. Considering the mere poetry of the part, the fact of Lear's great age might otherwise have escaped us.

Do you not think, sir, that a touch of lumbago, with—in the later scenes—a violent attack of gout, as indicated by flannel swathings, would also considerably assist the moral majesty of Lear, elevated as it unquestionably is by your capital ploy?[7]

Enough of the public went along with the mood that Forrest's run was a flop. After just a few weeks he was playing for virtually nothing, and the engagement came to a swift end. It was the first comprehensive defeat of his life.

Macready heard of Forrest's reception in Newcastle, where he was trudging through another provincial tour, and he read confirmation in the papers of the American's "disastrous and total failure in Macbeth." When he had seen Forrest perform, he noted, the experience was very dull but not otherwise offensive; "but in Macbeth he seems to have provoked the patience of the audience. I am truly sorry for him (without wishing him *great* success) and deeply sorry for his wife."[8]

At the beginning of March, Macready traveled down to London to spend his fifty-third birthday with his family, and he called on the Forrests at their Regent Street lodgings to invite them to the party. There is no record of whether they accepted, but later Macready remembered that over the next few months Forrest "returned mine and my wife's several visits, and met me on friendly terms *outwardly*," as if nothing had changed.[9] What is certain is that Forrest told Macready he had finally engaged to appear in Paris, where he was sure he would be better appreciated. "I fancy *not*," Macready thought.[10] Forrest had been trying to put together his own production at the Théâtre Odéon in Paris: as the actor he asked to be his stage manager later recalled, the negotiations were broken off as a result of the insolvency of the theatre's owner, and Forrest never did act in France. It was an embarrassing comedown: he had told his friends that he had set his heart on performing in the country that had aided America's glorious struggle for independence, and to herald his appearance flattering pieces had been placed in the French press.

However civil he was in public, in private Forrest was becoming increasingly furious. He was not an envious man, but he was rock solid in his conviction that he was the greatest actor in the world. Unlike Macready, he rarely found fault with his own performances. "I never acted better in my life—I never before achieved such a performance of 'Lear,' " he once wrote to a friend. "What a pity, it could not have been photographed! I mean the entire representation of the character, with all its power—with all its changeful passions—with all its unspeakable subtleties."[11] He had never submitted to being snubbed, even before the years of playing heroes to adoring fans had rubbed off on him, and he resented, with mounting self-righteousness, what he saw as a gross injustice. No matter that the majority of the American press had favored him over Macready; no matter that Macready himself had been attacked for years by the partisan English papers. Forrest's pride needed a grand enemy, and there was only one candidate.

He brooded over the pieces of the supposed plot. Macready, he knew, was the intimate friend of John Forster, the man who had written him down so spitefully on his last visit; besides, he also recalled, they were both cronies of Charles Dickens, the great America-baiter. On this visit, Forster's *Examiner* barely noticed the American's performances: its two squibs were based on secondhand information, and though the first passed on the news—arch enough, admittedly—that Forrest's style had apparently undergone a "clear improvement," the second was both brief and contemptuous. "Our old friend, Mr Forrest, afforded great amusement to the public, by his performance of Macbeth," it sneered. "Indeed our best comic actors do not often excite so great a quantity of mirth. The change from an inaudible murmur to a thunder of sound, was enormous; but the grand feature was the combat, in which he stood scraping his sword against that of Macduff. We were at a loss to know what this gesture meant, till an enlightened critic in the gallery shouted out, 'that's right, sharpen it!' "[12] This was enough to persuade Forrest that Forster had poisoned the press against him at his friend Macready's behest. Or so he said later.*

---

* Forrest was likely helped to his conclusion by Macready's enemies: one candidate is Henry Wikoff, Forrest's grand tour companion, who told his friend that everything Forster wrote was at Macready's charge (see *New York Herald,* April 26, 1849).

Then there was the suspicious fact that Macready had been in Paris when he was so rudely snubbed. Forrest only needed one more piece of circumstantial evidence, and it came via another close associate of Macready's, Edward Bulwer Lytton. Forrest wrote to Bulwer Lytton for permission to perform, for a nightly fee, two of his plays. The writer refused, but offered terms of fifty guineas for twenty nights. Forrest smelled a rat: since Bulwer Lytton had replied on March 4 and Forrest's engagement was for three nights a week and due to end on April 7, it was impossible for him to get his money's worth out of the deal.[13]

The names lined up: the Eminent, he concluded, had clearly stabbed him in the back. Or again, so he later claimed.

Was he right? Almost certainly not. There was clearly something uncivil about John Mitchell's refusal to meet with him, and it was easy to conjecture that the manager might have consulted Macready about Forrest's likely prospects in Paris. But Mitchell later categorically swore that at no point did Macready, "in any manner direct or indirect, with me personally, or to my knowledge with any other person, attempt to interfere with, or prevent, any arrangement, that Mr. Forrest might have desired to make with me for his appearance at Paris."[14] The truth is that Mitchell's enterprise was billed as the English Theatre in Paris: it would have been self-defeating to give the stage to an American, particularly one who wanted to prove that American tragedians were at least as good as English and then go home. Why Mitchell avoided Forrest, he kept to himself: most likely, he did not want to get into his reasons for excluding him.

As for Bulwer Lytton and Forster, it seems highly likely that after Macready came back from America he had complained to his friends about his head-to-head bouts with Forrest. He certainly told Catherine: in stark contrast to her earlier letters, she happily reported to her husband that Forrest had been spotted on stage foaming at the mouth to a disgusting extent.[15] Yet Forster had already shown himself perfectly happy to condemn Forrest without the slightest hint from Macready, or rather, despite all Macready's representations to the contrary; in any case, Forster was laid up with rheumatic fever during the American's engagement and missed the entire thing, and though it is certainly possible that he suborned deputies or spoon-fed a friendly editor, he had too many enemies in the press to marshal a full-scale campaign against anyone. Bulwer Lytton, meanwhile, was merely sticking to his usual policy and his standard fee: as a leading writer, he felt obliged to set an example by insisting on licensing his plays only for long runs. The principle was especially important just then because he was piloting a bill through Parliament to shore up writers' royalties. It must also have crossed his mind that Forrest had turned a vast profit from performing his plays across America free of copyright.

The most outlandish charge that Forrest later leveled at Macready was that he had personally orchestrated the whole opposition to him at the theatre and in the press. That must be untrue. Aside from the fact that he was away nearly the whole time, Macready had never attracted a fan club like Kean's Wolves, and he had never cozied up to journalists. In any case, he was too proud to play the hypocrite and call on Forrest if he had been maneuvering against him.

Who, then, was behind the dissent? There are two answers. The first is that Macready's school of acting had become the only show in town. Largely thanks to the Eminent's example, tastes had changed since Forrest's last trip: Victorians increasingly wanted Shakespeare played with reasoned artistry, and the American looked like a throwback to a more florid age.

The second answer lay in the world outside the theatre, a place where most actors seldom looked. In November, James Polk had been elected president on his slogan "Fifty-four Forty or Fight," and the English press was thick with battle cries: within months the London *Times* reported that the Foreign Office had informed the American envoy "that the English Government is perfectly prepared to make war immediately upon the United States, and to strike great blows at the first outbreak of hostilities."[16] Meanwhile the repudiation scandal was still rumbling on. *Punch* was busy caricaturing Americans as insolent "Yankee-Noodles" who shook their fists and pistols across the Atlantic and taught Grandmother Britannia to suck eggs, and in one number it managed to snare the twin demons of repudiation and expansionism with a single barb. America, it revealed, wanted to toss England for Oregon, and it was only prevented from making a proposition to that effect by the fear of having to borrow a dollar for the purpose.[17] When

One of a series of sourly condescending cartoons printed by the satirical London magazine Punch *in response to the threat of a new Anglo-American war. In each case the United States is portrayed as a scrappy little upstart towered over by its venerable English elders.*
Punch, *vol. X, p. 119, March 14, 1846.*

"WHAT? YOU YOUNG YANKEE-NOODLE, STRIKE YOUR OWN FATHER!"

Forrest tried out *Metamora,* his Indian tragedy, the entire press derided it as an orgy of senseless butchery and the *Observer* saw its chance. "What a pity," it crowed, "he could not be let loose upon the drab-colored swindlers of Pennsylvania."[18]

There was one problem with the hypothesis that Forrest was the victim of anti-Americanism: his costar and compatriot Charlotte Cushman had made an instant and spectacular hit. From her first night, she was hailed as the finest actress in the English-speaking world: the papers leaped over themselves to panegyrize her as the possessor of a godlike gift, a dizzying admixture of earnestness, intensity, sensitivity, and passion that put her beyond the reach of England's most accomplished actresses. Critics likened her to the great Sarah Siddons, and the *Sun,* forgetting it had used the same line about Forrest, declared that she had made the most impressive debut since Kean.[19] Forrest was outraged that a minor American actor had stolen his crown: he sat thunder-faced backstage while the audience roared her name, and he refused to lead her out. "Damn Miss Cushman, she can go to hell!" he exploded.[20] In a week, Charlotte went from eating chops in a bedsit to entertaining in splendor in Bond Street, and she was still starring at the Princess's long after Forrest had left to lick his wounds.

For a while, Forrest was convinced that Macready had maneuvered against him to elevate Cushman. The Englishman, after all, was her idol: she had been mesmerized by him as a child, she had thrown away a career as a manager to act with him during his last American trip, and she dated her discovery of true acting to their first night together on stage. Charlotte had sent Macready flowers and poems, published sonnets to him in the papers, and reverently kissed his hand, a liberty that sent him into his usual frenzy of propriety, though for once he worried unnecessarily, because Cushman, a large, angular woman who, some said, looked peculiarly like her mentor, turned out to have well-developed Sapphic tendencies. It was on Macready's advice that she had come to England to practice her craft, and the Englishman had furnished her with letters of introduction to the London literati: it was, Forrest told one actor, "by *them* he was crushed, as the means to exalt *her.*"[21]*

There was undoubtedly no love lost between the two Americans. Forrest charged Cushman with Macreadyism, which to him meant mannered, mechanical acting; once he labeled her "Macready in petticoats."[22] Charlotte called Forrest a butcher and refused to meet him at dinner; she was also far from convinced that he had been as universally admired on his first trip to London as he claimed. It appeared, she wrote home, that last time around Alfred Bunn had manipulated the press in his favor: "Now he has no such support. The papers cut him all to pieces."[23] But Cushman had no need to put Forrest down in her own cause, and Macready, even if he had had a taste for such intrigues, certainly had no interest in so doing: on her arrival in England, Cushman was canny enough to refuse to play second fiddle to her mentor, which infuriated him enough to leave her to

---

* Cushman was not the only American actress who professed herself indebted to Macready for his advice. Another was the wonderful Anna Cora Mowatt, a runaway child bride who turned to the stage when her elderly husband lost his fortune; a New York blue blood by birth, she became the first notable female American playwright as well as a successful comic actress. Macready threw a dinner to introduce her to his influential friends and, she gratefully acknowledged, promoted her interests with alacrity.

make her own way. In any case, Forrest quickly realized that talking up his compatriot's success was only a recipe for humiliation.

Yet Cushman's triumph does not refute the charge of anti-Americanism among Forrest's detractors. London cheered her because it had discovered an exceptional new talent in its own image and, perhaps, because she was a woman and a debutante. It booed Forrest because he was billed as the *American* Tragedian, the representative of his nation, and because he was famous for his nationalistic politics. Forrest had set himself up as the Great American, and London was only too happy to pull him down.

FOR THE NEXT year, Forrest avoided the capital and toured Britain and Ireland, where he was far better received. In Cork the papers lauded him as the foremost living actor, a man lit by the divine fire of genius, and the audiences cheered the roof off, especially when he acted the rebel against English tyranny: indeed, he identified so passionately with his characters' struggles that it hardly seemed like acting at all. On his last night, he came out for his call, boomed out the hope that "the dark cloud that overhangs this fair country will soon pass away; that a happier and brighter day will beam on her," and bowed himself out to an earshattering roar.[24] On March 1 he moved on to Edinburgh, and the next day he took advantage of a night off to see his old friend, now his arch rival, in *Hamlet.*

It was Macready's first night and the theatre was packed. He entered to a tempest of applause, though the figure he cut was hardly heroic. He wore a dress waisted under his armpits and a hat with a huge sable plume. His gloves were too big; his undershirt, of amber-colored satin, looked simply dirty. John Coleman, who was on stage with him, declared that "with his gaunt, angular figure; his grizzled hair; his blue-black beard, close-shaven to his square jaws, unsoftened by a trace of pigment; his irregular features; his extraordinary nose, unlike anything else in the shape of a nose I have ever seen; and his long, lean neck, he appeared positively grotesque." But, he added, "when he spoke, he made music—brightened, illumined, irradiated the atmosphere, and became transformed into the very beau ideal of the most poetic, subtle, intellectual, dramatic, and truly human Prince of Denmark I have ever seen."[25]

Macready, too, felt he was acting at his best, and he began to relax, sensing he was carrying the audience with him.

Then he reached the players' scene. He gave Hamlet's famous directions to the actors, he told Horatio that he had set *The Mousetrap* to catch the conscience of the King, and as the court entered he muttered to him the simple line:

"They are coming to the play. I must be idle. Get you a place."[26]

Modern editions of *Hamlet* still disagree about the meaning of the phrase "be idle." One camp glosses Hamlet's meaning as "seem to have nothing on my mind," another as "act foolish, pretend to be crazy." The two senses are similar to those of the word "distracted"—having one's attention diverted, or being affected with madness.

Both are dramatically possible, but the second gloss is a better fit. Hamlet has already put on an antic disposition before the court; Polonius has reported him as mad; the King and Queen have charged Rosencrantz and Guildenstern to find out what afflicts him. Now, as the march plays and the trumpet and drums sound in the court, the King turns to Hamlet.

"How fares our cousin Hamlet?" he asks.

"Excellent, i'faith," Hamlet replies: "of the chameleon's dish. I eat the air, promise-crammed. You cannot feed capons so."

Hamlet is playing on the meaning of the word "fares," and he responds as if Claudius has inquired what he had for dinner. Chameleons, as well as being able, like Hamlet, to change their hue, were commonly believed to feed on air. That offers him another pun, on the homonym "heir." Hamlet implies that he is being fed an equally thin diet: Claudius is filling him with empty promises that he will succeed to the throne. Perhaps there is a suggestion, too, that he is eating himself up in his horror at his situation. To Hamlet there is sense behind the line, but he does not expect Claudius to catch on to the innuendo, and its aim is clearly to make him appear crazed. Claudius's response suggests it has worked: "I have nothing with this answer, Hamlet," he replies; "these words are not mine." In other words, he does not understand what Hamlet is saying, because the Prince's answer seems to have no connection with his question.

During the rest of the scene, moreover, Hamlet hardly makes an effort to be unobtrusive. He jeers at Polonius, makes obscene puns to

Ophelia, pointedly remarks that his mother looks cheerful considering her husband has just died, and interrupts the play with barbed comments. "You are as good as a chorus, my lord," says Ophelia. The reading that Hamlet's line—"I must be idle"—marks his resumption of his feigned madness is, then, at least highly plausible and most likely correct. Macready certainly thought so. As the court entered he walked rapidly back and forth across the stage, bobbed his head from side to side, pulled out his handkerchief, took it by the corner and twirled it in the air while dancing a little hopping jig.

At that point, before the next speech had started, an almighty hiss came from a box to the right of the stage—a hiss, said Coleman, like the exhaust from a steam engine. Macready bowed derisively and waved his handkerchief even harder. The audience booed back at the hisser, the play came to a standstill, and Macready, livid with rage, struggling to stay in character, staggered back and sank into a chair.

"Turn him out!" came a cry from the students' gallery above the box; eventually a burly figure stood up and slowly turned away. Macready took hold of himself and launched back into action.

The next day the whole of Edinburgh was abuzz with rumors that the hisser was none other than the American Tragedian. Macready, standing in the footlights, had not made him out, but John Coleman had seen him distinctly: "The square brow, the majestic head, the dark eyes flashing forth defiance, the pallor of the white face enhanced by his black beard, which contrasted strongly with his turned-down white collar, he looked exactly as he used to look in *The Gladiator* when he said, 'Let them come, we are prepared!' "[27] At first Macready refused to believe it: Forrest, he told the manager Murray, was too much of a gentleman to betray himself so publicly.[28] But the next day it was beyond doubt. Three men who had been sitting in the American's box told an actor that the hisser was Forrest. Another audience member told the manager that the hisser was Forrest. A police officer came in during the rehearsal and said the hisser was Forrest, and the police record for the night confirmed it. That day the *Scotsman* alluded to the incident. "We should not have thought it worthwhile to mention such a circumstance," it mentioned, "had it not been reported, though we scarcely think it credible, that the offender was a brother actor, and one, too, who probably considers himself a rival."[29]

Lest any doubt remained, the high sheriff of Edinburgh later summed up the evidence: "There was but *one* hiss—and one hisser. Forrest was the hisser—Forrest's was the hiss."[30]

All of Macready's long-nursed animus against his profession burst out against the American actor.

"I feel glad that it is not an Englishman," he piously declared, suddenly patriotic—"but no Englishman would have done a thing so base. . . . I do not think that such an action has its parallel in all theatrical history! The low-minded ruffian! That man would commit a murder, *if he dare*."[31]

That evening Forrest coolly walked into the theatre again. He had dressed carefully for his part in his best dress suit and a pair of kid gloves, he had sprinkled himself with cologne, and he went in search of the editor of the *Scotsman*. He found him in his usual seat in the upper boxes, fixed his eyes on him, gritted his teeth, and asked if he was the writer of the article in his paper.

The newspaperman shrank a little.

"I am not," he replied.

"It is fortunate for you that you are not," Forrest said, glaring, "for had you been, by the living God I would have flung you over the balcony into the pit."[32]

By March 12 the scandal had filtered down to London. The *Times* reprinted the *Scotsman*'s report under the headline "Professional Jealousy," and added, belittlingly, "We believe that Mr. Forrest, an American actor, is the party supposed."[33] The *Edinburgh Weekly Chronicle,* which was firmly in Forrest's camp, published an enormously long piece two days later in which it attempted to justify the hiss and called the *Times*'s comment an "unjustifiable and inexcusable" slur motivated by favoritism and malice. Macready's hand, it added, was clearly behind it.

Perhaps the matter might have rested there. Forrest could have gone on performing to admiring regional crowds; the whole thing might have dispersed in a cloud of doubt. But it was not in Forrest's nature to let anything lie. He bridled at the accusation of underhanded behavior, and he took on the challenge like the man of action he was. The *Scotsman* refused to insert his letter answering its charges, but since the article had now surfaced in the London press—"doubtless," thought Forrest, "sent thither for insertion, from the same malignant motives which governed its writer"—he felt called upon to reply in the most public manner possible: a long letter to the editor of the *Times,* which he sent via a friend, along with strict instructions to ensure it was printed verbatim and a request that twenty copies of the paper be forwarded to him.[34]

It was not a conciliatory piece of correspondence. "There are two legitimate modes of evincing approbation and disapprobation in the Theatre," Forrest launched off:

> one, expressive of approval, by the clapping of hands, and the other by hisses, to mark dissent. And, as well-timed and hearty applause is the first meed of the actor who deserves well, so also is hissing a salutary and wholesome corrective of the abuses of the stage; and it was against one of those abuses that my dissent was given. . . . The truth is, that Mr. Macready thought fit to introduce a fancy dance into his performance of Hamlet, which I thought and still think, a desecration of the scene. . . .
>
> That a man may manifest his opinion, after the recognized mode, according to the best of his judgment, when actuated by proper motives and for justifiable ends, is a right which, until now, I never heard questioned, and I contend that that right extends equally to an actor as to any other man, in his capacity as a spectator. For, from the nature of his studies, he is much better qualified to judge of a theatrical performance, than any soi-disant critic, who has never himself been an actor. . . .
>
> As to the pitiful charge of "professional jealousy," preferred against me, I dismiss it with the contempt it merits, confidently relying upon all those of the profession with whom I have been associated, for a refutation of the slander.[35]

Behind Forrest's bombast and pique lay the differences between two styles of acting, styles now inseparable from their nations: to the American, Macready's flamboyant handkerchief action—Forrest later labeled it his *"pas de mouchoir"*—was an effeminate travesty of the manly dignity of a star. But sibilations, like vegetables, were dying out as vehicles of dramatic criticism, and though Forrest was hardly the first actor to be hissed in London, and Macready was not the last to be hissed in Edinburgh, Forrest's self-defense was built on shaky ground. In any case, when all was said and done the peculiar history of hissing and the different readings of *Hamlet* were beside the point. The plain fact was that never before had one actor stood up and hissed another in full view of the stage. Macready had never hissed Kean, Kean had never hissed Kemble, and the star of one nation had certainly never hissed the star of another. The act was probably unplanned; once done, it had to be defended, for Forrest was not about to admit he was in the wrong.

Macready read Forrest's letter—Forster showed him the paper—the day it was printed. "This seems to me," he wrote, "to be the seal of his character. Many have been indisposed to believe such malignity and such folly, and many have refused to believe it. But here stands self-confessed this citizen of the United States, to whom the greatest harm that I can do, I will: which is to give him the full benefit of his noble, tasteful, and critical qualities, and 'leave him alone with his glory.' "[36] It was a doleful end to a once cheerful friendship.

The controversy spread across the Atlantic and rumbled on long after Forrest went home in August. The reaction of the American newspapers was divided, largely along class lines: one half commended Forrest's independent spirit, while the rest strongly censured his lapse of manners. At the inevitable homecoming banquet in New York, the honor of proposing Forrest's health was given to William Cullen Bryant, the poet and editor of the *Evening Post*. But Bryant was also a friend of Macready's, and he slipped Forrest a piece of advice masquerading as praise. The American tragedian, he declared, had never fallen prey to the follies that tempted other men of his profession: "In the intense competitions of the stage, Mr. Forrest has obeyed a native instinct in treating his rivals with generosity, and, when beset by calumny and intrigue, has known how to preserve the magnanimous silence of conscious greatness."

Perhaps he might have once; not now. Forrest stood up and pointedly replied that he was sure his audience would pardon him if he broke that silence. England's theatrical cliques, he boomed, had machinated against him, and their hireling scribblers had treated him with malice:

"Even before I had appeared I was threatened with critical castigation, and some of the very journals which, upon my former appearance in London, applauded me to the echo, now assailed me with bitterest denunciations. Criticism was degraded from its high office, —degraded into mere caviling, accompanied by very pertinent allusions to Pennsylvania bonds, repudiation, and democracy." At the mention of repudiation nervous laughter and defiant cheers broke out in the hall.[37]

Forrest did not mention Macready by name, but he did not need to. He had brought home a burning grudge; he shared it with anyone who would listen, and it seeped out into the press, where it assumed the ridiculous dignity of a minor international incident. It would be wrong to suggest that Forrest demonized Macready to cover up his failure and explain his actions in Edinburgh: wrong because he had persuaded himself it was the truth. His friends took up his cause with a vengeance, and they were still nursing their anger two years later when Macready returned to the United States.

The battle lines were drawn, but still no one suspected that a petty feud that became public knowledge over a single line from Shakespeare would soon leave dozens dying on New York's streets.

CHAPTER 9

Of Men and Sheep

HISTORY, SAID MARX, repeats itself, first as tragedy, then as farce. The Shakespeare Riots proved the contrary: they were rehearsed as farce and played out as tragedy.

It was a cold, blustery November afternoon when William Charles Macready checked into Jones's Hotel in Philadelphia. The year was 1848, and he was in the second month of his farewell tour of America. He had finally accepted that the palmy days of the English drama were over, and he had embarked on a last round of engagements prior to retiring from the stage.

Shortly after arriving, Macready set out for a walk with a friend and saw Edwin Forrest coming toward him. Forrest, as usual, was in town to put on a show at the rival theatre. He was bigger than ever: with his bulging neck and shaggy, bristly hair he looked like a mature and territorial bull. Macready's companion exchanged a greeting with the actor; the Englishman looked the other way and walked on.

Two days later, on November 20, Macready made his way to the Arch Street theatre to open his engagement. As always the play was *Macbeth*. A huge and restless crowd had gathered outside; a fellow actor told him there would be a row, and he prepared himself to meet the worst. He walked on stage to a collision of applause and jeers; the tumult eventually died down, but each surge of applause brought a countersurge of hisses, and every time he reached a crucial line the opposition, which clearly knew its Shakespeare, took care to drown it out.

At the end of the first act, the Bard came to his aid.

"I dare do all that may become a man." Macready emphatically pointed at the rebels, to his supporters' delight: "Who dares do more is none."

At the start of the third act, a light shower of copper pennies fell on the stage, closely pursued by a bouquet from his supporters. In the fifth act, the commotion started up again and a rotten egg landed at his feet. With an almost cheerful relish, as if he was relieved to have his worst fears confirmed, Macready finished the play in his most forceful style, went back for his curtain call and, with characteristic courage and tactlessness, made a speech.

At New York and Boston, he said when he finally obtained a hearing, he had been warned that an organized opposition was in force against him; but there, as here, he had expressed his perfect confidence in the good feeling of the American public, and he was happy and grateful to find he was not disappointed.

"I have had," he pressed on between outbursts, "long acquaintance with, and I might say I have studied, the American character, and I am convinced it is incapable of sanctioning such gross injustice."

"Nine cheers for Macready!" a supporter called, though they were answered with more cheers—three or four feeble ones, Macready claimed—for Forrest.

He recorded the rest in his diary:

I observed that, in my country, it was an invariable principle of justice not to condemn a man unheard, and that their laws were similar to ours. There had been an impression widely and most industriously disseminated that I had shown hostility in my own country to an American actor. I declared upon my "sacred honour" that, not only were the assertions so made false in the aggregate, but that in all the circumstances carefully compiled there was not for a single one the smallest shadow of foundation. That I had been hissed in a public theatre by an American actor, an act which I believed no other American would have committed, and which I was certain no European actor would have been guilty of. That up to that period I had shown none but kindly feelings towards that person, and had never since then publicly expressed an unkind one.

At the mention of the hiss a great hubbub started, and when Macready insisted on his professional benevolence, fights broke out in the boxes, luckily drowning out most of his comments on the character of his opponents. What he tried to say was that he was sure the rest of the audience would agree they had only disgraced themselves:

> Under such unheard-of outrages as these, so unworthy of a civilized community (pointing to the filthy remains of the egg which lay upon the stage) I could not but feel grateful for the sense of the indignation which they had shown; that I should always remember the spirit in which they had resisted such proceedings, and in speaking of them should testify my gratitude for their generous sympathy; that I was perfectly ready if they desired to relinquish my engagement from that night (*No, No, No!*); and that, under any circumstances, I should recollect with satisfaction and pride the support they had so cordially rendered. Again and again I thanked them and retired.[1]

With the applause and jeers still ringing in his ears he was escorted back to his hotel by the recorder, the city's criminal judge, in case an attempt might be made to assault him.

After a sleepless night, Macready got up to read the papers and discovered to his astonishment that only one had condemned the disturbance; two ignored it and another seemed to think it was perfectly commonplace and unobjectionable. The *Public Ledger*, at least, called the previous evening's events "the most disgraceful that we ever saw in a theatre," but the following day it printed a "Card" from Edwin Forrest that finally shocked Macready out of his complacency.

This was what Forrest wrote:

> Mr. Macready, in his speech, last night, to the audience assembled at the Arch Street Theatre, made allusion, I understand, to "an Amer-

Forrest, aged forty-two, in a daguerreotype taken by an unknown American photographer in 1848. Cincinnati Art Museum, Gift of Mrs. James M. Landy in memory of James M. Landy.

ican actor" who had the temerity, on one occasion, "*openly* to hiss him." This is true, and by the way, the *only* truth which I have been enabled to gather from the whole scope of his address. But why say "an American actor?" Why not openly charge me with the act? for I did it, and publicly avowed it in the Times newspaper of London, and at the same time, asserted my right to do so.

On the occasion alluded to, Mr. Macready introduced a fancy dance into his performance of Hamlet, which I designated as a pas de mouchoir, and which I hissed, for I thought it a desecration of the scene, and the audience thought so too, for in a few nights after-wards, when Mr. Macready repeated the part of Hamlet with the same "tom-foolery," the intelligent audience of Edinburgh greeted it with a universal hiss.

Mr. Macready is stated to have said last night, that up to the time of this act on my part, he had "never entertained towards me a feeling of unkindness." I unhesitatingly pronounce this to be a wilful and unblushing falsehood. I most solemnly aver and do believe, that Mr. Macready, instigated by his narrow, envious mind, and his self-ish fears, did *secretly*—not openly—suborn several writers for the English press, to write me down. Among them was one Forster, a "toady" of the *eminent tragedian*—one who is ever ready to do his dirty work—and this Forster, at the bidding of his patron, attacked me in print even before I had appeared upon the London boards, and continued his abuse of me at every opportunity afterwards.

I assert, also, and solemnly believe, that Mr. Macready connived when his friends went to the theatre in London to hiss me, and did hiss me, with the purpose of driving me from the stage—and all this happened many months before the affair at Edinburgh, to which Mr. Macready refers, and in relation to which he jesuitically remarks, that "until that act, he never entertained towards me a feeling of unkind-ness." Pah! Mr. Macready has no feeling of kindness for any actor who is likely, by his talent, to stand in the way. His whole course as man-ager and as actor proves this—there is nothing in him but self—self—self—and his own countrymen, the English actors, know this well. Mr. Macready has a very lively imagination, and often draws upon it for his facts. He said in a speech at New York, that there, also, there was an "organized opposition" to him, which is likewise false. There was no opposition manifested towards him there—for I was in the city at the time, and was careful to watch every movement with regard to such a matter. Many of my friends called upon me when Mr. Macready was announced to perform, and proposed to drive him from the stage for his conduct towards me in London. My advice was, do nothing—let the superannuated driveller alone—to oppose him would be but to make him of some importance. My friends agreed with me it was, at least, the most dignified course to pursue, and it was immediately adopted. With regard to "an organized opposition to him" in Boston, this is, I believe, equally false, but perhaps in charity to the poor old man, I should impute these "chimeras dire," rather to the disturbed state of his guilty conscience, than to any de-sire on his part wilfully to misrepresent.[2]

Though Forrest was right that Macready had met with no open hostility in New York or Boston, he knew perfectly well that a demonstration had been planned against his rival in Philadelphia.* There is no evidence that he personally orchestrated it, and on balance it seems unlikely that he did, but there is enough to suggest that he encouraged his friends to lay into Macready in the papers. The most vicious dressing-down, splashed across several columns of the *Boston Mail,* rehashed all of Forrest's grievances and added a few new flourishes. "Mr. McReady," the ingenious writer declared, had *"acted openly towards Mr. Forrest as his determined foe."* The Englishman—the piece went on—was behind the snub Forrest had received in Paris, he or his friends hired the men who hissed Forrest in London, he hypocritically invited Forrest to dinner to cover his tracks, he prevailed on Bulwer Lytton to bar Forrest from performing Bulwer Lytton's plays, and he wound Forster up and sent him off to ensure that the American was outrageously assailed by the press; McReady, the writer imaginatively added, was a part owner of the *Examiner* and had some evil hold on its editor.[†] Forrest's hiss, he further claimed, was echoed by the entire Edinburgh audience, and they hissed again after he had left town, but McReady had convinced the London papers that Forrest was the sole hisser. The Englishman had presented himself to the world as a persecuted man, whereas it was really Forrest who had met with persecution at every step—"in Paris, in London, in Edinburgh, and in London a second time." There was but one reason for his meanness to his rival—for *"his inhospitality, his crushing influence, his vindictive opposition, and his steadfast determination to ruin the prospects of that gentleman in England"*: jealousy. These, the writer concluded, were the simple facts: let the Englishman deny them if he wanted; and for good measure he advised the pigheaded McReady to restrain himself from writing "a black book about American manners, &c., *à la Trollope* and others" when he got home.[3]

Forrest was clearly behind the piece. *"We speak by card, and write upon the very best information, viz. the highest authority,"* the writer proclaimed,

* "I have not seen any one who has seen the 'superannuated,' " Kate had written to him from New York a month earlier, "but *'there's a good time coming'* for him in Philadelphia." After reading one of Macready's speeches she wrote again: "I suppose he thinks himself safe now—but the Ides of March are not over" (Anon, *Report of the Forrest Divorce Case* [New York, 1852], 75–76).

[†] Forster had recently been appointed editor of the *Examiner;* Macready never had any financial interest in the paper.

and his editor told an actor that Forrest would "endorse all that the article in question stated."[4] Forrest had been so stung by the criticism of his hiss that he had elaborated his suspicions into one overarching justification, and his determination to prove himself right had overwhelmed his attachment to the facts.

Forrest's fiercest supporters applauded his Card as a truly American piece of straight-shooting, but the majority of the papers roundly condemned it—the *New York Herald,* which hardly had a delicate stomach, called it brutal, ungentlemanly, and disgraceful—and even his friends were taken aback by its intemperance. The *Democratic Review* gently advised him to curb his anger; Evert Augustus Duyckinck, a leading light of Young America, the Democratic-aligned campaign for a national literature, predicted that Forrest's "extraordinary performance" was in such bad taste that the public would cold-shoulder him.[5] Several writers noted the flaws in Forrest's reasoning. He was, indeed, in danger of boxing himself into a corner: the more he insisted that Macready had conspired against him long before the hiss, the more it appeared that he hissed in anger, rather than, as he claimed, in a spirit of disinterested criticism.

The disapprobation only stiffened Forrest's spine, and his temper was not improved when the excitement brought on his old malady, intense headaches followed by stabbing chest pains, which made acting a horror. In private he began to talk up the contest in zealously nationalistic terms. "The theatrical excitement is yet great," he wrote to Kate. "There are now two parties, the American and the English, and I have no doubt the former will triumph." And, he added to his English-born wife, "Englishmen must be *cuffed* into a proper conduct towards us; a milder treatment would not reach the disease." He was convinced that Macready had only escaped being driven fully off the stage because he had packed the theatre with police officers and English factory workers: "I think Mac has received his death blow *professionally,* in this country," he exulted. "The feeling manifested against him here will spread over the whole continent."[6]

The news of Forrest's now notorious Card spread across the Atlantic, where the papers took up the cudgels on the Englishman's behalf. "The placards posted by the dregs of London in the windows of the vilest pot-houses" were polite compared to Forrest's production, the London *Times* huffed.[7] Macready's allies were ecstatic: they were sure the American's reputation had been irreparably damaged. Dickens wrote to his friend asking whether it was true that he had paid Forrest five thousand pounds to publish his diatribe. If so, he declared, he had got it cheap: "It certainly was worth £10,000 to you and I question whether £20,000 would have compensated him for eating such a wagonload of dirt." Everyone in London, he added, was disgusted.[8] Macready himself was equally sure that the Card would rebound on its author, but for the first time he seriously began to worry about his personal safety. "*Oh! Mr. Forrest!!!*" he exclaimed, after numerous outbursts at his rival's staggering and atrocious villainy. "I felt the blow he had struck upon his own head, but yet was uncertain how far the low class under his influence might be affected by it. *Sent for three dozen of the papers instantly!*"[9] He was half convinced that Forrest would set his b'hoys on him; if the ruffian could arrange his assassination he would rejoice, he scribbled, and if he could get away with killing him with his bare hands he would gladly do that too.

The Macready show, though, had to go on. He ordered the theatre's treasurer to mount a guard of ten police officers behind the scenes—at least then he could put up a fight, or at worst beat a retreat—and, as determined as his rival actor to prove himself right before the world, he sat down to write his own retaliatory notice. It was quickly printed and handed out that night at the theatre doors.

TO THE PUBLIC OF PHILADELPHIA

In a Card published in the Public Ledger and other morning papers of this day, Mr. Forrest having avowed himself the author of the statements, which Mr. Macready has solemnly pledged his honour to be without the least foundation, Mr. Macready cannot be wanting in self-respect so far as to bandy words on the subject, but as the circulation of such statements is manifestly calculated to prejudice Mr. Macready in the opinion of the American Public, and affect both his professional interests and his estimation in society, Mr. Macready respectfully requests the public to suspend their judgment upon the question, until the decision of a Legal Tribunal, before which he will

Of Men and Sheep ❧ 173

immediately take measures to bring it, and before which he will prove his veracity, hitherto unquestioned, shall place the truth beyond doubt.

Reluctant as he is to notice further Mr. Forrest's Card, Mr. Macready has to observe, that when Mr. Forrest appeared at the Princess's Theatre in London, he himself was absent some hundred miles from that city, and was ignorant of his engagement until after it had begun; that not one single notice on Mr. Forrest's acting appeared in the Examiner during that engagement (as its files will prove), Mr. Forster, the distinguished Editor, whom Mr. Macready has the honour to call his friend, having been confined to his bed with a rheumatic fever during the whole period, and some weeks before and after.*

For the other aspersions upon Mr. Macready, published in the Boston Mail, and now, as it is understood, avowed by Mr. Forrest, Mr. Macready will without delay appeal for legal redress.[10]

Macready emptied his purse of its valuables, commended himself to God, squared his shoulders, and set off to play *Othello,* which Forrest had also chosen for that night. While he was dressing he was told that the public mood had turned: in the event, the single shout in Forrest's favor was quickly drowned in rounds of cheers. He instantly knew he had made a mistake in issuing his notice; still, he had made a public pledge, and he sent off a sheaf of letters to England, to Bulwer Lytton and Forster, to Fonblanque, the proprietor of the *Examiner,* to the Paris promoter Mitchell, to the high sheriff of Edinburgh, and to Murray, the manager of the Edinburgh theatre, requesting corroboration of his statement.

The rest of his run went without a hitch. In *Hamlet* the *pas de mouchoir,* which he acted with particular care on his last night, was cheered to the echo, and afterward Macready could not resist declaring how deeply grateful he was for the "truly noble and generous earnestness" with which his supporters had defended him, a stranger, from the grossest outrage and injustice. He bowed his thanks again and again, and

---

* As Macready later admitted, the *Examiner* had printed a few barbed remarks on Forrest, though not a full-length "notice" or review. Forrest seized on the admission as evidence of Macready's duplicity, and it was on that basis that the banners were unfurled in Astor Place declaring that Macready had been proved a liar.

took his leave to rounds of acclaim. Yet for all the support he received, he was mortified to find himself swept up in such an unseemly squabble, and his temper began to turn on America. Despite Dickens's best arguments, Macready had crossed the Atlantic with the firm intention of emigrating to the United States on his retirement; his plan was to settle in Cambridge, Massachusetts.[11] The Oregon problem had finally been resolved—the two countries had agreed on the old compromise of the Forty-ninth Parallel—and the end of the U.S.-Mexican War, which Macready, like his friend Charles Sumner, abhorred as an unconstitutional act of aggression, had removed another obstacle. Slavery still appalled him, though perhaps it seemed sufficiently far removed from the life of a private New England gentleman. Even the news that Forrest had been publicly fêted after the hiss had not swayed him; now, though, he exclaimed during one tantrum, he would prefer a dungeon or a hovel in any other country to a fortune in America. "I find the bile has been accumulating," he noted in a more self-aware moment.[12]

For the second time, Macready went south for the winter, taking in Baltimore and Washington en route to Richmond and Charleston, giving more ill-judged speeches in which he thanked his audiences for supporting art "irrespective of clime, or race, or faction" and demonstrating that the taunts about his premature decline were misplaced.[13] Once again the south proved a respite from the factionalism of the northeast, and this time society manifestly threw its weight behind the Englishman. In New Orleans, where he played nearly every night for a month to enormous audiences, friendly papers lauded him as the prince of actors: his Othello, the *Picayune* declared, was the most brilliant thing on the stage, so great that it would redeem the profession from ten times its vices.[14] For his benefit, at his patrons' request, the tickets were auctioned off at fantastic prices, and the pièce de résistance was a spectacular public dinner thrown in his honor shortly before he left.

It was held in the grand banqueting hall of the ornate Verandah Hotel. Macready was seated between a general and several judges and in front of a specially commissioned portrait of himself. The lights danced, the cooled wines flowed, and when dessert was brought in, a confectionery model of Shakespeare's house in Stratford was placed before the guest of honor, along with a confectionery Temple of Thespis on which his favorite characters were emblazoned in icing. The real reward, though, came with the speeches; Macready could have written them himself. The list of official toasts included not just Genius, Shakespeare, and the Drama but Edward Bulwer Lytton, the same Bulwer Lytton who had supposedly snubbed Forrest. Then the general drank the health of Macready: "Our distinguished guest, whose fine taste, splendid art, and zealous devotion to his profession, united with all the qualities of the gentleman and the scholar, have made him the pillar of the drama of his age, and entitled him to the respect and homage of all lovers of the art." The last two toasts were even more finely calibrated to vindicate Macready and, by implication, to censure Forrest. The first was to Charlotte Cushman and Mrs. Mowatt, "the representatives of the American drama in England. —Their generous reception by an English public shows that national distinctions and prejudices can never prevent or restrain the admiration and applause which true genius and merit must ever extort." The second was to Great Britain and the United States: "With a common language—a common literature—a common drama—may no discord or hostility ever interrupt the friendly intercourse between them—the mother and the daughter."

Macready responded with the best speech he ever made. It was dignified, earnest, and cordial. He spoke out against narrow-minded nationalism, a fault he was careful to find in the English as well as Americans. Manifest Destiny, he averred, was a noble mission: only the "low-minded, the narrow-hearted Englishman" would begrudge America's resolve to spread freedom of opinion and "the first great principle of good government, 'the greatest possible happiness of the greatest possible number,'" across the earth, though he gently but passionately insisted that it should make its case by the power of opinion, not by arms. In stirring words, he proclaimed that the unequivocal proof of Britain's greatness was America: England, he vowed, could trace no glory beyond that of giving birth to such a people. And he concluded with a hymn to the two countries' shared culture, epitomized, of course, by its greatest mind: "Coextensive with the spread of the Anglo-Saxon race will be the humanizing influence of our literature and our arts; and from the remote Columbia river to the distant peak of Darien, the words of Shakespeare may be instruments of civilization, inculcating one large and binding charity among all, who are made wiser in his precepts, who learn humanity from his living pictures of human passion, and glow with raptures unfelt before at the thrilling music of his magic verse." Undoubtedly he believed it, at the time: the soaring idealist and the self-absorbed scourge were two sides of the same complex man.[15]

Macready must have hoped his troubles were over, but when he moved on to Cincinnati he was soon brought back to earth. *Hamlet* was the first night's business, and in the *Mousetrap* scene, after his *pas de mouchoir,* just after the King, frighted with false fire, had been lighted away, the raw carcass of half a sheep came flying down from the gallery and thudded onto the center of the stage. Macready carried on, so astonished he hardly knew what to think, but afterward he knew: it was, he declared, an incident that "for disgusting brutality, indecent outrage, and malevolent barbarism, must be without parallel in the theatre of any civilized community."[16] His feelings toward the town were not improved when he got into an argument about the low standard of acting with the sozzled manager, who threatened to take a club to him. Whether the sheep-thrower was expressing an opinion of Macready's ability, or whether, as one writer believed, his gesture was "a mere ebullition of amiable vivacity," no one discovered, but it sent Macready into a renewed orgy of disgust.[17] He had been wrong about America all along, he decided. It was a land of blackguards and underbred curs, and Dickens's aversion was altogether too feeble: "with me it becomes *loathing!*"[18]

New York was nearing again, and Forrest's friends were equally hopped up. As they read the widely published reports of the New Orleans banquet—Forrest must have thought the adopted home of his youth had knifed him in the back—they grew more determined than ever to teach the Englishman a lesson. The press, meanwhile, ratcheted up the rhetoric. The conservative papers were full of praise for Macready's speech, and Forrest's sympathizers fought their corner. "We are among those who despise Mr. Macready, with an earnestness of contempt which language cannot express; we believe him to be craven-hearted, egotistical, cold, selfish, and inflated—a mere machine as an actor, and no more entitled to be called a genius than the organ pipes which thunder out the diapason," one thrust back.[19] Neutral papers scolded the two actors to patch things up for the sake of their reputations, profession, friends, and countries, though the *Herald,* always eager for a good fight, egged them on. "Go it, my chickens!" it crowed: the old cockfighter's cry.[20] Forrest, meanwhile, had spent the last few months sending off to the Pittsburgh *Post* a series of enormously long letters, which were reprinted in full in the New York papers. He ran through his grievances yet again, taking issue with Forster's reviews in obsessive detail, citing instances of Macready's abusive treatment of his fellow actors and calling his rival a liar in every way short of using the word. On April 23—Shakespeare's birthday— Forrest began his engagement at the Broadway Theatre, and the next day his final communiqué ran down two long columns of the *Herald.*

Macready arrived in New York two days later and gave a series of Shakespearean readings to the city's public-school teachers, a habit he had adopted in England. The Park Theatre, his usual home, had burned down a few months earlier: a sheaf of playbills had fluttered into a gas jet and the deflagration had reduced the building, the preeminent theatre in the New World for forty years, to ashes in an hour. Instead Macready had opted to appear at the new Astor Place Theatre, which had half the seats but charged double the price and was popularly known as the Opera House, the designedly highbrow name under which it had opened eighteen months earlier. No doubt Macready was not displeased by its exclusive atmosphere, but in truth he had little choice: Forrest had commandeered the only real alternative.

The Astor Place had been leased on Macready's behalf by William Niblo, the society pleasure-garden impresario, and James Hackett, a gentlemanly actor, best known as the American Falstaff, who was a longstanding enemy of Forrest's. Niblo and Hackett had put together an unusually capable company, which given the competition was no mean feat, because down at the Bowery the enterprising Tom Hamblin had capitalized on the excitement to launch his own Shakespearean season. It was still not exceptional for two or even three of the city's half-dozen proper theatres to schedule the Bard on the same night. "Shakespeare, like every other exile, finds a refuge and a home in glorious America," the *Herald* had declared the previous year; the appetite for his plays was still going strong.[21] It was, though, singular that on May 7, the day of Macready's debut, all three theatres, with almost ten thousand seats among them, announced the same play: *Macbeth.*

Before then there was one final surprise. On April 30, between hearing rumors that Forrest's friends were preparing to start a row and receiving letters helpfully advising him to challenge his rival to a duel in Canada, Macready read in the papers that Forrest had repudiated his wife without cause assigned. The separation had taken place on the day Macready arrived in town.

THE TROUBLE AT West Twenty-second Street had started soon after Forrest brought his English bride home.

At first it was a giddy time. The newlyweds were met at the gangplank by such a crowd of well-wishers that Kate hid behind her husband's broad back until he pulled her into his arms, gave her a loud smack on the cheek, and passed her proudly around. For months she was astonished and a little alarmed by the ecstatic cheering that met him wherever he went: a handsome star was one thing, but she had not realized she was marrying a national mascot.

Kate adjusted to sharing her husband with his public, but they soon turned out to have very different ideas of what marriage was about. Barely a year after their wedding, Kate's father, mother, and sisters followed her across the Atlantic, and a strong whiff of bohemianism came with them. The Sinclairs installed themselves in the Forrests' home, and while Edwin was off performing, John Sinclair threw wild parties nearly every night. In the mornings, the housekeeper informed Forrest, she had found his parents-in-law passed out in the parlor: Kate's father on the carpet, her mother behind the door. Forrest, whose notions of domestic felicity were inherited from a puritan mother and three puritan sisters—none of the sisters ever married—informed Kate that her family had to go. She put her foot down: if they went, she tearfully swore, she would too, and in desperation Forrest swept her off on a long tour and instructed a friend to bribe his in-laws to make themselves scarce.

Kate was what was then pejoratively known as a bluestocking or an advanced woman. She was highly intelligent, a progressive thinker, and, in private, a subtle and powerful advocate for women's rights; the sepulchral ideal of middle-class American wifehood must have struck her cold. Fanny Trollope captured the routine with scalpel precision. Trollope's exemplary woman is college educated, marries early, and immediately vanishes into domestic insignificance. "She has a very handsome house," Trollope itemized; "she has very handsome drawing-rooms, very handsomely furnished . . . she is always very handsomely dressed; and, moreover, she is very handsome herself." She dresses, eats breakfast in silence while her husband reads the papers, then puts on her bonnet and drives to an identical house, where she sits with several other women, very like herself, sewing clothes for the poor. Alternatively, out of sheer tedium, she goes four or five times a day to chapel, where the clergyman supplies the attention wanting from her husband, and she becomes fanatically religious. At three she returns home, takes off her bonnet, puts on her apron, looks in the kitchen, checks the table, and sits down to await her spouse. "He comes, shakes hands with her, spits, and dines. The conversation is not much, and ten minutes suffices for the dinner." In the evening she receives a young missionary and her sewing circle for tea. "And so ends her day."[22] Trollope was barely straining the truth: compared to their sisters in England, educated American women were notably less prominent in society, and even when a married couple entertained at home, the wife vanished for good at the end of the meal while the men sat with coffee and cigars and went out on the town, a custom that Macready found barbaric.*

Kate had been brought up among artistic circles where self-expression was encouraged. She liked attention, and Forrest's male friends were cut from the same plain patriarchal cloth as he. One explained to her that if a man took a mistress his wife should examine her heart and discover where she had failed; men, he pointedly added, loved women as much for their helplessness as their beauty. ("Intellect snugly put out of the question," she replied, before sweetly but comprehensively demolishing his arguments.[23]) Unsurprisingly, when Forrest was away Kate took to inviting more congenial figures, artistic men and outspoken women, to their

---

* Under the surface, plenty of "respectable" women were not as innocent as their husbands liked to think. By the late 1840s ice cream parlors were the latest focus of panic: according to moral watchdogs, they were no less than assignation houses, where married women met married men over a banana split before heading to one of the notorious brownstones off Broadway which were disguised, for the convenience of both sexes, as the combined premises of dressmakers' shops and dentists' surgeries.

house, and to her husband's democratic dismay she became a fixture among the fashionable crowd.

For several years, despite the long separations and the sorrow laid on them by their childlessness, they patched up their differences and remained happy. When Forrest went on tour they wrote solicitous letters to each other almost every day. Kate sewed her husband's costumes, packed his trunks, copied his parts, sent transcripts of his speeches to newspapers and his reviews to theatre managers, and recorded his every performance in a great ledger, complete with the name of the play and its writer, its date, time, and place, its attendance and receipts, and its reception by audience and press.

By 1847 Forrest had accepted that he would be left without an heir, and he set about building a monument to his love for his wife and his profession—or, cynics suggested, to himself and his vanity. He bought—with typical canniness, at a foreclosure sale—a large piece of land in a picturesque declivity on the banks of the Hudson, sixteen miles upriver from New York, and started building a fortress. Fonthill Castle was a bluff Norman-Gothic structure that would not have looked out of place on a craggy outcrop of the Rhine or the backdrop to a blue-fire melodrama. It was formed from six buttressed octagonal towers of dark hammer-dressed granite topped with embrasured battlements. The heavy door swung open on a great hall with dark oak vaulting springing from gilded corbels carved as theatrical masks. Aside from Kate's room, which was finished with rose-colored white-veined marble and Gothic windows with delicately entwining leads, it was Forrest in stone and wood. Outside he chiseled a nook, inside which he sealed three significant mementos: a sample of American coinage, a copy of Shakespeare, and a document that explained the castle's purpose:

> In building this house, I am impelled by no vain desire to occupy a grand mansion for the gratification of self-love; but my object is to build a desirable, spacious, and comfortable abode for myself and my wife, to serve us during our natural lives, and at our death to endow the building with a sufficient yearly income, so that a certain number of decayed or superannuated actors and actresses of Ameri-

can birth (*all foreigners to be strictly excluded*) may inhabit the mansion
and enjoy the grounds thereunto belonging, so long as they live. . . .

The parenthesized command somewhat diluted the romantic gesture to
his English-born wife, but Fonthill might have been a poignant memorial to an unhappily childless man.[24]

Edwin and Kate never moved into their castle. In the spring of 1848,
while the first blocks of New York stone were being levered into place,
the Forrests traveled to Cincinnati, where the tragedian was booked to
appear at his old friend Sol Smith's theatre, and checked into the City
Hotel. One day Forrest went out with Smith to have his portrait painted,
but the portraitist was missing and Forrest returned early to his room.

As he opened the door, he saw his wife standing in front of the sofa,
between the knees of one of his fellow actors. George Jamieson was tall
and good-looking, and he had his hands on Kate. Jamieson wisely made
a sharp exit from the building while Forrest was still suspended in disbelief.

"What is the meaning of this?" he demanded when he came to, and
Kate tremulously replied that Jamieson had been pointing out her
phrenological developments. Phrenology was a fashionable craze at the
time, and the explanation had some credibility, or at least plausibility, because the couple had an appointment with a phrenologist later that day.

Forrest was too astonished to be furious, and he chose to believe that
his wife was just being giddy and imprudent. The next January, though,
while Kate was out at a party thrown by her sister Margaret, he un-
locked the bottom drawer of her bureau with a duplicate key; inside, he
found a sheaf of letters. One was a florid declaration of love, and it was in
Jamieson's hand.

The letter, addressed to "Sweetest Consuelo," is such high-flown nonsense that Jamieson sounds more like a lovesick schoolboy than a successful adulterer. Consuelo was the heroine of an eponymous novel by George
Sand, and Forrest rushed out to get a copy. He discovered that Sand's
heroine, though bohemian, was irreproachably chaste, and yet he still suspected the worst. That night he paced his library until two in the morning, and when Kate came home he pulled her inside. Perhaps to retain the

advantage, perhaps because he could not bring himself to speak of it, he kept the Consuelo letter to himself: instead he railed against Kate's sister, whom he loathed as a licentious socialite and had banned from his house. His wife was more loyal to her sister than to him, he shouted: Margaret was poisoning her against him and dragging her into her evil ways.

"It's a lie!" Kate indignantly answered, and that was the end.

"If a man had said that to me," Forrest growled, "he should die. I cannot live with a woman who says it."

Kate went to bed crying at six. The morning after she checked the papers in her bureau and started back.

"Forrest has got my letters!" she exclaimed. According to the housekeeper, she opened another drawer and threw two more documents on the fire, then came downstairs with another bundle and burned that too.*

Forrest interviewed the servants and discovered that Kate had been entertaining her friends in a manner of which her parents would have approved. Singing, drinking, and smoking had gone on through the nights, the rooms were left in a mess, and Kate had allegedly been found lying on a sofa with one man and in bed with another, sitting on a third's knee, and kissing a fourth. A fifth gentleman caller had purportedly been hidden in the house for three days, and one of the servants had given birth to a child by one of Kate's regular guests.

Forrest retreated into his library, where he admitted his wife only when she brought his breakfast or coals for the fire. He must have wished his mother were alive to advise him: Rebecca had died two years earlier, and with her had gone the voice of common sense that kept her son from indulging his growing conviction that a web of injustice and lies was tightening around him. One night he wrote out a solemn oath declaring that Kate had never betrayed her marriage vows; she tearfully signed, but it was too late. Whether or not he believed that she had been unfaithful, he was certain that she had comported herself in a way no wife of his should, and a few weeks later he casually announced that he was going to close their house. Kate packed her belongings in a daze and arranged to stay with a friend. Before she left, she asked for two me-

---

* Kate later denied that this incident, and indeed the scene with Jamieson, ever happened. As with Forrest's suspicions of Macready's enmity in London and Paris, she claimed he invented the whole story to justify his inordinate response to a minor disagreement.

mentos: one was the portrait of her husband that had hung side by side with hers in their parlor; the other, equally calculated to please him, was a volume of Shakespeare. "Mrs Edwin Forrest, from Edwin Forrest," he wrote in the front of the *Collected Works,* a sad diminution of his usual inscription, "From her lover and husband, Edwin Forrest." They drove through the streets, Forrest's portrait propped up beside his wife, and he left her at her new door without a word.

During the sensational divorce trial that ended their marriage, Kate's lawyer, Charles O'Conor, claimed that the root of the whole problem was the Macready affair: Kate, he explained, had taken her countryman's side against her husband. In fact, the reverse was true: throughout the actors' feud, Kate wrote to Edwin encouraging him to stand up to his rival. She called Macready "the great superannuated phenomenon" in one letter, "the old woman" in another. "So far well enough *pour le commencement,* but I hope they are following the matter up to-night," she wrote after the first row in Philadelphia, and when Forrest issued his contentious Card she immediately backed him up.[25] "The public required it," she declared, "as your treatment in England has never been clearly understood since your return . . . what more than all the rest I like about your card is its simple, bold, and *unmistakeable* language." Her loyalties could hardly have been clearer: "I hope you are well, my own blessed Edwin, and that you will *give it* to the 'superannuated,' " she encouraged him, and added: "I shall assuredly not die happy unless he gets punished in some way for the annoyance he has caused you."[26]

Despite that evidence, O'Conor insisted that Kate had strongly disapproved of the Edinburgh hiss, and that prior to Macready's arrival in America she had remonstrated with her husband about the intemperate language he used when he talked of the Englishman. Forrest, Kate declared in her deposition, "frequently became very angry with me about this, as he attributed the part I took in the matter to my English feeling." Her husband, she added, "was wrought up to such a state of excitement about Macready, that his friends feared lest he should utterly lose his reason," and he had vowed to everyone that he would have his rival driven from the stage.[27] *Forrest vs. Forrest* became such a farrago of charges and countercharges that the truth barely showed its face: Kate's counsel also alleged that Forrest had left money in Boston and New Orleans to be used against Macready, but there is no evidence that he attempted to mount an opposition in either city; if he did, it was a signal failure. Most likely O'Conor had taken a leaf out of Forrest's book and exaggerated a slender difference into one of the many pretexts he tried out in his client's defense.

Whatever the true cause of the separation, it had three immediate effects. It made Forrest more hostile than ever toward the fashionable circles his wife moved in, it cut his last tie with England, and it left him more bitter and self-righteous than ever. Forrest's impetuous temper had begun to harden into an indurate rage. "Yes, let me own that I have a religion of Hate," he later avowed. "I have a hatred of Oppression in whatever shape it may appear—a hatred of hypocrisy, falsehood, and injustice—a hatred of bad and wicked men and women, and a hatred of my enemies, for whom I have no forgiveness excepting through their own repentance of the injuries they have done me."[28]

Forrest was in no mood to prevent the humiliation of his English rival, and nor were his supporters. Several, indeed, had ambitions far more explosive than merely salving their friend's honor: ambitions that, if fulfilled, could change the face of America. And New York City was the keg to which the whole crooked powder trail finally led.

CHAPTER 10

A Night at the Opera, and Another in Hell

A T THE CLOSE of the social season in 1849, Manhattan's elite
threw itself an epic fancy-dress ball. It was a suitably theatrical climax to the year's whirl, not least because the costumes were supplied by
Monsieur Dejonge, the former costumer to the incinerated Park Theatre.
New York was still a mercantile town at heart, and it knew a bargain
when it saw one.

The leading families vied to procure the choicest ensembles for their
daughters, and three days before the appointed night, pyramids of tin
trunks and black boxes began to arrive at their doors. Messrs. Dibblee
and Barker, ladies' hairdressers of Broadway, brought out their best wigs
and curls, while Medhurst's, the gentleman's barbers, drooped with false
beards and mustaches.

So much beauty and fashion demanded a dazzling backdrop. At the
entrance to the ballroom, a huge Gothic arch sprang up, painted to imi-
tate granite and draped with blue and pink muslin trimmed with silver
stars. At ten o'clock the first guests slipped through the celestial curtains
into an immense room lined with flaming Persian columns. Festoons of
green leaves hung between them, and more swung up to the ceiling,
where they met in the center and formed a great green tent. Twelve giant
chandeliers lit the length of the hall, and at the end, in front of the orchestra, three more arches wrapped in blue, white, and pink trimming framed
three transparencies on which evergreens and flowers wove around three
painted words:

BEAUTY   LOVE   PLEASURE

As the band struck up, the room filled with twirling nuns and mar-
quises, harem concubines and knights, Alpine milkmaids and pirates,
Marie Antoinettes and archers, and all the motley contents of the old
Park's wardrobe. The dances stepped off with sedate marches, moved
through old-fashioned quadrilles and cotillions, heated up with the
once-daring waltz and broke out into the new Hungarian polka which
sent petticoats twirling above ankles and, thundered one traditionalist,
was "one of the most indecent and disreputable movements in dancing
that can be seen in any society throughout the civilized world." The
show went on till dawn, and the efforts were rewarded when the *Herald*
came out with an exhaustive description of every outfit stretched across
several columns. At the foot of the page was a short, shaming list
headed "Ladies Not in Costume," though even their outfits were a riot
of brocade and tulle, silk flowers, ruffles, and lace.[1]

New York had suddenly become conspicuously, inescapably rich. In
1842, the *Sun* published the original Rich List, which laid out the
pedigree and estimated the wealth of every citizen worth more than
$100,000; the list quickly ran through several editions, each fatter than
the last. By mid-century, Nathanial Parker Willis put a number on the
city's elite—"the upper ten thousand"—and the term stuck, albeit in-
numerately abbreviated to the Upper Ten. As trade chased wealth uptown, the money retreated into the famed Fifteenth Ward, a district of
ornate Italianate brownstone mansions and silver bell-pulls that spread
north from Houston Street to Fourteenth Street and east from Sixth Avenue to the Bowery, where the days were divided into opportunities
for display. During the morning visiting hour, carriages lined with
damask, embellished with escutcheoned panels, and ridden by liveried
coachmen plied between houses furnished with silk and ormolu, Italian
sculpture, and old masters in the most expensive European taste. Promenade hour, when genteel women threw off their dark concealing shawls
and blazed out with the latest fashions prescribed by the *Monthly Magazine of the Courts of London and Paris,* became a ritual of social one-
upmanship. Dinnertime, once a simple affair at which the head of the
house forked out the food, was thoroughly Frenchified: waiters served

pageants of courses on Sèvres porcelain, a spectacle so unrepublican that the Upper Ten also became known as the Porcelain Class.

Extravagance bred extravagance, and even modest men of commerce built themselves lavish mansions and lived on the brink of a money pit. Wealth, or at least the reputation of wealth, was the password to the new New York, and the avalanche of freshly minted money that hit the city in the 1840s chased the old plain ways into the shadows. The flamboyant new balls were the most visible sign that things had changed. Fancy dress had always been frowned on as frivolous and extravagant—frowned on almost as much as the licentious anonymity of masked balls, which were still banned on penalty of a $1,000 fine, or $500 if the hosts informed on themselves—but now it became a conveniently expensive way to keep out the hoi polloi. Even worse, an increasing number of balls sported an all-male guest list: these were held in the high-ceilinged Broadway parlor houses of high-class courtesans, went on until dawn, and invariably descended into orgies, while the carriages of prominent merchants, lawyers, and public figures waited conspicuously outside.

Not everyone in the Upper Ten was happy with the new dispensation. The old patricians, the Dutch Knickerbockers and the Yankee Codfish Aristocracy, looked down their noses at the vulgar nouveaux riches, the shopkeeping and stockjobbing aristocrats, the brusque sons and daughters of butchers and bakers hiding behind shiny silks and flashing jewels.* Yet the city's elite had discovered how to survive in a democracy. Old names needed new money, while for the new rich, wealth alone was not enough. Breeding, beauty, and style, the most expensive commodities of all, marked you out from the next millionaire, and given enough cash, they could be bought. In the end the rich flocked together, and eventually even parvenus like department-store owners and ironwork tycoons were admitted to the old parlors and the new clubs.

The Upper Ten's red-plush life might not have been so incendiary had it not been accompanied by an explosion of poverty in the city's

---

* The Codfish Aristocracy were the scions of old New England families that had made their first fortunes in the fisheries or the merchant fleet; many had moved to New York and made a second fortune from manufacturing. At first there was little love lost between the pleasure-loving Dutch stock and the puritanical Yankees, though shared interests had gradually thrown them together.

lower wards. The old artisan class had been hit hard by the long depression and decimated by the replacement of the apprentice system, which provided room and board as well as training in a trade, with mass production, which drove skilled mechanics and craftsmen into wage slavery and the bulging working class. As if that were not enough, they also had to contend with something entirely new.

Mass immigration hit America in the 1840s, and it soared again after the Irish potato famine, the industrial and agricultural troubles in Germany, and the failed European revolutions of 1848. By the end of the decade, two thousand ships, crammed with more than two hundred thousand immigrants, were arriving each year in New York alone. Pale faces stared over salty rails at the city that curved before them as if through a fish-eye lens; sometimes they stared for days, as they waited for a berth along the docks that lined the East River and the Hudson for four miles. The numbers were almost unimaginable. Twenty-two thousand four hundred and fifty migrants, the population of a decent-sized city, landed in April 1849; on May 2, fifty-two ships sailed into New York's port carrying 6,350 new arrivals.[2] The rickety piers sagged and occasionally collapsed beneath the weight of crates, porters, and carts.

The poor huddled masses permanently changed America from a thinly populated, largely Protestant nation into a multicultural melting pot. But that affirmative concept belonged to the future; meanwhile, New York bore the brunt of an unfathomably fast transformation. Many immigrants passed through to the frontier, but enough stayed so that, when their numbers combined with those of internal migrants, the city's permanent population grew by more than two hundred thousand during the 1840s. By 1850 it had passed the half-million mark, making it three times the size of its nearest rival, even without counting the neighboring city of Brooklyn which, with nearly a hundred thousand residents, was itself the seventh most populous city in the Union and would soon be the third.*

As more immigrants arrived and wages plummeted, tens of thousands disappeared below the subsistence line. Polarization plowed the city into starkly different tracts. Behind the docks of lower Manhattan,

---

* Brooklyn was not incorporated into New York City until 1898.

where most immigrants settled within walking distance of the shipyards, ironworks, abattoirs, and textile factories where they lined up
for casual work, old mansions and warehouses were turned into airless,
windowless tenements and their old inhabitants became slum landlords
to poor families paying the highest per-square-foot rent in the world.
Shoddy wooden lean-tos blocked backyards and alleys, genuinely penniless newcomers slept in the streets, and America discovered mass
urban poverty on its doorstep for the first time.

New York's slums were puny compared to the giant pools of misery
that stagnated across great swaths of London. But one corner of Manhattan, which matched London's rookeries in everything but extent,
became the most notorious slum in nineteenth-century America. The
Five Points was a miniature Seven Dials, an intersection of alleys a few
short blocks northeast of City Hall Park, built over a spring-fed lake
that had become a toxic run-off for tanneries, breweries, and slaughter-
houses. The landfill had left the ground marshy and the dank clap-
boarded shacks slowly sank, along with the tenants—often two dozen,
in one case a hundred—crammed inside.*

Five Points stank. The worst alleys were an ankle-deep mash of
human, animal, and industrial waste that defeated even the city's roaming tribes of ornery and overfed pigs. Brown water came up from the
wells, and when cholera hit the city it found a third of its victims in the
little Points.† The whole dismal spectacle has long entered New York
lore, with the Old Brewery, a rotten frame building, abutted by a passage called Murderer's Alley and undermined by a tangle of tunnels
ending in concealed trapdoors, as its house of horrors. The Brewery was
home to several hundred of the city's most desperate souls who, it was
rumored, occupied themselves with incest, murder, robbery, prostitution, shrieking brawls, and drunken orgies. Dozens more hid out in its

---

* The Points were long ago bulldozed into infamy: one section was wittily replaced by Foley Square
and the columns of the New York County and U.S. courthouses. The intersection was at the spot
where Baxter Street and Worth Street now meet.

† Evangelical ministers promised the plague would pass over God-fearing houses and attack those
weakened by vice, a prophecy that was fulfilled not so much by prayer as by the ability of their well-
to-do congregations to flee town. While many New Yorkers confronted the sheer scale of poverty for
the first time, others thought that an infinitely wise and just God had sent the plague to drain off
society's scum (Edwin G. Burrows and Mike Wallace, *Gotham* [New York, 1999], 589–94).

catacomb of underground cells and seldom saw the light of day; twenty-six were said to live in one basement room fifteen feet square, and a little girl, who had been stabbed for a penny, was buried in the corner.[3] Some of the most lurid stories owe more to legend than reality: many Five Pointers were the respectable poor—shoemakers, tailors, masons, or cigar-makers who had fallen on hard times—and there was a camaraderie that went beyond the gangs of scavenging children and the celebrated Hot Corn Girls, pretty, barefoot, and dressed in spotted calico. But the tenements of the Five Points were undoubtedly dangerous places to call home. Thieves and gamblers shuffled greasy cards around tallow candles in basement oyster dens; bare-breasted prostitutes retailed themselves on the threshold (sometimes picketed by members of the Female Moral Reform Society reading Scripture), and pulled passing sailors or loafers into the corner of a straitened immigrant's home or a single-room brothel where mothers and daughters received their customers *en famille.*[4] The cannier operators filled their victims with firewater and compromised them just enough to make them easy prey for "panel thieves" who jumped out from behind a false wall, stole the clients' clothes, punched them in the head if they resisted, and kicked them out into the street, where they were swept up into the local prison, a building quaintly modeled in the Egyptian style, quaintly named, in the wake of countless suicides, the Tombs, and anything but quaint inside.

In the prurient nineteenth-century way, the Five Points became a magnet for slum tourists, the same hardy types who made a beeline for prisons, madhouses, and reform schools, and its fame spread around the world. The most celebrated visitor of all was Charles Dickens: in *American Notes,* the Points figured as a vision of hell, where rotten staircases led up to windowless rooms in which heaps of rags stirred into the shapes of huddled, scared women sleeping on the floor. Dickens's last port of call was Almack's, a raucous drinking and dancing room with red bombazine curtains and sanded floorboards which was named, probably more in a spirit of self-satire than aspiration, after the famous ballroom of London's aristocracy. Almack's was run by Pete Williams, a theatre-lover who loathed Macready and was among Forrest's greatest cheerleaders, and after the great writer's visit, probably in the same ironic spirit, it was renamed Dickens's Place.

Williams was one of the Points' few African-American entrepreneurs: by the time of Dickens's Stygian ramble the population was predominantly Irish. By the late 1840s, more than a hundred thousand Irish were arriving in New York each year, mostly on the overcrowded, unseaworthy, and disease-ridden vessels that became known as coffin ships because one in ten voyagers perished at sea. Once on land, many of the survivors were suckered by runners, drawn from the last wave of immigrants, who led their countrymen to squalid boardinghouses where they were robbed and thrown out, or who sold them fake railroad and boat tickets to the interior. Most ended up in the Five Points, and the change that came over them in dead-end tenements like Brick-Bat Mansions or the Gates of Hell unnerved the rest of the city and astonished visitors. "In my part of the country, when you meet an Irishman, you find a first-rate gentleman; but these are worse than savages; they are too mean to swab hell's kitchen," declared Davy Crockett.[5]

Many native-born Americans, particularly working men and women who found themselves priced out of a job, began to resent the new arrivals with a passion, almost as much as they resented Britain's disastrous Irish policies for foisting so much hardship upon them. Immigrants, they railed—and by "immigrants" they meant poor Irish—marched off the ship, took a detour to a grog-shop, and ended up among the burgeoning population of Blackwell's Island, where the workhouse, penitentiary, hospital, and lunatic asylum quickly became overburdened.* "No Irish Need Apply" signs appeared in shop windows and at factory gates, echoing proscriptions against free blacks.[6] "It is," complained George Foster, an urban geographer who specialized in sensationalism, "a terrible food for any nation to digest, such an immense mass of moral and physical filth and putrefaction . . . huddled together, writhing like loathsome reptiles, in a pestilential and noxious atmosphere." Immigration, he concluded, was "a gigantic moral phenomenon whose proportions strike terror to the soul."[7]

At least since 1798, when John Adams's administration refused asylum to the leaders of the Young Irishmen rebellion on the grounds that they were malcontents who would stir up trouble, the United States

* Blackwell's Island is now called Roosevelt Island.

had held an equivocal attitude toward the Irish.* On the one hand, they had cheered the Revolution; suffering under British rule themselves, they deserved American support; and they made up most of the great pool of cheap labor that built the country's canals, docks, roads, aqueducts, and railroads. On the other hand, unlike German immigrants they insisted on ganging together and getting involved in firebrand politics. But what distinguished the new arrivals from their predecessors was not just their extreme poverty or lack of skills: it was religion. Most were Roman Catholic, and their traditions seemed to threaten the American (that is, the white Anglo-Saxon Protestant) way of life. Nativists set up platforms in Irish strongholds and delivered harangues against the Catholic church, spreading the story that the Irish owed fealty to a foreign potentate—the pope—who controlled their minds and was conspiring to take over the country. Popular novels painted the bishop of Rome as the Antichrist and the Roman church as the Whore of Babylon. Fictional memoirs promised titillating revelations about life inside convents, a trend that peaked with the anonymous *Awful Disclosures of Maria Monk,* a salacious swirl of flagellation, affairs between priests and nuns, and infanticide. The most zealous nativists spied an agent of destruction in every Catholic who stepped off a boat. "The first foreigner named in history was the Devil, who migrated from Hades to the Garden of Eden, thereby bringing ruin and misery upon the world," preached a paper called *The Yellow Flower and Native Blossom*—subtitle *We'll Make All Rome Howl*—in its first edition.[8]

New York life was lived on the sidewalks, and it was inevitable that so much religious and economic tension would erupt onto the streets. Nativists attacked churches and stoned bishops' houses and convents; Catholics banded together for protection; and loose neighborhood groups coalesced into America's first full-fledged gangs.

Not all New York's gangs were formed with violent intent. In an age of increasing working-class powerlessness, gang membership was a source of solidarity and a badge of pride, and some gangs were relatively innocent associations of "sporting men," free-living bachelors from the

---

* Adams's real fear was that they would become foot soldiers for Jeffersonian democracy, and when he was elected president Jefferson duly let them in.

same street or trade, butchers, mechanics, shipbuilders, and cartmen whose lives revolved around boardinghouses, saloons, and brothels, some of whom met to go to the theatre, often to see Edwin Forrest act it up at the Bowery. Many gangs grew up around the famous volunteer fire companies; their stations became unofficial after-work social clubs, thronged with unemployed youths who hung around polishing the engines, helped to pull them to a fire, raised false alarms to provide an excuse for a run, fixed races by sabotaging their rivals' equipment, fought other companies for fun or to stop them reaching a burning building first, and generally basked in the reflected glory of the shiny brass machines. This was the world of the rude boys or b'hoys—the Irish inflection became the norm in the 1840s—who swaggered down the Bowery in their best tough-guy style, adopted their own slang—"blow-out" and "go on a bender" were terms first heard on the Bowery, as were "chum," "pal," and "kick the bucket"—and thumbed their noses at the sober propriety of their bourgeois employers.[9]* Not all of the b'hoys were gang members, and even those who were were often stout-hearted, hardworking men, but enough caused enough trouble that their reputation spread quick and wide.

Among the real head-bashing gangs some devoted themselves to crime, running moonshining, gambling, or protection rackets; and some, like the Irish Roach Guards, Shirt Tails, and Plug Uglies, fought each other, as well as their declared rivals, to protect their turf. But the most fearsome of all were in the business of ethnic violence. The largest and fiercest nativist gang, the Bowery Boys, was the arch enemy of the Irish Dead Rabbits.[†] The Boys marched into the Five Points, stomped on heads, gouged out eyes, and burned down houses; the Rabbits surfaced with their mascot, a bunny skewered on a pike, and their arsenal of brickbats and bludgeons, brass nails, and hobnailed boots—or, in the case of the notorious Hell-Cat Maggie, a set of filed teeth—and they engaged in running battles for two or three days at a time.

---

* They were also known as Soap-locks, from their plastered-down hair and long sidelocks, or Buttenders, from the cigar stub permanently jammed in the corner of their mouths.

† The Bowery Boys was the name of a specific gang; "b'hoys" was the term for the wider, multiethnic, working-class subculture of young men who frequented the Bowery. Since the Bowery Boys were also b'hoys, the two have often been confused.

There was one thing that Irish, nativists, gangsters, and b'hoys all had in common: a deep-seated hatred of England. The Irish Kerryonians existed solely to attack anything and anyone English, while the True Blue Americans stood on street corners in long black coats and stovepipe hats like gloomy hellfire preachers and predicted the annihilation of the British Empire by fire and sword. By the late 1840s, though, the epithet "English" had become such a useful term of abuse that it was applied by association to the whole Upper Ten, the "shallow-pated, milk-hearted sucklings of foppery and fashion" who aped European tastes, and the gangs were chafing to wreak vengeance on both the obnoxious country and class.[10]

NEW YORK'S STREETWISE politicians were not slow to see how useful a biddable gang might be; to firm up their powers of patronage, they began to buy up the saloons, dance halls, and gambling dens where the b'hoys gathered. In 1834, called the Year of the Riots, when the mayor was directly elected for the first time, militant Democrats invaded the Whig campaign office, ripped down banners, tore up ballots, and attacked their opponents with clubs and knives. In a creative burst of revenge, the Whigs built a huge model of the *Constitution,* a frigate famed for its role in the War of 1812, mounted it on wheels, decked it out in the party colors, and manned it with seamen who pulled it down the Bowery and into the Five Points accompanied by marching bands and a thousand employees who had been given the afternoon off to shout anti-Irish slogans. Three days of rioting climaxed when a rumor that the Democrats were headed for the Arsenal sent the Whigs running to get there first. Five hundred broke in and armed themselves, twenty thousand from both camps massed outside, and disaster was averted only by the appearance of twelve hundred troops.

Increased immigration widened the partisan divide. Fresh immigrants meant fresh ballots to be bought, and Tammany Hall, the Democrats' headquarters in New York, saw a new avenue open, an avenue lined with pliant, cheering voters. Copying the boardinghouse touts, the Democrats sent runners sporting emerald green neckties to round up new arrivals and usher them to their offices, where a welcoming committee sat beamingly at the ready. Tammany took them in hand, explained their rights, arranged their naturalization, gave them a small job with a big title, and harvested their votes. It worked: almost every Irishman in the city voted Democrat, and by 1848 more than a quarter of the votes cast in New York's elections were cast by Irishmen.

Tammany's strategy, though, brought a backlash in the form of flag-waving nativists. At first their outfits were a ragbag of splinter groups—the Protestant Association, the Native American Democratic Association, the Native Sons of America, the Patriotic Order of Sons of America, the American Brotherhood—but they quickly coalesced into a movement with real clout. The American Nativist party boasted a three-plank manifesto, which proposed to extend the qualifying period for naturalization to twenty-one years, ban immigrants from public office, and campaign against foreign interference in public life. Working-class agitation had been fighting the tide of economic history: the turbulent shiploads of immigrants seemed easier to turn back, or at least easier to label as the source of all woes. "The day must come," feared one nativist, "when most of our offices will be held by foreigners—men who have no sympathy with the spirit of our institutions, who have done aught to secure the blessings they enjoy, and instead of governing ourselves, we shall be governed by men, many of whom, but a few short years previously, scarcely knew of our existence."[11] New York's nativists swept the city elections in 1844—though one rally was brought to a halt by Irish-women who packed paving stones in their stockings and swung them as impromptu maces—and the Democrats and Whigs vowed to win back power at any cost. Both parties marched paupers and prisoners from workhouses and jails to the ballot and bribed them to vote, sometimes several times in the same day, and more votes were routinely counted than there were voters in the city. Roads were dug up for the sole purpose of paying supporters to fill them in again; flaming handbills appeared on walls proclaiming that the consequence of voting for one party would be the end of civilization, or masquerading as messages from orphans and widows declaring that the candidate of the other party had pilfered their savings; and the newspapers stoked the fires by accusing their political opponents of arson, burglary, and adultery. By the early 1840s, tough Democratic ward heelers and their gangs had shouldered power from the old committees of shopkeepers and merchants; the Sixth Ward, which included the Five Points, became known as the Bloody Sixth, and black eyes, torn coats, and bashed hats were badges of honor at Dooley's Long-Room, a bar where the local Democrats gathered.

The most successful ward heeler of all was "Captain" Isaiah Rynders, a close friend of Edwin Forrest. Rynders, a onetime gambler on the Mississippi riverboats—the only thing he had captained was a sloop—bore the scars from numerous fights with bowie knives, pistols, and one red-hot poker, though like Mark Twain's river pilot he could also quote scenes of Shakespeare from memory. When he arrived in New York, he took over a string of saloons, ran protection for brothels and gambling houses, and entered politics by founding the Empire Club. The business of the club, which was housed above a saloon on Park Row, was to secure votes by mounting intimidating parades and knocking out opponents—often literally, because among its membership were some of the city's most noted pugilists. Rynders added to his influence by establishing his own company of Guards, who marched to target practice equipped with muskets and tailor-made uniforms. At election time he armed his outfit with bludgeons and knives and placed it at the service of the Democrats, but the party paid the price when he burst into Tammany Hall with two thousand supporters and took over the whole show. Within a few years, Rynders had made himself the boss of the Sixth Ward.

EVEN ISAIAH RYNDERS was not the most unprincipled of the Sixth Ward rabble-rousers. That honor went to a flame-haired urban legend named Edward Zane Carroll Judson, who was known to everyone as Ned Buntline. Like Rynders, Buntline would be deeply implicated in the Astor Place riots.

Ned Buntline was one of the most colorful sleazeballs in American history. A short, stocky man with blue eyes, toffee-apple cheeks, bushy red whiskers, and bunched shoulders, he is best known to history as the man who fashioned William C. Cody, a frontiersman who enlisted in the Civil War when drunk and never saw action, into Buffalo Bill, the greatest scout in the West and a drum-beater for the temperance movement. Buntline's Buffalo Bill stories were just a small part of his prodigious output of paperback dime novels, which also stretched to macho-patriotic seafaring adventures and muckraking exposés of city life and reportedly made him the best-paid writer in America. His own life, though, was more outlandish than his most far-fetched plot.

E.Z.C. Judson ran away to sea at thirteen, seduced and abandoned four girls, or so he later boasted, before he was fourteen, made midshipman in the navy when he was fifteen, sailed around the Mediterranean, skirmished in the Seminole War, and fought ten duels. At eighteen—the stories continued—he was cleared by court-martial of killing an English sailor with a cutlass stroke to the back of the head in a bar brawl, but in return he was leaned on to resign his commission.[12] He turned to seducing a beautiful girl from Florida—he later claimed she was a Cuban duchess—and having pretended to convert to Catholicism he married her and moved to Nashville, where he worked through her dowry, left her without food or clothes, distracted himself with affairs and, while she was dying in childbirth, shot through the eye a man whose teenage wife was his latest conquest. He was hauled off to court, where the dead man's brother burst in, fired at him, and missed—three times. With bullets dancing around him, Judson escaped into a nearby hotel where he hid on the fourth floor until he was discovered. He jumped out of a window, aiming for the porch roof, and landed in the street, in the process breaking his arm and leaving him with a lifelong limp which he wore as a badge of pride. He was carried off to prison. Later that night, the outraged citizens of Nashville overpowered the jailer, dragged Judson to the town square, and hanged him from the rail of a clothing store awning, but a passing coal merchant cut him down and he was carried back to the lockup. Three months later, after his trial collapsed, he escaped town disguised as a woman; eventually, after deserting various other conquests and possibly entering into a sham marriage, he fetched up in New York City, where he capitalized on his talent for self-publicity and turned his hand to journalism.

Buntline, as he now called himself, came up with a brilliant ploy to make himself appear respectable, turn a healthy profit from publishing salacious gossip, and run a tidy sideline in blackmail at the same time. He cranked out a scandal sheet called *Ned Buntline's Own* and styled himself the Friend of the Working Man, the unmasker of fashionable vice and corruption. His *Own* took a stand against the city's brothels and gambling dens, though he took care to list their exact locations for the aid of the curious. An editor who was not guided by the highest principles, he carefully explained, might easily extort large sums from people who feared exposure, and the madams and their gentlemen frequenters who took the hint suddenly vanished from print. Ned played the reform card so well that he bamboozled plenty of well-meaning New Yorkers who never suspected he was among the most enthusiastic patrons of the same brothels and gambling houses that he anathematized. He even posed successfully as a temperance advocate, and one night, after an all-day barhop followed by a dousing with soda water, he delivered a temperance speech to the United Daughters of America stone drunk.

Ned's Own was funded by Buntline's latest father-in-law, an Englishman by birth. Ned lived in his house in Abingdon Place; when his victims came calling, he barricaded himself in with an array of pistols, muskets, bowie knives, and cutlasses selected from the weapons closet in his study.[13] Annie, his wife, allegedly contracted a venereal disease on their wedding night. After one of his regular fights, his father-in-law bailed him out just in time for him to see her give birth; Ned knelt weeping beside her, swore never to take another drink—his father-in-law made him put it in writing—and disappeared on a two-day bender. Throughout his marriage, he kept at least one mistress—by one count, he had seven on the go at the same time—though he threw them over as soon as they found he had reneged on paying their rent, and when one pestered him with desperate appeals for a few dollars he tried to get her jailed.

Occasionally Ned's paltering caught up with him. One high-class courtesan named Kate Hastings, whose name Ned published after she refused to submit to his blackmail, darted out of her carriage while he was strolling down Broadway, grabbed him by the collar, and struck him on the head, then drew a whip from her skirt and cowhided him until he ran away. Ned charged her with assault and battery, but when the case came to court Kate produced a letter, written to her by Buntline, in which he called her an "infernal dirty bitch" and threatened to have her shot if she waylaid him again. Kate pleaded guilty and was fined six cents, and Ned received a dressing-down from the judge.[14]

Buntline, though, had a trump card: he had set himself up as the champion of nativism. His *Own* bristled with attacks on the beggarly Scots, the felonious English, and the viperly Irish, and one day he sailed his yacht into the harbor and shot the Stars and Stripes from a cannon across the bows of an English steamer. The Irish, he editorialized, had proved their bad character by living in sin with blacks in the Five Points, and every gang of burglars in New York was made up of foreigners, mostly Englishmen. The nativist Bowery gangs adopted Ned, and in no time he established himself as Generalissimo of the Order of United Americans, a brotherhood that met in secret and engaged in strange rituals. He started muttering to anyone who would listen about a new American revolution, which would reclaim America for Americans and be led by Ned Buntline, the second Father of his Country, the King of the B'hoys.

Around the same time, Isaiah Rynders hired him as his deputy. The fact that Rynders was a Democrat and Buntline was a nativist was neither here nor there. They understood each other perfectly. They were both in politics for the money and the power, and when Buntline became the ringleader of nativist politics in New York Rynders defected from Tammany Hall and joined him, for as long as it suited his purpose.

FOR YEARS, WITH the true city dweller's talent for compartmentalization, most New Yorkers scarcely registered the growing power of the gangs. Gradually, though, the wave of crime seeped into the smarter parts of town, and respectable citizens began to complain that the city was awash with "courtesans . . . thieves, pocket-book droppers, burners, watch-stuffers, hack-bucks, mock-auction men, gamblers, dance-house keepers, grog-shop keepers [and] pick-pockets."[15] Bullies stalked Broadway, women were harassed, muggings were on the rise, and the upper classes took to packing pocket pistols. But it was the combination of militant gangs and reckless demagogic leaders like Rynders and Buntline that finally shook them out of their torpor. "Dreadful Condition of New York!" the *Herald*'s front page screamed in 1844: "Both Parties Arming for the Election. No Police—No City Government— Triumph of the Mob Spirit and Club Law."[16] "Reign of Terror! Anarchy!

Revolution!" shouted the *Courier and Enquirer,* which lavishly declared that the bloodthirsty spirit sweeping the city would have disgraced revolutionary Paris.[17] Another paper called for the seditionaries to be shot down like dogs, while the city's recorder decried the new mobs as engines of brute force that bold and bad men were manipulating to gratify private revenge.[18]

That was why the word "riot" suddenly took on an altogether more sinister meaning than before. There had always been riots in New York. There were riots in 1788, when medical students snatched bodies from newly dug graves for dissection, and riots when a wealthy citizen was acquitted, against all the evidence, of raping an impoverished sewing girl. There were four "hog riots," led by working women defending their right to keep pigs in the streets despite complaints about the animals' grunting, rutting, and shitting. There was a riot over the price of flour, during which five thousand protestors tore down a warehouse, stoned the mayor, and hurled hundreds of barrels into the street, thus intensifying the shortage. There were repeated anti-abolition riots, in the course of which numerous houses, churches, and brothels were razed. In the past, such disturbances had been tolerated as an exercise in letting off steam, but now the city seemed to be falling apart, even, said alarmists, to be on the edge of savagery, and the rumble of the European revolutions set alarm bells ringing even louder in the parlors of the Upper Ten. It was time to take a stand.

THE FACT THAT the showdown took place in a theatre was not as outlandish as it appears today. The theatres had always been the great democratic gathering places, the only arenas where the people's voice was louder than the elite's, where the poor could sit in judgment on the wealthy folk below. The prospect of the Upper Ten retreating into its own realm of kid gloves and white vests, politicians like Isaiah Rynders declaimed, was the most public affront possible to the people, the most blatant instance yet of the elite turning in on itself and hoarding the fruits of cheap labor, when it was precisely low wages that had pushed ordinary New Yorkers to the poverty line.

To the Upper Ten, the Astor Place Opera House was an attempt to gain some control over their city. They were no longer willing to put up with being hit on the head with a rotten pippin, a shower of nuts, chunks of gingerbread, or any of the other gifts that cascaded down from the gallery.[19] They were certainly not willing to set foot on the crepitant layer of peanut shells that covered the floors of the increasingly raucous Bowery theatres. At the great Bowery Theatre itself, social commentators shuddered, the pit had turned into stamping, shrieking, catcalling pandemonium, while the gallery rang with the yells, screams, oaths, and obscene songs of "rowdies, fancy men, working girls of doubtful reputation," and "the lower species of public prostitutes, accompanied by their 'lovyers,' or such victims as they have been able to pick up," all fueled by cheap spirits from the punch room.[20] The quintessence of East Side character was concentrated within its walls: in the intermissions, families tucked into pork chops and playfully shied the bones at the heads of acquaintances in the pit, while the actors made a sure point of a piece of moral wisdom by bellowing it at the top of their lungs from the front of the stage and then grandstanding to the audience. "Isn't that so, boys?" they'd ask, with a wink, and the response was so deafening that babies started to wail and delayed the play even more.[21] By 1845 even Walt Whitman professed himself completely nauseated by the vulgarity and bad taste of the Bowery, while George Foster recorded a typical conversation in the lobby:

"Helloa Bill, your eyes, how are you?" says one of the b'hoys to his friend, whom he encounters in the crowd, at the same time raising his Herculean hand above the other's head, and crushing his hat down over his eyes and ears. The other sputters, and chokes, and struggles, and at last gets his head out of his hat; and, hitting his friend a tunk in the ribs without being at all discomposed or out of humor, says, "pretty well,—you! how are you! Is Lize along?" "Yes. Your gal here?" says the other. "Yes, in coorse, she ain't nothin shorter," replies the first. "Well, then spose we go and saloon our women!"[22]

The storm was somewhat stilled when a great actor played Shakespeare: the b'hoys still loved the Bard and they shouted out prompts, and expected thanks for them, when actors flubbed their lines. But at the Bowery, Shakespeare had become more interactive than ever: at one

Christmas performance of *Richard III* three hundred b'hoys climbed onto the stage, tried on Richard's crown, swung his sword, swelled the number of soldiers during the Battle of Bosworth Field, formed a ring for Richard and Richmond's fight and, when one of the actors looked as if he might tire, pushed him back into the fray until the duel had lasted for fifteen minutes.[23]

Down at the National on Chatham Street, things were even rougher.[24] Fanny Trollope had once risked her dignity by braving its doors, and she was rewarded with the sight of a mother breastfeeding in the front row of a dress box.[25] Now a Bowery b'hoy called Mose and his g'hal, Lize, had taken up residence on the stage. Mose was the Paul Bunyan of the Bowery: a giant red-haired sporting fireman who gallantly fought entire rival companies single-handedly, heroically pulled infants out of burning buildings, saved cigar girls from depraved aristocrats, and drank barrels of beer in one gulp: a figure big enough to counterbalance the reduced circumstances of his class. The opening

Frank Chanfrau as Mose, the ultimate b'hoy. In this print from 1848, Mose is posing in his fireman's uniform, while behind him other members of his fire company are working their engine. At right, one trainee b'hoy is sitting on a hydrant, doubtless to prevent a rival team from seizing it. Courtesy of the Library of Congress.

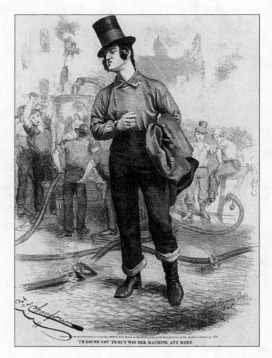

"I'M BOUND NOT TO RUN WID HER MACHINE ANY MORE."

night set the pattern for years of plays in the same vein, several of which were adapted from Ned Buntline's dime novels:*

> [Mose] stood there in his red shirt, with his fire coat thrown over his arm, [his] stovepipe hat . . . drawn down over one eye, his trousers tucked into his boots, a stump of a cigar pointing up from his lips to his eye, the soap locks plastered flat on his temples, and his jaw protruded into a half-beastly, half-human expression of contemptuous ferocity. . . . Taking the cigar stump from his mouth and turning half-way round to spit, he said:
>
> "I ain't a goin' to run wid dat mercheen no more!" Instantly there arose such a yell of recognition as had never been heard in the little house before.[26]

Mose, of course, never would stop running with the machine of one fire company or another. It was not just his pumping walk and blend of belligerence and sentiment that made him an authentic blast of the Bowery: the character was modeled on Moses Humphrey, a printer at the *Sun* and a volunteer rope man for Engine Company 40, and he was played by Frank Chanfrau, whose brother, a stalwart of the rival Engine 15, had ended Humphrey's reign as the unconquered champion of the streets by beating him senseless while a thousand of their supporters fought each other in sympathy. The novelty of seeing themselves on stage sent the b'hoys wild, and every night they gathered over midnight butter-cakes and coffee, or something stronger, to size up the play against the real thing.

To the Upper Ten, it was the final sign that rowdiness had become an endemic working-class disease. The elite stopped differentiating between sporting b'hoys and full-fledged gangsters, and they began to loathe the sight of workingmen parading around town with their insolent air of independence. They no longer called them fellow Americans; now they were the lower ranks, the common people, or even the

---

* Many were also modeled on *Life in London,* the scurrilous old tour through the Regency's fleshpots. To the censorious, that ancestry emphasized the kinship between bawdy Regency London and mid-century New York, which seemed to have taken on the mantle of the new Babylon. This time, though, the heroes were not slumming toffs but Bowery Boys, romanticized to the brims of their stovepipes, celebrating rather than condescending to street culture.

swarthy, horn-handed beasts. What was needed was a whole new theatre, not a box or a seat under cover at the back of the pit, and quite deliberately New York's exclusives set about introducing a European-style opera aristocracy—an Astor-ocracy, one wag said—to the United States. When the Astor Place Opera House opened, the same sparkling eyes lined the soft velvet sofas every night and swept the boxes with pearl opera glasses, while debutantes adjusted their bouquets and ringlets at the end of each act and peered over the railings to see which suitor had left his seat, or cast their eyes demurely down and listened for the expected footsteps outside the door. The opera was about being seen, not about opera, and the new theatre had an intoxicating air of whispered pleasantries and rustling silks which made fashionable hearts beat fast.

Opera exclusiveness was a mainstay of European aristocracies, but it was something quite alien to New York. Still more controversially, the Upper Ten had not just followed the European custom and retained the boxes for the season: they had replaced the entire pit with a parquette of armchairs which could be purchased only by subscription, a provocative move that had never even been countenanced at the Queen's Opera in London, where it was thought very bold to replace a few rows of pit benches with high-priced stalls. The dress code, an "etiquette of toilet" which required the purchase of an expensive dress and thus the use of a carriage, weeded out even more people, and if anyone plain-mannered and plain-dressed trespassed in the lobby, their self-styled betters made sure to be plain rude. As the carriages disgorged the gossamer costumes, the real-life Mose and Lize, strolling down the Bowery on their way to a tangy Irish entertainment at the beery Vauxhall Gardens, found themselves outcasts in a foreign world. In 1849, a minstrel show put working-class outrage in the mouths of blackface satirists, thus saving (white) face:

> De Astor Opera is anoder nice place;
> If *you* go thar, jest wash your face!
> Put on your "kids," and fix up neat,
> For dis am de spot of de *eliteet*![27]

For all the conflict between capitalists and workers and the heightened class consciousness imported from revolutionary Europe, it is possible to overstate the element of class struggle in mid-century New York. Fashionable society was nothing like as hard to break into as in London: even Philip Hone, the acknowledged arbiter of social standards for the bon ton, was the son of a joiner who made his fortune as an auctioneer, retired at forty, and came back from a grand tour with a new set of manners. Moreover, for all the fuss over the Astor Place, grand opera had a hard time establishing itself in New York. The previous opera house was converted by a flamboyant Italian restaurateur called Ferdinando Palmo from a public bath: it quickly went bust, and Palmo, having lost his Café of a Thousand Columns down to the last pot and kettle, was reduced to advertising himself as a cook and barman for hire. The merchant class suspected that opera society was still a bit rich for the New World, and there were not enough Maecenases among the fashionable to prevent the balcony from being thrown open to ordinary theatregoers. "Unfortunately we of ourselves are not sufficiently numerous to support an Opera, so we have been forced to admit the People," one patrician woman was heard to lament in 1848.[28] Even so, they had failed to sustain a full season, which was why the Astor Place had been downgraded to a commonplace theatre and was available for the much more bourgeois business of Shakespeare when Macready arrived.

Yet in 1849, the year after the United States won its first foreign war and pushed further west, after the Communist Manifesto was published and the French monarchy was ousted by a democratic insurgency that triggered revolutions across Europe, a crucial point in time seemed to have arrived. New Yorkers read that their city was on the cusp of history: it would be the preeminent metropolis of the world, and it was up to its citizens to decide what shape it would take.

The city's tub-thumping politicians seized their moment. The appearance of the leading representative of English culture, the supercilious maltreater of the American Tragedian, at the elite opera house was a golden opportunity to attack both England and the Upper Ten in one fell swoop. Macready, Rynders spelled out to his cohorts, was a jumped-up aristocratic puppet whose strings needed a swift snip, and it was the duty of every republican to resist the prospect of an English-style elite establishing itself in America. "England hates because she fears the young giant of the West, and she knows that the easiest way to rob him of his strength, is to accustom him to the luxury and artificial existence that has made her so weak in her old age," another of Forrest's supporters warned, typically gendering America as masculine and Britain as feminine.[29] Ned Buntline, naturally, took things to another level. "If they mean to have a war, let it begin here!" he agitated in his *Own* as Macready approached New York: let the people, he added, give the Englishman what their ancestors had dealt out to the Redcoats at Lexington.[30]

On Monday, May 7, Isaiah Rynders bought fifty tickets to Macready's first night; altogether, thanks to the zealousness of his co-conspirators—led by Andrew Stevens, the jeweler whose Hoboken excursion had started the whole plot—five hundred were handed out to the b'hoys. Inside the theatre, Edward Strahan, a fiery Tammany orator, led the cheers for Forrest, and the amphitheatre rang with cries against the Codfish Aristocracy.* Rynders placed himself in the second tier of boxes and complacently surveyed the action, and after the curtain fell Hiram Fuller, the editor of the *Evening Mirror,* ran into him in the lobby.

"Are you the leader of this party?" Fuller asked.

"Which party?" Rynders replied.

"Oh, the peace party, of course," Fuller laughingly answered.

Rynders told him it was none of his business, asked him to repeat his remarks to an associate, and while he was distracted gave him a glancing blow to the left side of his head.

"Damn you, I have flattened your face for you," he shouted as the journalist was led out by a friend to find some iced water.

Rynders and his Guards rode the omnibus to the Broadway Theatre, where Forrest had just finished performing.

"We have put hell to Macready; he has never had such a reception before," the Captain crowed to his friends.

One of the slogans shouted down from the Astor Place amphitheatre had linked Macready with abolition, which some Americans still saw as a nefarious English plot. "Three cheers for Macready, Nigger Douglass, and Pete Williams" was the cry: Williams was the owner of Dickens's Place, while Frederick Douglass, a former slave who was now a powerful

---

* The Codfish families were famously Anglophile and notorious for adopting English manners and pronunciations. Most also shared a puritan distaste for the theatre, but to the b'hoys the term had come to refer to any cold-blooded type who had made a fortune in business.

voice for abolition, had been seen walking arm-in-arm down Broadway—on the fashionable side—with two white women two days before. Douglass was in town for the annual anniversary week of the great moral and religious societies, and all over the city crowds of activists were packing the wooden pews of the public meetinghouses. Isaiah Rynders decided to press home his advantage. The evening after his performance in Astor Place, the Captain and a hundred of his thugs burst into the Tabernacle, where the Anti-Slavery Society was in session, and took possession of the platform. From the upper tier, the Hutchinsons, a famous close-harmony family quartet, started singing psalms, and Rynders's troops gradually stopped their stamping, whistling, and hooting. The infuriated Captain strode up the aisle, told the psalmists to stop their damn singing, and instructed a "scientist" among his gang to lecture the meeting on the close connection between the "nigger" and the "monkey." That accomplished, he turned to Douglass and challenged him to reply, though when he found himself thoroughly outdebated Rynders hastily adjourned the meeting.[31]

The next day Ned Buntline went calling on Edwin Forrest at his Chelsea home.

"You know there is going to be a muss," he explained to a fellow journalist on the way, "and I want to see Forrest, to see if he is right or wrong, for I consider myself the leader of the native American party in this matter, and if Forrest is right, I mean to see him through."[32] Forrest was away from home, but he would no doubt have given Buntline the same answer he had given Rynders. "Two wrongs do not make a right," he had said with a frown—but, he significantly added, "Let the people do as they please."[33]

It was a busy week in New York City. On Tuesday, at five minutes to noon, the official returns of the mayoral election were read out at City Hall, after a campaign during which the gangs had toppled yet more ballot boxes. The Democrats had been bitterly split by feuding factions, and Caleb S. Woodhull, the Whig candidate, won by a large majority. The Whigs were closely associated with the city's Silk Stockings, the old-money patrician class, and Rynders and his Tammany cohorts were mightily roiled.

However improbable the sequence of triggers that tripped into place that May in 1849 must have seemed, they surely created the conditions for the perfect riot. A personal, a local, and an international feud had all converged in one fraught moment. Macready's determination to make the theatre respectable had made him the archetype of the Victorian Englishman. Forrest's frontier populism had made him the hero of the new America. The theatre's central place in both British and American culture had thrust the two actors onto an international stage, the competitiveness of their profession had fostered a jealous rivalry, and years of being stars had excised a sense of proportion from both men. English abuse had worn America's patience thin, and American expansionism and indebtedness had raised England's hackles. The wealth of New York's elite had incensed its increasingly impoverished workers, and the power of the gangs had made organized violence a demonstrable threat. Even Forrest's marital troubles and the election of an inexperienced Whig mayor had added to the crisis. Not least of all, America's conflicted relationship with its heritage had split the nation into two opposing camps, and both were determined to claim Shakespeare as their own. A feud that started with Hamlet and a hiss had become a contest to decide who controlled American culture. It was absurd that two Shakespearean actors fomented one of the worst riots in American history, but it would have been even more astonishing if peace had suddenly set in.

CHAPTER II

America Rules England Tonight!

A<small>T ELEVEN O'CLOCK</small> on the morning of May 10, 1849, Mayor Woodhull convened a crisis meeting at his office in City Hall.

It was a fresh-washed spring day, the high sun drying the mud left by a long spell of driving rain, the dust clouds not yet rising. William Niblo, the manager of the Astor Place Theatre, made his way downtown with his partner, James Hackett. Major General Charles Sandford, the commander of the New York County militia, walked over from his nearby law practice. The three-hundred-pound figure of George Matsell, the chief of police, tacked through the doorway, and the group was completed by John Westerveld, the sheriff; Frederick Tallmadge, the recorder; and the city's police justices.

Spread on the table were the baffling documents of a most peculiar case. The first piece of evidence was the letter that had been delivered to Macready that Tuesday evening and published in Wednesday's papers. It was not idly worded. The public assurance that the actor would be sustained by the forces of order was a thinly veiled challenge to the authorities, and as the Whig mayor cast his eyes down the list of the forty-eight signatories it did not escape his notice that nearly all were prominent uptown Whigs.[1] There was a plurality of lawyers and judges, a preponderance of merchants and editors, and a scattering of writers, bankers, brokers, congressmen, and senators' sons: men like Washington Irving, now the grand old man of American letters; Samuel Ruggles, the developer of Union Square and Gramercy Park; and Henry Raymond, the cofounder of *The New York Times*.* There was no doubting society's loyalties. Macready, Philip Hone declared, was a gentleman and a scholar, whereas Forrest was "a vulgar, arrogant loafer, with a pack of kindred rowdies at his heels," and his vile band of retainers was threatening to disgrace the city. But there was also a larger issue at stake: now that the Whigs were in power, they were not inclined to let their opponents' gangs terrorize the city. "This cannot end here," Hone added after Monday's riot: "the respectable part of our citizens will never consent to be put down by a mob raised to serve the purpose of such a fellow as Forrest."[2]

Unsurprisingly, as Mayor Woodhull well noted, the Whig papers agreed. The *Tribune* called Monday's display a "wanton, tyrannous and scoundrelly outrage": to suppose, it scoffed, that because a man had paid a dollar he could terrify his fellow spectators, put a stop to the play, destroy the furniture, endanger the performers' lives, and deprive a man of the means to make his living, all in the name of liberty, was "to evince an intensity of stupidity and ruffianism which even 'Mose' should be ashamed of."[3] Never mind that actors had been driven off the stage with the collusion of the press on numerous previous occasions: this was another age and another man's mob, and the *Courier and Enquirer*—the same *Courier* that had organized the Wood riot back in 1843—appealed to Macready to perform again as a matter of justice, thereby allowing his friends the opportunity to redress his wrongs and prove that thugs did not make the law. It also conclusively named Forrest as the orchestrator and paymaster of Monday's debacle, thus adding the shame of inflicting "a thorough and lasting disgrace upon the American character" to that of "bad acting and unmanly conduct," though it quickly retracted the allegation when Forrest's lawyer threatened to sue for libel.[4]

Next came Macready's reply to the letter, which was printed in the

---

* Only four were Democrats. One—at the head of the list—was Ambrose L. Jordan, the attorney general of New York State. The other three, Evert A. Duyckinck, Cornelius Mathews, and Herman Melville, were more surprising inclusions: they were leaders of Young America, the Democratic-aligned group which proselytized for an American national literature. But all three came from genteel old families, and they had grown increasingly disillusioned with the gangland politics of Tammany Hall. Besides, Young America did not approve of Forrest. Duyckinck declared that he tramped and staggered like an ox in the shambles: "If a bull could act, he would act like Forrest" (Perry Miller, *The Raven and the Whale: Poe, Melville and the New York Literary Scene* [Baltimore and London, 1956], 164). English or not, Macready was much more in their mold.

papers the same day. Though he made a becoming show of his difficulty in answering his petitioners, Macready could only meet such a high-minded appeal with a high-minded response, and he duly gave one:

Under the unprovoked indignities offered to me in the Astor Place Theatre, it was certainly my desire and my fixed purpose, to avail myself of the legal right thus offered me, and withdraw at once from my engagement contracted there.

In leaving this country which has been endeared to my recollection by long and strong attachments, I should not have done you the injustice of associating the American character with the ill-deeds of persons, unhappily too frequently to be found in every large community: and in the same spirit which would preserve me from a hasty and inconsiderate judgment upon the late occurrence, I assent to your request, honoring and feeling grateful for the sentiment that has dictated it.

Not everyone took the affair so seriously: the *Herald* declared that it was all the fault of that "talented little Cockney" Dickens, for prejudicing his friend Forster against America.[5] Overnight, though, the city had been blanketed by two hundred posters that raised the stakes with a blatant appeal to national prejudice:

WORKING MEN,

SHALL

AMERICANS

OR

ENGLISH RULE

IN THIS CITY?

The Crew of the British steamer have

Threatened all Americans who shall dare to express their

opinions this night, at the

ENGLISH ARISTOCRATIC OPERA HOUSE!

We advocate no violence, but a free expression of opinion

to all public men.

WORKINGMEN! FREEMEN!

STAND BY YOUR
LAWFUL RIGHTS!
American Committee.

More mischievous handbills were pasted next to them, this time decrying Americans, in giant letters, as "Low Curs" and calling upon Englishmen to sustain their countrymen by mounting their own show of force in Astor Place. They were signed "John Bull," the English equivalent of Uncle Sam, but it was later discovered that both publications were printed in the same office on Ann Street, and both were delivered to the public house at 28 Park Row from which Isaiah Rynders ran his Empire Club. On Wednesday, Rynders and half a dozen of his henchmen were seen going down into the cellar, and one of the group hung a sample poster on the wall and stepped back to admire it.

"There, that's an American bill," he declared, "and I'd like to see any goddamn English son of a bitch express an objection to it. He'll get a toothache that will last him all his life."

"That's the talk," Rynders approved. "Now boys, take a drink."[6]

Ned Buntline was not in the room, but he was heavily rumored to be the American Committee's leader, if not its entire board.

The involvement of the British steamer was a complete fabrication, but the posters had the intended effect, and the newspapers that Thursday morning were full of dire speculations. Meanwhile, with spectacular timing, the *Herald* added another twist of paper to the fire: virtually a whole page was taken up by Macready's "Replies from England," the fruits of his requests for evidence proving his innocence of the charges leveled at him by Forrest. There were letters from Bulwer Lytton, spluttering with outrage at the very idea that Macready had vetoed Forrest's performing his plays, from Fonblanque, the editor of the *Examiner,* vowing that Macready's only intercessions had been in favor of the American tragedian, from Mitchell, the Paris manager, swearing that Macready had in no way sought to turn him against his rival, and from a host of officials and actors insisting that Macready had no hand in fomenting the opposition in London and that Forrest, and only Forrest, had hissed Macready in Edinburgh. Macready had been persuaded to call off his threatened court case; he had intended his pamphlet for private circulation, but after Monday night's scenes he had decided to vindicate himself by making its contents public.

"The Great Theatrical War—Macready Yet in the Field," the *Herald* headlined.[7]

The last item on the table was the playbill, announcing that Macready would repeat *Macbeth* that night, which Niblo and Hackett had pasted around town. *Macbeth* was again announced at the Bowery; at the Broadway, Forrest chose to fight back with *The Gladiator.*

Mayor Woodhull sat in his new office and wondered what to do. He asked Niblo and Hackett whether they would close the theatre: the bills were up, they replied, and the show must go on. Woodhull took another look at the names ranged against him and decided not to argue.

Police Chief Matsell spoke up. His eight-hundred-strong force, he was certain, would not be able to suppress a full-scale insurrection: the military would be needed. Matsell was no fool: he knew that half the precincts were in the pockets of the ward politicians who appointed his men. Besides, he was not above a little graft himself.[8] On Monday he had been stationed in the Astor Place gallery with half a dozen officers, but he had magnanimously declined to enter the fray, in order, some thought, not to upset his paymasters. At the same time he was well aware that he was despised by the b'hoys, and the prospect of giving them a bloody hiding while screening himself behind a file of soldiers must have filled him with grim satisfaction.

Woodhull took a deep breath and signed the fateful edict. "Having reason to apprehend a serious riot this evening," it read, "which will require more force to preserve the peace than is possessed by the police, Major General Sandford is requested to hold a sufficient military force in readiness to meet the apprehended emergency."[9]

Sandford went to work. First, he issued orders to the 7th Regiment of the New York State militia—the National Guard—to muster at the Artillery drill rooms at Centre Market, on Centre Street between Grand Street and Broome Street. Next he summoned a troop of light artillery from the Washington Greys, the 8th Regiment, to the Arsenal, together with two six-pound field pieces and two companies of infantry from the 6th Regiment, the Governor's Guard, to protect the guns. Finally he ordered two troops of horse belonging to the 7th and

8th Regiments and two companies of hussars to assemble at the Arsenal yard.*

Later the call-up of the military became the subject of searching questions. It was a provocative move: the volunteer militiamen had always been reluctant to act against their fellow citizens, but unlike the police, who were equipped only with short clubs, they were armed with lethal force. Yet Woodhull never issued a proclamation warning the citizenry to stay away from Astor Place. Was the call-up a legitimate strategy to maintain law and order, a red rag to the b'hoys, or the flustered action of an inexperienced chief magistrate? If the troops had to be called out, should they have taken the ground earlier? Would a warning merely have heightened the tension, or was the Upper Ten determined to provoke a showdown and lance the boil of b'hoydom once and for all?

AFTER THE MEETING Niblo and Hackett strolled back to the theatre, where they found Macready in the midst of a rehearsal. With his usual supererogation he had insisted on running through every line again, even though the play had not changed since three nights before. The two managers, following the mayor's instructions, set the carpenters and stagehands to board up the lower windows of the theatre with thick wooden planks.

Across in Abingdon Place, Ned Buntline emerged from his father-in-law's house resplendent in a tall hat and a blue frock coat shining with gilt buttons. Ned mounted a light wagon, took a boy with him to hold the reins, and rode up and down the Bowery, jumping out to issue instructions to his nativist troops. Down in the Five Points, the Tammany Irish were also stirring for action. Macready had pulled off the impossi-

---

* The 7th Regiment of the New York State Militia traced its origins to the British navy's decapitation of the American helmsman during its blockade of New York's harbor prior to the War of 1812; when his headless corpse was put on display, a mass rally provoked a surge in enlistments. The first state militia unit to refer to itself as the National Guard, it had already quelled numerous public disturbances in its previous incarnation as the 27th Regiment, New York State Artillery, though none approached the Astor Place riot in scale. It was an elite unit in more than one way: it was also known as the Silk Stocking Regiment because of the roster of socially prominent members among its officers, a trend that became even more pronounced after the riot. The hussars, from the 5th Regiment, were attached to the brigade of General George P. Morris, the poet and founder of the *Mirror* and *Home Journal,* New York newspapers for well-bred ladies, and the man who had officially welcomed Dickens to the Boz Ball.

ble: he had united Irishmen and nativists, Tammany Hall and the Order of United Americans, the Five Points and the Bowery under one banner.

The prospect of a showdown brought out knots of people who had no ax to grind but saw plenty of fun, or money, to be had. Having been caught by surprise on Monday, Macready's supporters were determined that this time the tickets would end up in the right hands, and the news quickly spread that they were signing up recruits. William Doyle, a ship's caulker, presented himself first at the Astor Place Theatre and then at the Wall Street office of one of Macready's public sponsors and offered the services of twenty-five hard-fisted men from the shipyards in return for a handsome reward. If they could not put down the opposition in any other way, he promised, they would throw it out the window. Doyle's speculation was unsuccessful, but Bill "Sparks" Parks, a mason, Robert Long, a former barkeeper, and Charles Tappan, a plumber who had recently been arrested for burglary, hit the jackpot. The three called on Moses H. Grinnell and Duncan C. Pell, another two of the signatories to the letter delivered to Macready, and spun a story about a large party of men from Fulton Market who were keen to support the English actor. Grinnell unsuspectingly handed over twelve tickets for the parquette; in the afternoon, Pell met the trio on the corner of Ninth Street and Broadway and took them to the box office, where he supplied them with a hundred amphitheatre tickets. They kept three for themselves and left the rest to be sold at a discount in bars. Isaiah Rynders had run out of money after his ticket-buying spree on Monday, but he borrowed fifty dollars from one of Forrest's friends and snapped up as many as he could.

A little after noon a regular muss-loving Bowery b'hoy called John Ripley was walking back from dinner to his machinist's shop when he was called into Jim McNulty's Saloon, at the corner of Chatham Square and Doyers Street, and handed a pair of tickets. Ripley was already familiar with the drill: on Monday he had taken a coworker to the theatre and kicked up a storm in the gallery. This time he was given more precise instructions: go early, get seats in the front row, and look out for danger, as a plan was afoot to throw enough gunpowder into the great gas chandelier to blow it up and start a stampede. Ripley, though, also happened to be a corporal in the 7th Regiment. At four o'clock, just as he was getting ready to leave for Astor Place, the company sergeant marched in and read out his orders. Ripley handed his ticket to his workmate, went home, put on his uniform, picked up his musket, and reported for duty, ready to preserve the peace he had been instrumental in breaking three days earlier. Whether from the short notice or more cases of split loyalties, only two hundred and ten muskets mustered, more than a hundred short of the full contingent. With their white trousers, their black helmets topped with a short white plume, and their gray coatees finished with white fringed epaulettes, white cross-belts, black frogging, and three rows of brass buttons, the Greyjackets, as they were popularly known, were still a splendid sight.

In the afternoon the wind changed to the east and storm clouds scudded across the sky.

Andrew Stevens hastily consulted with his fellow intriguers and headed for the Broadway Theatre to talk to Edwin Forrest. The actor's friends, he represented, felt strongly that it would be wise for him to disassociate himself from the coming trouble by publicly asking his partisans to refrain from getting involved. According to Stevens, Forrest was boiling with resentment at the treasonous behavior of his rival's backers, and he peremptorily refused.[10]

At twenty to six, William Charles Macready set out from the New York Hotel. Looking down Astor Place he saw the Harlem streetcar pull up on the Bowery and discharge a carload of policemen, and he noticed more officers in front of the theatre. "This is a useful precaution!" he observed to himself. After all the humiliation and suspense, he was seized with an almost giddy spirit of defiance.

At six o'clock, Chief Matsell made his way to the theatre and met with his officers. Three hundred and twenty-five policemen were at the scene, just over a third of the full force. Two hundred were stationed inside the theatre, ranged along the lobbies, stairs, parquette, balconies, and amphitheatre, identifiable by the stars pinned to their coats from which their popular name derived. Of those outside, seventy-five were posted in the nearby mansion and stables of Mrs. Langdon, a granddaughter of John Jacob Astor, leaving just fifty in the streets.

Ned Buntline wheeled home in time for supper and read out the latest pugnacious piece about the affair which he had drawn up for his

Own. As the family rose from the table he asked his brother-in-law Frank to take a walk with him, and a few minutes later he reappeared in a light-colored monkey jacket—a short, tight sailor's coat—and a white Tom Hyer cap, named after the nativist prizefighter who had beaten the Irishman James Sullivan to become the American champion three months earlier. Frank recognized both as his own. Annie, Ned's wife, asked where he was going.

"To John Graham's house," replied Ned, referring to one of his regular associates who lived nearby. "I have to consult him on some important business."

Annie was pregnant and unwell and she begged him to stay at home. Ned brushed her aside and walked out with Frank in tow. At Twelfth Street he stopped short. "Let's go down to the Opera House," he proposed. "There's going to be some great sport there tonight." They passed Graham's house, made off down Broadway, and stopped outside Weller's barroom. Ned drew Frank to one side. Some gamblers who were his enemies might be there, he warned, and he slipped Frank one of two six-barreled, self-cocking revolvers he had pocketed earlier, telling him to watch his back. After a fortifying drink, the two headed off to Astor Place, and in the street Ned nudged Frank again.

"I have got William's Roman sword with me," he said between his teeth, and he parted his jacket to reveal a large double-edged sword in a red sheath which he had borrowed from another brother-in-law. "It will make such a show," he breathed, his eyes glinting.

By seven o'clock the streets leading to the theatre were jammed with noisy young men, many sporting the red uniforms of volunteer firemen. Several members of the Rynders Guard were there, though Rynders himself stayed safely away, and tickets were still being pressed into hands.

The doors opened and the b'hoys rushed inside. Most did not get far. The tickets issued by Macready's friends had a special mark on the back, and anyone lacking the seal of approval was told the house was sold out. Within minutes, a placard was put up announcing that the amphitheatre was full, and dozens of Forrest's partisans were pushed back by the police and shut outside.

"I will go in or have my money back, or I will give you hell for it!"

threatened one furious ticket holder. They were being kept out, others shouted, because they were not from the white kid gentry. The exclusives, they could plainly see, were being waved in; some were even ushered through the stage door. It appeared that the house had been deliberately oversold to allow the managers to weed out the undesirables, and now the b'hoys had fraud to add to their list of grievances.

The doors were barred and a line of police took up their positions in front. The crowds continued to cram into the surrounding area, and by eight o'clock between ten thousand and twenty thousand demonstrators formed a dense mass of top hats that waved down Broadway and along Astor Place, through Eighth Street, Lafayette Place, and the Bowery, and across the large expanse of open ground where the last four thoroughfares intersected.[11]

A number of uptowners had come out to witness the proceedings, and to one side of the crowd a bespectacled middle-aged man was earnestly expostulating with a knot of protestors.

"We can't live, sir, under such a state of things," he reasoned. "The mob must be put down."

"Damn you to hell!" roared a tall, burly man who overheard him. "America rules England tonight, by Jesus!"

Macready retreated into his dressing room and the familiar anxieties of a performance night. His hairdresser's tardiness ruffled his nerves, but finally he was ready for his call. He went on, as pertinacious as ever— "with full assurance, confidence and cheerfulness," he later declared—to a rousing reception from his friends and an outbreak of fist shaking, groaning, hissing, and abuse from the front rows of the parquette and the amphitheatre. The troublemakers were thinner on the ground this time, but enough had slipped in that yet again the first act went on in pantomime.

Macready laughed as carelessly as he could at his hecklers and pointed them out, with Macbeth's truncheon, to the police. His supporters stood up and called for the malcontents to be arrested.

"Go on! See if you dare!" they jeered back.

One of Macready's men leaned a blackboard against the front of the stage: "The friends of order will remain silent," the chalked message directed. As the plan caught on, the Eminent's men—there were only seven women in the audience—quietly sat down, and the protestors found themselves exposed. In the stage-left box Chief Matsell, the recorder, and the police justices held a conference. Though, thus far, the intimidation was notably less violent than on Monday, other considerations had come into play: there was a new mayor, and his supporters had loudly criticized the chief's earlier inaction. Besides, this time it was the b'hoys who were outnumbered, not the police. The conferees concluded that the peace had been breached, and on Matsell's order his stars swooped on the troublemakers, dragged them out, and locked them up in a storeroom under the parquette. Every arrest brought a new round of cheers from Macready's supporters and a new howl of outrage from Forrest's, who furiously shouted that their civil rights were being trampled to pieces. Among the earliest to be arrested were the three men who had extracted the tickets from Macready's friends: one, Robert Long, threatened to set fire to the theatre and kill his captor unless his handcuffs were removed. He was not entirely bluffing. First the prisoners tried to kick down the wall, and when that failed they swept up a heap of shavings and straw left over from some packing crates and lit a bonfire. The flames started licking at the ceiling beams; the prisoners cried "Fire!" and banged at the door. Smoke started to seep into the auditorium and rumors spread that the building was burning; the officers on guard charged into the storeroom, stamped out the flames, and clapped the incendiaries in irons.

The second act went off better: a few passages were even audible. Then, on the stage, Macready heard a terrible noise coming from outside.

A LITTLE EARLIER, Ned Buntline and his brother-in-law Frank had arrived on the scene, and after a circuit of the theatre they stopped on Eighth Street. By now it was a dark, overcast night, and Ned could not make out his troops.

"Are there any Americans here?" he shouted.

"I am a Northern Liberty boy," one youth answered.

"I am Ned Buntline," Ned announced, "and you want a nucleus to this body." Earlier in the day he had arranged for an engine company's ladders and hooks to be stashed around the corner, and he explained his plan: they would make out there was a fire, scale the walls, and drive the audience out. The young nativist was not convinced: the whole scene was so disorganized that he thought it would be impossible to raise the cry. Ned decided it would be quicker to start a real fire, unaware that his comrades inside had already beaten him to it.

By now Buntline's boys had started to recognize him, and he hit on a better idea. A sewer was in mid-construction near the theatre, and heaps of cobblestones were lying around where the street had been dug up. Ned stationed himself out of harm's way, between two trees opposite the north entrance to the theatre, and rallied his troops. "It is a shame that Americans should be used so!" he declared in a low, urgent voice: the military preparations were an insult, and it was the boys' democratic duty to resist them. With his hand cupping his mouth, he issued his orders, and relays of his ragged army—perhaps two hundred strong by now, many of them teenage fire engine fanatics who were keen to prove their worth as trainee rowdies—went off to fetch armfuls of stones and pass them around.

"Now, boys, for a shower!" one gang stalwart shouted, but Ned was determined to make an impact and not everyone had their ammunition.

"Hold, boys, till you are all ready!" he intervened.

On his command a volley of stones flew at the theatre, and every few minutes another followed, methodically pounding the doors and smashing the windows from the Bowery end toward Broadway.

"Put out the lights!" someone cried, and a new volley knocked out the streetlamps. Most of the surrounding houses had already gone dark: the pale moon and the shafts of light shining through the upper windows of the theatre cast an eerie pallor on the scene.

The assault had begun to dislodge the planks nailed up inside the tall lower windows, and the best shots were rewarded with an almighty cheer.

"Fight! Fight! Tear it down!" Buntline's troops chanted. "Burn the damned den of the aristocracy!"

"You can't go in there without kid gloves on!" a burly b'hoy shouted. "I paid for a ticket and they wouldn't let me in, because I hadn't kid gloves and a white vest, damn 'em!"

"I luxuriate in the scene!" a more fastidious nativist declared. "Hurrah! I will have nothing to do with breaking windows, but I luxuriate in the scene!"

Many of the stones were directed at the police; dozens of them were injured, and they retreated into the lobby. One insider—perhaps the theatre's resident caretaker—thrust a hosepipe through a window and sprayed the mob with water, which brought hoots of derision and a concentrated barrage.

Ned Buntline saw his moment. He charged up and down, swinging his Roman broadsword and rallying his teenage army to renew their attack.

"Let's see Ned Forrest put through!" he whooped. Cheers rang out for the American tragedian, followed by groans for Macready.

One of Buntline's nativists pushed through the crowd and warned him that he was being watched closely by a police officer, the captain of the Thirteenth Ward. Even in the gloom Ned was not hard to spot: he had taken to wearing a full red beard, a patriarchal figuration that was his new pride and joy. Buntline thought better of his heroics and asked his brother-in-law to take his sword.

"Not for twenty thousand dollars," Frank retorted. Ned pulled him off toward the Bowery.

"They will not arrest you, but they may me—you take the sword," he wheedled, and Frank gave in. He slipped it under his coat, and in exchange he handed Ned back his six-barreled revolver. Ned told him to wait at Weller's and headed back to his post.

Inside the theatre, the lobbies were strewn with stone, glass, and broken boards. One plank had been driven off with such concerted force that it sailed across the fop's gallery—the passage at the back of the balcony—and plummeted through the audience, where it was only held back by the balustrade from falling into the parquette. One gallery rowdy poked his head through a broken window and yelled that Forrest's supporters were being rounded up and arrested, a report that built into a rumor that the police inside were murdering the rebels.

"Don't back down!" Ned Buntline cried. Chunks of stone started flying into the auditorium through the unboarded upper windows: one hit the great chandelier and sent the parquette scrambling beneath a shower of crystal shards.

Macready carried on with his usual stiff upper lip, and when one anxious actor suggested he might cut part of *Macbeth* he turned on him sharply.

222   The Shakespeare Riots

"I have consented to do this thing," he snapped. "I have placed myself here, and whatever the consequences I must go through with it. The audience have paid for it, and the law compels me to give it; they would have cause for riot if all is not properly done."[12] As ever he was determined to defend his propriety, even at the hazard of his life, or the lives of those around him.

Outside, teams of b'hoys had turned themselves into battering rams and were hurling themselves against the entrance. After three or four attempts, one door burst open and a shout went up to rush the theatre, but before the raiding party had time to form, a phalanx of police charged out swinging their clubs. In the initial surprise, they pushed the crowd back and dragged several stone throwers inside.

"Hit the stars!" the rioters shouted, and many of Matsell's men were badly battered. One of Buntline's henchmen seized an officer's badge in a struggle and held it aloft.

"Victory! Victory! Three cheers for victory!" he cried. In desperation, the police captains ordered their men to hide their stars.

By now, the heavy brigade had arrived. A group of Short Boys, a shadowy but terrifying gang of hoodlums, had placed themselves among the mob and were cooperating with Buntline's band.

"Stand by, Short Boys, don't let them arrest you!" they hollered at one another.

"You sons of bitches!" one screamed as a policeman grabbed him by the collar, and he raised his fist to strike him with a stone. Another officer grasped the rioter by the wrist and made him release his grip, which sent the stone flying at the first policeman's neck.

"Don't let them take them! Rescue them!" Buntline's boys shouted, and they dragged several of their comrades from the grasp of the police. The mob was gaining the upper hand.

TOWARD NINE O'CLOCK, Sheriff Westerveld sent General Sandford's aide—who was also the general's son—to the drill rooms with an urgent request for the military's assistance. The general, who was still dressed in his black business suit, distributed a thousand rounds of ball cartridge to the infantry, summoned the cavalry, and gave the order to march. The troops moved off, Sandford at the right of the forty-strong cavalry, Brigadier General William Hall at the right of the infantry, and filed along Broadway to Astor Place.

Rumors of their approach reached Ned Buntline, who primed his own crew to step up the attack. "Now, boys, whatever you have to do must be done quickly, as the military are coming," he hurriedly urged.

There was no time. Shortly after nine, the militia marched into view. Sandford looked around in disbelief: nothing in his thirty-five years as an officer had prepared him for a scene like this. A dense, seething crowd packed the streets for blocks; as the troops pushed through, hisses, hoots, and curses filled the air. The mob had scented victory, and the appearance of uniformed soldiers unleashed a wave of fury. The hussars, mounted on white horses and armed only with sabers, wheeled first into the midst of the fray, but before they could gain any ground showers of stones flew at them out of the dark. The horses, trained for parade duty rather than crowd control, reared under the assault. Several riders were pulled to the ground; the rest were driven off, their faces streaming with blood. Behind them, the regular thud of the infantry's boots broke up as they pushed blindly through, with knots of b'hoys, Irish now as well as nativists, attacking them from either side with stones and screaming abuse.

Ned Buntline was still waving his arms and urging on his boys.

"The ground you stand on is your own: you have a right to it, and I will assist you in defending your rights!" he shouted, and added: "You need not be alarmed—they have nothing but blank cartridge—no one will be hurt." But Ned's night of glory was to be cut short: Matsell's men had finally wised up to his antics, and on one of their sorties they headed for him.

"What am I being arrested for?" Buntline blustered. "I am a member of the working press. This is an insult. I will make the authorities suffer for this—my wife is about to be confined." For all his bravado, he failed to put up a fight, and he was handcuffed and marched inside. By now the improvised lockup in the basement was close-packed with a hundred b'hoys, not all friends of Ned's. Several began to shout abuse at him, and he begged not to be thrown inside. No one listened, but the diversion gave him time to signal to Marcus Cicero Stanley, a fellow journalist and partner in Ned's *Own.* Catching Ned's drift, Stanley rubbed up against him, and reaching into his pockets Ned slipped him his pair of revolvers.

General Sandford, a short man in a dark suit, was less conspicuous than his uniformed troops; he made it through the nucleus of the mob, dismounted, and struggled back to take charge of the infantry. On his order, a detachment pushed through to the rear of the theatre on Eighth Street, defiled two-by-two across the street, turned back to back, and slowly parted the crowd toward Broadway and the Bowery.

Mayor Woodhull finally arrived on the scene and made his way into the theatre. He found Chief Matsell, Recorder Tallmadge, and Sheriff Westerveld under siege: the mob, they warned him, could not be kept out much longer. General Hall, bleeding from wounds inflicted by stones, came in and repeatedly told the mayor that his men would leave the ground unless he gave the order to fire: they would not stand being stoned to death with arms in their hands.

"Not yet, General. Wait a little," Woodhull stalled. Within minutes he took to his heels and ran for cover to the New York Hotel, where he stayed for the rest of the night.

The noise from the street was turning into a steady howl as Macready left the stage after the banquet scene and went to his dressing room to change. He found it flooded: a hail of stones had broken the pipes.

General Sandford summoned Matsell and the sheriff to join him outside. At his request, two lines of police officers moved in behind the troops who had cleared Eighth Street and took their place. The troops marched into Broadway and around into Astor Place, where Sandford ordered them to repeat the operation. This time, though, the press of the crowd was so fierce that the soldiers struggled to get through, and nearly the whole front rank was knocked down by another bombardment of stones and carried bleeding into the theatre. Eventually the remaining troops pushed the mob back, and there was a comparative lull just as the fifth act began.

Macready pointed all his years of pent-up defiance at his unseen enemies. "I flung my whole soul into every word I uttered," he boasted to his diary, "exciting the audience to a sympathy even with the glowing words of fiction, while those dreadful deeds of real crime and outrage were roaring at intervals in our ears and rising to madness all round us."[13] The Englishman's resolve astonished and enthralled his audience, but in truth, with the fierce yells and the crashing stones it did not take a leap of the imagination to conjure up an army bearing down on the Thane's castle. Even more strikingly, as Forrest had found on Monday, several lines might have been written for the night.

> I will not be afraid of death and bane,
> Till Birnam *forest* come to Dunsinane,

Macready defiantly growled, and a yell of recognition swept through the theatre. He had another up his sleeve:

"Our castle's strength / " he mocked, "Will laugh a siege to scorn," and for once the audience laughed in sympathy with the great villain. No one chose to worry that the forest was about to arrive, or that the castle was about to come crashing down, and when the tyrant was slain it was the still-standing actor whom they cheered. One critic, no doubt swept away in the excitement, declared he had never seen the fifth act of *Macbeth* so splendidly and perfectly performed.[14]

Macready came out for his curtain call, emphatically bowed his thanks, signaled his sympathy to the audience, and quitted the American stage.

OUTSIDE, RESURGENT VIOLENCE had put the troops back on the defensive. A rush at the entrance forced them to the sidewalk; a fierce hail of stones rattled off their muskets and sent up a shower of sparks. Pistols flashed in the crowd; a captain was shot in the leg, though he noticed his injury only when he found his boots spilling blood.

"Down with the Codfish guards!" one rioter shouted: the soldiers, others angrily echoed, were the tools of the Upper Ten.

It was now clear that the military would be forced from the scene if the order to fire was not given: even John Ripley, who was part of the line holding the entrance, wondered what was taking so long. Finally Recorder Tallmadge, his staff of office raised against the barrage, threw himself into the mob.

"Disperse, or you will be fired on!" he shouted. "Fall back or we will fire!"

"Fire, damn you, if you dare!" a voice jeered back.

From the front line, Generals Sandford and Hall echoed the recorder's warning. Few heard them; the response from those who did was a hail of stones, which knocked down Sandford and several of his soldiers.

"Charge bayonets!" Sandford ordered, but the mob was so close upon them that there was no room to mount a charge, and instead the b'hoys grabbed several of the soldiers' muskets and again forced them back.

That was it: the sheriff gave the order to fire.

"Fire over their heads! Aim at the side of Mrs. Langdon's house!" General Hall shouted, just as he was shot in the face and felled by stones that struck him on the elbows and back.

A scattering of flashes, a sulfurous flare, and the bullets flew, first from a few pieces, then, as the order went along the line, in a fiercer second round, and a third heavier still. Smoke filled the air and stung the soldiers' eyes.

While some protestors continue to throw stones, others panic as the infantry, with their backs to the theatre, open fire. This print by Nathaniel Currier was published shortly after the riot. Courtesy of the Library of Congress.

Muskets were notoriously inaccurate at any range above a hundred yards. One bullet pranged through the sash window of a nearby house and whistled past two women inside. Two perforated the wooden wall of an oyster shanty on the corner of Lafayette Place, one grazing the face of an old African-American woman who was lying in bed. Ten sprayed into a public house on Eighth Street; one pierced the door, and two whistled through a window and buried themselves in a closet, just clearing the heads of a family of children who were cowering under their sheets. Several bystanders had equally lucky escapes: one bullet tore through an overcoat, another through a hat. Most, though, pitted Mrs. Langdon's walls—and the bodies of several onlookers who were standing in front on a pile of boards to improve their line of sight. John Leverich, a varnisher and polisher, was stooping down to help one man who had been shot in the groin when another, who had been shot in the head, fell against him and smothered his face with blood. George Gedney, a thirty-four-year-old Wall Street broker who had told his wife he was going out for a stroll, was standing behind the railings with one hand in his pocket and the other on his cane: at the first discharge he crumpled to the ground. A piano maker and two others picked him up, found his head covered in blood, and banged on the front door.

"We have a wounded man," they called; "no one will come in but us."

The man who answered the door tried to shut it against them, and when they refused to budge he called for help. A policeman came up behind him and clubbed the piano maker on the head.

Inside the theatre, the afterpiece—a farce—had started up. The audience had been more shaken than hurt—the threatened gunpowder had never appeared—and to some the report of the muskets sounded like a round of firecrackers. But as the dead and wounded were carried in, one killed by a shot through the head, and laid out on the velvet benches, the spectators finally panicked and streamed out into Eighth Street, and at last the curtain fell.

In the confusion not all of the muskets had fired, and after the initial shock the leaders of the mob surged forward.

"They have only blank cartridges!" they jeered, taking up Ned Buntline's line, and unable to see the bloody scenes behind them. "Give it to them again!" The fiercest volley of stones yet came arching through the air. For now Macready had been forgotten: the military was the foe.

The infantry reloaded their muskets.

"Fire, you damned sons of bitches; you durs'n't fire!" one rioter cried, tearing open his red flannel shirt and pointing at his breast. "Take the life out of a free-born American for a bloody British actor? Do it; ay, you darsn't!"

After more unheeded warnings, a new volley was ordered. This time General Hall gave the command to fire low, though again few heard him. Two men fell to the ground at the head of the crowd, one shot through the arm, the other killed by a bullet through the cheek, and gradually, through the crowds and the smoke, the rioters realized they were faced with live ammunition. The troops pushed them back, but again they rallied and surged forward with a fresh barrage of stones. The order to fire was given again, and several more fell dead. As the muskets went off, a Harlem Rail Road car pulled up on the Bowery to let out Asa Collins, a forty-five-year-old real estate agent, near his house at Fifth Avenue and Eighth Street: he was shot through the heart with his foot on the top step. Screams of pain and rage filled the misty night air.

Still the hail of stones kept coming, though less thickly now. Sandford sent to the Arsenal for the light artillery and the detachment of the 6th Regiment; at half past eleven they wheeled onto the ground and set up two brass cannon loaded with grapeshot, one facing the Bowery and the other raking Broadway. The crowds were warned that the cannon would be lit if they failed to disperse, and finally, gradually, the remaining groups melted away.

More than fifty soldiers and at least as many civilians had been wounded; more than twenty citizens lay dead or dying. The b'hoys carried their comrades through the streets, crying revenge on their assassins. A twenty-year-old apprentice with a musket ball lodged in his leg was refused admission at a doctor's house and was dragged, bleeding, to a drugstore at the corner of Broadway and Bleecker. On Broadway, a team of men pulled a wagon laden with dead and wounded; another crowd followed, bearing a corpse on a stretcher improvised from a shutter. A butcher with a bullet through his head died in agony at Chilton's drugstore, at the corner of Eighth Street and Third Avenue, where eight badly wounded soldiers and several police officers were also brought in. At another drugstore, on Eighth Street and Broadway, two victims died of their wounds during the night. At the Vauxhall Saloon, a man lay dying on a billiard table with a gunshot wound to his stomach, gasping for breath and begging for laudanum. On an adjacent table, another man was stretched out, still warm but already dead. At the Fifteenth Ward Station House, eight corpses were laid out. An Irish laborer, shot in the throat, was slumped on a bench. Next to him lay the body of George Gedney, the Wall Street broker. His brother-in-law found him there with his brains spilling out of his skull: he had gone looking for another brother-in-law, a member of the National Guard who had fired on the crowd, and when the soldier heard the news he nearly went out of his wits. A third man had his whole skullcap blown off. On the floor were five more corpses: one shot in the breast, another in the neck, a third in the abdomen; one was a mechanic, another an elderly man whose name nobody knew.

The lists of the injured were almost as horrifying. A nine-year-old boy was shot through the thigh on the corner of Lafayette Place; another small boy was shot in the foot. A soldier had his jawbone broken by a paving stone. At the City Hospital, eleven wounded were brought in. A twenty-four-year-old man was shot through the eye; the bullet had lodged behind his ear. A merchant from New Brunswick had a bullet in his right lung, a Massachusetts shoemaker had been shot in the stomach, a seventeen-year-old Irish oysterman was shot in the leg, and an eating-house keeper had been shot twice, in the shoulder and neck. Bridget Fagan, a thirty-year-old Irish housekeeper, was lying on a mattress with a grisly gunshot wound to her right knee. Her husband knelt beside her. They had been walking arm in arm two blocks from the theatre, window-shopping for shirts, and when the military fired she crumpled against him like a child. Her leg was amputated a few days later, and a few days after that she died.

Every saloon, cigar shop, and oyster cellar near the theatre was a blur of angry faces fuming about the atrocity of killing American citizens on behalf of English actors. Isaiah Rynders was at a tavern near Canal Street when he was told about the shootings; he rushed up to Astor Place, took in the scene, and started his own tour of the bars. At Charles Abel's public house on Broadway he burst in with two of his entourage. "I would like to whip some damn son of a bitch," he fumed. There were none there, Abel replied, and Rynders told him to go to hell. "I'll die first," Abel shot back, and Rynders launched into a diatribe at the cowardly soldiers and the murderous authorities. An even wilder voice chimed in and vowed to burn down the theatre and kill the soldiers, and one injured infantryman was nearly ripped apart on his way home before gentler voices intervened.

A posse of b'hoys set off to track down Macready at his hotel—it was later alleged that Rynders tried to slip them in by claiming he had left a trunk inside—but they were driven off by a line of waiters armed with gilt trays. Macready, though, had never gone back to his room. After the play he had been surrounded by his friends while he was still half dressed and persuaded to don a disguise fashioned from one actor's coat and another's cap, which had to be cut up the back to fit on his large head. Since the stage door was barred, he jumped down into the orchestra, climbed up into the parquette, and slipped, hunched over, among the stream of spectators who were making their way out between the lines of police on Eighth Street. Robert Emmet, a judge and the son of one of Macready's first American friends, accompanied him and nearly blew his cover.[15] "You are walking too fast," Macready whispered several times in his ear. They crossed the police line, threaded through the crowd onto Broadway, and made for Emmet's house. For several hours, Macready sat in front of the fire, smoking a cigar, thinking of the anguish his family would suffer if he were murdered and wondering how such a thing could happen in America, the country he had thought to make his home.

Emmet dispatched his son to a livery stable to order a coach and a good pair of horses for four o'clock, with the explanation that the passenger was a doctor making a call on a gentleman who lived near New Rochelle. The deception was just as well, because he passed an omnibus driving furiously down the street chased by an enraged crowd. "Macready's in that omnibus!" one of the pursuers shouted. "They've killed twenty of us, and by God we'll kill him!"[16]

The clock struck four, the coach pulled up, and in the fresh morning air Macready rolled down Fifth Avenue, passing butchers' and gardeners' carts and laborers starting early for work. At New Rochelle, he boarded the train for Boston. His friend's precautions may have saved his life, because the train had already been swept by another mob at the Twenty-seventh Street terminus.

CHAPTER 12

Exit, Pursued by a B'hoy

THERE IS AN uncanny stillness about a theatre the morning after an opening night, when the seats are shadowed by lively fading ghosts, and the days of bustle and suspense give way to a subdued apprehension about what the next nights will bring. So it was with New York City, as dawn gently broke on Friday, May 11.

Inside the Astor Place Theatre, though, the show was still not over. Hundreds of soldiers were pacing around or resting on the plush velvet seats with their muskets propped at their sides. A few b'hoys had even slipped inside among the plainclothes police officers and were helping themselves to the refreshments. Corporal John Ripley, who knew them well, kept his distance: instead he slipped into the lobby, only to run into more Boweryites, this time cuffed in irons and about to be marched away. His former friends looked contemptuously at his gray jacket and gilt buttons and warned him not to show his face in the Bowery if he valued his life. At five o'clock, Ripley's regiment mustered outside, and fifteen or twenty more b'hoys stormed up to him and ripped open their shirts.

"Shoot me! You shot my friend," they taunted, and they kept swearing and threatening until they were marched to the drill rooms to cool down. To the b'hoys, the volunteer soldiers had become the enemies of the people, and Ripley went into hiding for three months.

In the cool morning light, the full horror of the night's events became clear. Bullet holes pocked the brick and clapboard walls. Pools of blood laced with bits of brain and skull stained the pavement. Wives and mothers trickled in, picked their way over the field of stones, and asked after missing husbands and sons. Later in the day, at the Seventeenth Ward station, a train of hearses emerged and a thousand angry mourners set off in pursuit, some with tears streaming down their faces, most swearing revenge.

Rumors swept the town. A hundred had been killed, maybe more, among them several children. An armed mob was gathering at Vauxhall Gardens, a popular resort of the b'hoys just below Astor Place, ready to attack. Weapons had been bought in huge quantities: one gun seller reported that he had been asked for a loan of two thousand muskets. A hundred-and-fifty-strong Philadelphia gang known as the Killers, led by a famous desperado called the Panther, was coming to town on the night line.*

Uptown in the mansions of Union Square, where several of the signatories to the now famous letter lived, apprehension was eclipsed by grim satisfaction. The Macreadyites were taking no chances, and they spent the day barricading their houses. Samuel Ruggles bundled his sickly daughter out of town and convinced his wife's mother, who had not left her room for three months, to move into the parlor of his son-in-law George Templeton Strong; after helping them, Strong spent the day cleaning his pistols and moved a portrait of his own wife out of the line of fire. Yet, the breakfast tables agreed, it had all been worthwhile. The rabble had been taught a lesson, dearly bought but essential to establish that citizen-soldiers could sustain the law, and though the city had been disgraced, it had been defended against the Bowery insurgency. As the newspapers were brought in, their pages crowded with the sensational news, the Upper Ten were reassured to find that they overwhelmingly took their side. The riot, pronounced General Morris's *Home Journal,* was the most painful event in the history of New York, but it had almost certainly forestalled a much larger proof of the law's supremacy. The *Courier and Enquirer* went further: the quelling of the uprising, it declared, presented "a spectacle which exceeds in moral grandeur any that our country has exhibited since the declaration of our

---

* All were false alarms. A police officer was dispatched to remove the gun seller's muskets to the armory, but the loan request turned out to be an attempt to frame a politician for sedition.

independence of foreign thraldom," and it reassured its businessmen readers that the firm action taken by the authorities was "an excellent advertisement to the Capitalists of the old world, that they might send their property to New York and rely upon the certainty that it would be safe from the clutches of red republicanism, or chartists, or communionists of any description."*

Downtown on the Bowery and in the Five Points, the verdict was equally clear. The b'hoys skipped work at the shipyards and docks and gathered in knots at street corners, burning with outrage at the blood spilled by the authorities. In one bar, a Boweryite overwhelmed with anger broke down in tears, stripped to his shirt, and starting hitting out at anyone within the radius of his fists. Edwin Forrest summed up the Bowery feeling, self-righteously but accurately, in a letter to a friend: "This blood," he wrote, "will rest on the heads of the committee who insisted that Mr. Macready should perform in despite of the known wishes of the people to the contrary, and on the hands of the public authorities who were requested by many of the citizens to close the house, and thereby prevent any further demonstrations."[1] "The people" in this equation were the demonstrators who had forced Macready off the stage on Monday: it did not worry Forrest any more than it did the b'hoys that, inside the theatre, the Englishman's supporters had been in the majority.

Isaiah Rynders and his fellow ward heelers were desperate to turn the situation around. What had started as a show of strength had ended in a bloody rout, and their authority was on the line. In the middle of the night, they had rushed two new posters to the printers, and by early that morning these were plastered on the streets. The first may have been drawn up earlier, because Ned Buntline's fingerprints were all over it:

AMERICANS!!

AROUSE! THE GREAT CRISIS

HAS COME!!

Decide now whether English

ARISTOCRATS!!!

---

* As if to prove the point, the price of New York stocks shot up on the London money market, prompting the *Herald* to report, tongue firmly in cheek, that the whole debacle had been engineered by Wall Street (September 16, 1849).

AND

FOREIGN RULE!

shall triumph in this

AMERICA'S METROPOLIS,

or whether her own

SONS,

whose fathers once compelled the base-born miscreants

to succumb shall meanly lick the hand that strikes,

and allow themselves to be deprived of the liberty

of opinion so dear to every true American heart.

AMERICANS!!

come out! And dare to owe yourselves sons

of the iron hearts of '76!!

AMERICA.

The second was pithier, freshly written, and set in huge type:

TO THE PARK!

THE CITIZENS OF NEW YORK,

OPPOSED

TO THE DESTRUCTION OF HUMAN LIFE,

ARE REQUESTED TO ASSEMBLE IN THE PARK, AT 6 O'CLOCK

THIS EVENING!!

Friday, May 11, to express public opinion upon the

lamentable occurrence of last night.

Later in the day Mayor Woodhull held a conference with Samuel Ruggles and several more of Macready's supporters. The mayor responded with his own pasted-up proclamation, deploring the loss of life but reminding the city that the rule of law must and would be maintained, if necessary by the whole citizen-soldiery of the county, and requesting all New Yorkers to stay at home and avoid public assemblies.

Despite Woodhull's entreaties, thousands of b'hoys and g'hals converged on City Hall Park; by some counts the crowd was even larger than the previous night's.[2] Isaiah Rynders called the meeting to order, but before anyone could speak the hastily erected platform collapsed with a great crash and tumbled the Tammany grandees precipitously to the ground. They were not seriously hurt, but a nine-year-old boy was crushed under the falling timber and died at a nearby drugstore in great pain. "Such was the lively interest which everybody felt in himself and the meeting," the *Herald* reported, "that no notice was taken of the matter, and the interrupted business was immediately resumed."

Rynders brushed himself off, climbed on a table, called on the coroner's jury to find the mayor, the recorder, the sheriff, and General Sandford guilty of first-degree murder—"Hang them!" the crowd cried—and the meeting went ahead.

Edward Strahan, the Tammany orator who had led Monday night's barracking of Macready, read out nine full-throated resolutions declaring that peace-loving men like him could not stand by while the mayor murdered innocent Americans and trampled on their First Amendment rights.

"*Resolved,*" he boomed. "That we look upon the sacrifice of human lives in the vicinity of the Astor Place Opera House, last night, as the most wanton, unprovoked and murderous outrage ever perpetrated in the civilized world; and that the aiders, abettors, and instigators of that unparalleled crime, deserve, and shall receive the lasting censure and condemnation of this community.

"*Resolved,* That we mingle our tears and lamentations with the mourning friends and relatives of the men, women and children who have fallen victims to the pride, tyranny and inhumanity of those who, 'dressed in a little brief authority,' have shown a higher regard for the applause of those who courted a fatal issue, than for the lives of their fellow-citizens." The quotation, of course, was from Shakespeare.

"Rynders! Rynders!" the crowd chanted, and the Empire Club leader bounced back and outdid Strahan's harangue. Mass murder, he charged, had been perpetrated to revenge the aristocrats of the city on the peaceable and unarmed working classes—"to please an aristocratic Englishman, backed by a few sycophantic Americans . . . [who] would shoot down their brethren and fellow-citizens rather than be deprived of the pleasure of seeing him perform." Edwin Forrest (at the mention of his name the assembly roared its approval and sent up three cheers) was entirely innocent, whereas Macready, who was full of his country's prejudices from the top of his head to his feet—if he had any, the Captain quipped—had personally supervised the distribution of tickets to his supporters, and American soldiers had acted as the cowardly slaves of the queen of England.

"Murder! Murder!" the crowd roared.

The final speaker was Mike Walsh, the chieftain of another Tammany gang and a man with a well-honed talent for colorful abuse. The authorities, he bellowed, were worse than the czar of Russia, who at least fired blanks before shooting insurrectionists; if such a thing had happened in Paris, barricades would have gone up all over the city, and the recorder, sheriff, and mayor should be hanged a thousand times over.

"Hang them up! Hang them up!" the crowd chanted.

As he launched into an attack on the white-kid nabobs Walsh's voice shook with the genuine ring of revolution.

"I say, so help me God, if another shot is fired by these scoundrels, I will, with musket and bayonet in my hand . . ." he thundered, but the rest of the sentence was lost amid the pandemonium. "We owe it to ourselves, to our fellow citizens, and to society, if ever there is a repetition of this shooting, to arm ourselves, and to call upon every man to arm himself—" he resumed, but again, said the *Herald,* he was drowned out: "The tumult became great, and the excitement intense. Loud cries for vengeance rose from the crowd."[3]

Gradually the uproar fused into four words: "To the Opera House!"

WASHINGTON SQUARE, A few blocks from Astor Place, had meanwhile turned into a hotbed of military activity the likes of which had not been seen for generations. Four troops of horse artillery, a squadron of cavalry, and four regiments of infantry went through their drill, answered roll calls, and received rounds of ball cartridge, canister, and grapeshot; they were joined by a detachment of the Veteran Artillery pulling four pieces, including a twenty-four-pound howitzer. Dozens of bystanders gathered to watch, children trundled their hoops in the square, and across on Broadway the fashionables turned out for their regular promenade. New York was not easily deflected from its business. Soon, though, the crowds grew larger and rowdier, and the Broadway blue bloods retired to watch from their parlor windows.

Toward seven o'clock, the troops formed in marching order and filed along Eighth Street. At a quarter past seven, the cavalry and artillery turned onto Broadway, with a large body of infantry marching to the beat of its band in the rear. By now a crowd of thousands, mostly young men, stretched several blocks down Broadway and across to the Bowery.[4] Led by the dragoons and hussars walking their horses four abreast, the troops pushed through and encircled the theatre. They were met with jeers and hoots but little violence, though one boy was loudly applauded for throwing a stick at a restive horse. The surrounding streets were blocked off at each end by double lines of police backed up, ten or twelve feet behind, by double lines of soldiers, with a detachment of cavalry holding the space between; on Broadway, the omnibuses were forced to pull up and make a long detour. Another detachment of cavalry cleared the Bowery by forming a line spanning its width and riding up and down at full gallop. Four heavy pieces of artillery were set up to rake Broadway and Eighth Street in both directions; four more were trained on Waverly Place, Lafayette Place, and the open ground to the east of the theatre.

The Opera House was in the possession of the police, swelled to more than double their usual strength by a thousand special deputies sworn in during the day by Chief Matsell. Placards had been nailed on the doors: "The House Has Been Closed by Order of the Lessee," they announced. The vaults had been turned into makeshift prisons, the dressing rooms into surgical hospitals, and the boxes, parquette, and stage into campgrounds for bivouacking troops. Between the militia, police, and constables the forces at hand were nearly four thousand strong.

Soon the crowd was swollen by thousands surging up from City Hall Park. The yells grew louder and more threatening, and at half past eight, with the streets again in near darkness, the police made a charge at the most turbulent part of the mob and arrested several ringleaders. The deadly paving stones had been carted away, but a posse of b'hoys took possession of a marble merchant's yard that was handily located on the corner of the Bowery and Astor Place, and once again showers of stones, some slung in handkerchiefs, fell on the cavalry and knocked several off their horses. One band of b'hoys climbed onto the flat roofs of the houses at the corner of the Bowery and Eighth Street to get a clearer line. Taking Mike Walsh's earlier hint, another group built a barricade out of a wagon and some crates across Ninth Street, near Fourth Avenue, and put up a strong fight before it was stormed. At the same time the police cleared the marble yard and the roofs and made dozens of arrests. That only enraged the rest of the rioters: picking up stones on the run, they threw them with fresh force, and for the second night running the infantry was ordered to load. By now the authorities were determined to prevail at all costs: they knew that a rout would mark the end of their civil power.

"The next shower of stones will bring a return of lead!" shouted Recorder Tallmadge.

The muskets were leveled, but they were never fired. One soldier on Broadway accidentally dropped and discharged his weapon, which sent the crowd fleeing for cover, but on the Bowery the barrage subsided before the order was given. Instead the rioters took to lighting bonfires, which only made them more visible, and within an hour nearly all had been taken prisoner or scattered by a running charge.

By midnight, order was restored. Sam Ruggles and his son-in-law set out to reconnoiter the operations and were greatly pleased with what they saw. Everything looked in deadly earnest: the guns were loaded, matches lit, ready to sweep the streets with grapeshot at a second's notice. The mob had been in a fierce rage but now it was a good deal frightened, Strong recorded in his diary: "Some of the cavalry were badly hit with paving stones, but as soon as the Unwashed were informed that unless they forthwith took themselves off they'd be treated with a little artillery practice, they scampered."[5] A note of triumphalism began creeping into the conversations of the Upper Ten.

Over at the Broadway Theatre that night, Forrest had been playing King Lear. With the energies of his fiercest supporters redirected to the streets, and ordinary playgoers repelled by the violence that had been unleashed in his name, only fifty people turned up. The next day, as the military's show of strength curbed the appetite for rebellion, he acted the tragic-heroic Metamora to an almost empty house. It was his last performance in the city for three years.

FOR SEVERAL MORE days, the entire New York police force camped out in the Astor Place Theatre, their lights gleaming through the broken windows, their boots crunching the smashed glass, and patrolled the surrounding area. Troops continued to march through the streets. The whole 1st Division of the state militia was kept ready to muster at seven strokes of the City Hall bell, with the U.S. troops on Governor's Island and the Marine Corps at the Brooklyn Navy Yard held in reserve.

On Saturday the heavens opened, and all Sunday the rain poured in hard showers. To many in the riot-fatigued city it seemed like a blessing sent to dampen heated passions.

Isaiah Rynders draped the flag of the Empire Club in black crepe and advertised for his Guard to assemble "for the purpose of forming the corps to go on a drilling and target excursion. Every member is expected to be present, as this is the time for excursions for all Guards."[6] The threat was mere saber-rattling, or face-saving, and apart from a few stones flung by a few youths there was no more trouble.

On Saturday the coroner opened an inquest into the first confirmed deaths. Fifteen jurors—mostly small shopkeepers—were sworn in, and they set out in five carriages to view the bodies. At one house, on Twelfth Street near First Avenue, the former home of Matthew Cahill, an Irish laborer who had been shot through the chest, two plates filled with tobacco were perched on top of the coffin along with several short pipes. Three fat red-faced women sat nursing fat babies, and two empty liquor bottles stood on a table next to an Irishman who was keeping the mourners noisily entertained. At another house, in Sullivan Street, the supposed deceased opened the door and shared a laugh with the jurors at the court's mistake; he was not the week's only apparent revenant. On Monday, the jury delivered its verdict in the doleful surroundings of the Tombs. The authorities, it declared, had been justified in giving the order to fire, though it added that if a larger force of police had been present from the start, the military might not have been needed.

Eighteen men were the subjects of the inquest. By trade they were printers, sailors, clerks, grocers, ship's joiners, carpenters, cartmen, laborers, butchers, and waiters. One was fifteen, one sixteen, two seventeen, two nineteen, and most of the rest were in their early twenties. Excluding the ill-fated passersby, three fifths of the dead were native-born Americans and two fifths Irishmen. More victims died in the next days and weeks from their wounds. The total number of lives lost is impossible to fix with certainty: it was at least twenty-six and possibly as high as thirty, even discounting the rumor that the bodies of some gang members were spirited away by their fellows.[7] By any tally, it was by far the greatest loss of civilian life due to military action since the Revolution. Even on the field of battle, fewer American soldiers had been lost at the Battle of New Orleans or the siege and capture of Vera Cruz. Citizen militiamen had killed rioters before: four in the Providence race riots of 1831, at least six and perhaps ten in Philadelphia's Irish-nativist riots in 1844.[8] At least three citizens were shot dead by the militia in New York's Doctors Riot, but that incident, the only previous occasion in which New Yorkers had been killed by their own soldiers, had occurred sixty-one years earlier, before the state had even ratified the U.S. Constitution. Never in the nation's history had soldiers fired volley after volley at point-blank range into a civilian crowd.

Tuesday was a day of mass funerals, and trains of angry mourners weaved through every district of the city. By the end of the week, though, the sinking of the steamer *Empire* after a collision with a schooner on the Hudson, a calamitous fire in St. Louis, and the threat of large-scale flooding in New Orleans pushed the riot off the front pages, while fashionable society prepared to leave for the summer season at Saratoga Springs and Newport, just in time to avoid the pandemic of cholera that swept the city, killing more than five thousand people, forty percent of them Irish.

THE SHAKESPEARE RIOTS were over, but the reverberations rumbled on for years.

Altogether a hundred and thirteen rioters had been arrested. Among them were machinists, butchers, organ builders, bakers, coopers, brass finishers, printers, porters, rail makers, chair makers, gardeners, marble cutters, clerks, piano makers, masons, plumbers, shoemakers, coopers, sail makers, carpenters, bookbinders, and gunsmiths, and one newspaper editor. Several were well known to the police, but many, having been hauled off in the dark, could not be positively identified the morning after and were let go. Six more escaped from the station house, and just ten were put on trial that September.

It was said that no jury would dare convict them, and apocalyptic results—rule by the gun and the dissolution of society—were predicted if the case failed. When the judge was named, the Upper Ten were even more rattled. Charles P. Daly was a Democrat who was born on the Lower East Side of poor Irish immigrant parents. Early in life, he fled home after throwing an inkstand at his new stepmother, then struck his quill-maker master and, like Ned Buntline and Lorman Forrest, ran away to sea as a cabin boy. He was shipwrecked off Holland and shanghaied into the Dutch navy, and after making his way back to New York he signed up as a carpenter's apprentice and volunteer fireman before turning to law clerking. At twenty-two, he was made his firm's junior partner; after dabbling in politics—he joined Tammany Hall just as Forrest was invited to run for Congress—he worked his way up to the State Assembly at Albany, and he was still only twenty-eight when he was appointed a judge. The elite, though, need not have worried: Daly was fast becoming a member of the establishment, and his charge to the jury powerfully stated the distinction between liberty—a privilege, he proposed, that carried a duty of obedience to the democracy's laws—and unbridled license. New Yorkers discussed the passions and prejudices aroused by the case with unabated excitement, and the whole country watched to see what example the great metropolis would set.

The trial lasted for two long weeks. All the defendants produced witnesses who spoke to their previous good character—all, that is, except the star defendant.

Ned Buntline's tricks had finally caught up with him. The day after he was arrested he had managed to issue an Extra of the *Own* from his cell, a single sheet in which he insisted he had had nothing to do with the riot, had merely walked over to Astor Place from the bedside of his sick wife to see whether the reports that had reached him were true, and "without knowing a single man in the crowd, while standing in silence on the side-walk," having been on the scene only five minutes and just then turning around to go home, he was summarily arrested. "If the wife of my bosom, who is now on a sick-bed, dangerously ill, should die from this shock, there shall be more than one man held responsible for her murder!" he threatened.[9] He was released on bail of a thousand dollars and immediately served with divorce papers by Annie, rather undermining his claim of spousal outrage; he responded by postering the city with tales that his wife had illegally seized his newspaper property to prevent him from publishing an exposé about the nefarious activities of foreigners.[10] Within days, he was jailed again, for debt, and as soon as he was safely locked away his assistant editor Thomas Paterson, who was miserably underpaid under threat of blackmail, finally broke ranks and published a spectacular piece of character assassination in the form of a lengthy pamphlet entitled "The Private Life, Public Career, and Real Character of that Odious Rascal Ned Buntline!! As developed by his conduct to his past wife, present wife, and his various Paramours! Completely lifting up the Veil, and Unmasking to a Horror-stricken Community, his Debaucheries, Seductions, Adulteries, Revelings, Cruelties, Threats and Murders!!!"

Ned brought a case for slander against Paterson, but he already had another pending against himself, brought by Bennett of the *Herald* after Buntline had printed salacious rumors about his sister-in-law's sex life. By now Ned had antagonized nearly every newspaper editor in town, in addition to his father-in-law, whom he threatened by letter to shoot, probably for withdrawing some bail bonds. The papers danced on his grave, while Frank, his brother-in-law, testified that Ned had tried to blackmail him into refusing to take the stand by threatening to publish humiliating information about the family in the scandal sheet they had helped set up.

During the trial Ned barked out dire warnings about the consequences that would follow his conviction; there were alleged attempts at jury tampering, and Judge Daly received a series of anonymous letters warning that his life was in danger. But guilty verdicts rang out against each defendant, and when the sentences were handed down Ned could not resist getting to his feet for one last piece of grandstanding.

"I have been tried by a prejudiced jury," he sobbed to the crowds, "and, I might say, a prejudiced court. I can safely lay my hand upon my heart, and appeal to my God, that I am the victim of an unjust persecution." The press, he piously protested, had set out to crush him—he was a victim; he stood there a martyr, a man as gentle as a sucking dove.

Ned Buntline, the great rascal, the oracle of rowdyism, had run out of cards, and Daly glowered down on him from the height of the bench.

He was a recreant and a coward, the judge pronounced, who had shown the vanity to pose as a leader without the courage to expose himself as one: "There is," he concluded, "a withering meanness to your conduct." Buntline's fellow defendants received jail terms of one to three months; Ned was given the maximum sentence—a two-hundred-fifty-dollar fine and a year's hard labor on Blackwell's Island—and Daly declared that he had never so felt the inadequacy of the punishment within his power. On the same day, at the other end of City Hall, Annie was granted an unconditional divorce. As he was rowed across the East River in irons, shaved of his patriarchal beard, put in uniform, and set to digging out stones, Ned never stopped railing against the outrageous injustice, and he later turned the whole experience into a bad novel about a crusading journalist framed for leading a theatre riot and convicted by a corrupt judiciary. His spell in jail did him no harm with his b'hoys: on his release, he was driven home in an open barouche pulled by six white horses and flanked by a marching brass band playing "Hail to the Chief," and his Bowery comrades threw him a testimonial dinner. The influential Know-Nothing party emerged from his clandestine nativist societies, and Buntline resumed his role as New York's troublemaker-in-chief.

Some said Ned had been a straw man for the real conspirators. In January, Isaiah Rynders was tried for instigating the riot, but unlike Buntline, Rynders had been careful to keep his distance from the showdown, and with the help of his attorney John Van Buren, a fellow Tammanyite and the son of a president, he was acquitted.* Four others were tried alongside him and also acquitted; four more, including two of the trio who procured the tickets from Macready's friends and "Butt" Allen, one of the chair-throwers on the first night, failed to answer the summons and warrants were issued for their arrest, but their trials collapsed along with the rest. Only the third ticket-tout, Robert Long, was convicted, of arson in the third degree, for setting the fire under the theatre. Andrew Stevens, the leader of the expedition to the Elysian Fields, refused to give evidence to an investigation launched by the mayor: his role was uncovered only when he confessed three years later, in revenge

---

* In 1857, Rynders was appointed U.S. marshal of the Southern District of New York.

on Forrest, who had broken off their friendship on the suspicion that Stevens had fraudulently secured large loans in his name.

New York's fiercest gangs were left untouched by the trials. Even when Matsell's men arrested the odd gangster he was unlikely to be prosecuted by the politicized justice system, and the few who were convicted, even of murder, were invariably pardoned, especially if the victim was one of their own, and the felon had political influence or electioneering clout. Yet the sentences handed down at the trial drew a clear line: they were a warning from the Fifteenth Ward that whatever the gangs did on their own turf, they would not be permitted to invade the hallowed uptown ground. The threat of revolution receded, and the Astor Place riot stood as America's deadliest civil disturbance until the Draft Riots took over that unhappy title in 1863.* With the old common-law crime of riot now backed by the new force of precedent, those few May nights were instrumental in tipping the balance of society away from freedom of expression toward the protection of property, and from government by consent to government by force. They directly led to the first appearance on American streets of police officers trained in riot control and military drill, and to the authorization of the first lethal police weapon, a heavy twenty-two-inch club to be used in self-defense. The time when insurrectionist mobs could congregate for violent acts with impunity was over, and the Upper Ten slept easier in their beds.

Yet something had been lost. As New York continued to grow, the rift between the haves and have-nots became still more immense, and even well-off New Yorkers wondered whether it was the poor alone who represented the forces of disorder, who had destroyed the bonds of neighborly understanding on which mild government was built. In that sense, too, the riot had been a watershed: it was the first time that two classes of Americans had failed to resolve their conflicting rights without resorting to muskets and brickbats, and it confronted the nation with a new and shocking notion. The riot, wrote a reporter from Philadelphia, left behind it "a feeling to which this community has hitherto been a stranger—an opposition of classes—the rich and the

---

* The Draft Riots again united nativists and Irish immigrants against the rich, who could buy themselves out of military service during the Civil War for $300.

poor—white kids and no kids at all; in fact to speak right out, a feeling that there is now, in our country, in New York City, what every good patriot has hitherto felt it his duty to deny—a *high* class and a *low* class."[11] Even the genteel *Home Journal* felt compelled to remind its readers that "WEALTH, IN A REPUBLIC, SHOULD BE MINDFUL WHERE ITS LUXURIES OFFEND," and that one of its most offensive luxuries was "the *aristocratizing* of the pit."[12]

Opera society did its best to ignore the writing on the wall. The Astor Place Theatre was rebuilt and reopened that November, but it never washed off the stain of blood; it was sold the following year, and in 1854 it reopened as a library and lecture hall. The Upper Ten pushed further north and erected the Academy of Music at Fourteenth Street and Irving Place, the setting for the virtuoso survey of New York society with which Edith Wharton's *The Age of Innocence* opens. With four thousand seats, the Academy was the biggest opera house in the world, and its crimson auditorium sparkled like a giant jewelry box, but many of the seats were priced within reach of ordinary music-lovers, while the aristocracy was limited to eighteen boxes in which to display its wares. Yet that constraint, though it was billed as a democratic response to the riot, was itself an elitist statement: the old-money syndicate that built the Academy commandeered the boxes and kept out vulgar arrivistes like the Vanderbilts. New money fought back: a consortium of excluded millionaires built the even larger Metropolitan Opera, which boasted a hundred and twenty-two boxes floating over the stalls like golden boats.

In both buildings, there was a strange new sound from the audience: silence. No longer were interventions from the gallery tolerated; even hissing fell into desuetude. The working classes gravitated to the vaudeville houses where they were welcome, while the fashionable theatres weeded out the prostitutes, banned liquor, and drew in respectable families with advertisements for fountains of iced water. The Astor Place tragedy put an end to theatre riots, but it also marked the final passing of a whole way of life. First in London, and now in New York, the age of the theatres as meeting places for an entire society had come to an end, never to return.

To the public-minded middle classes, the riot at last brought home the shocking depth and extent of disaffection in their midst. They became obsessed with the image of New York City as a diseased organism, the cause of the illness being its failure to provide education and employment to its neediest citizens, the symptoms brutality and a love of disorder. Some advocated draining the lake of discontent by removing immigrants to the nation's interior; others identified rum shops and groggeries as the nurseries of villainy and campaigned for temperance, or at least a liquor tax; and still more campaigned against the newspapers for making speculations out of fomenting envy, gloating over vice, and fostering a rancorous hatred of anyone outside their clique. The Ladies Home Missionary Society bought the Old Brewery in 1852 and replaced it with the Five Points Mission; before the Brewery was pulled down, they conducted tours to bring its hidden horrors to light, though when the pastor they appointed showed more interest in creating jobs than in saving souls he was dismissed. The phenomenon of b'hoydom proved easier to deal with: by the 1860s, it had come to a natural end as new waves of immigration loaned the Bowery an increasingly cosmopolitan face—the Bowery Theatre became the Jewish Thalia, its front covered in Yiddish playbills—though the great avenue continued its slide into the Skid Row of later notoriety.

Another group of reform-minded social leaders, Whigs with a newly reinforced belief in compassionate, big-government conservatism, resurrected William Cullen Bryant's proposal to carve out the country's first great landscaped civic park, a breathing space that would provide a refuge from the slums and saloons of lower Manhattan and translate democratic ideas, as one of its designers declared, into Trees and Dirt. The year after the riot, both mayoral candidates pledged to green the heart of the city; in 1853, the authorities began buying up a vast strip of central Manhattan, in the process evicting sixteen hundred poor residents, including Irish pig farmers, German market gardeners, and a whole African-American village, and Central Park was born.[13] Paternalism, though, was not the only driving force: at least as crucial were the prestige of the city, the provision of a showground for society, and the effect on property values around the perimeter. Besides, the park was miles away from the Bowery and the Points, farther even than the Elysian Fields, and when it opened the elite was once again firmly in charge. Picnics were prohibited, tradesmen were banned from driving their families around in commercial wagons, and for a decade, more than half the park's visitors arrived in private carriages for the fashionable late-afternoon parade, the new version of the Broadway promenade. Only later in the century were the laborers who built the park permitted its free use: to reformers, it seemed that the lessons of the riot had been all too swiftly forgotten.[14]

Perhaps that was not surprising, given how cloudy its origins had been. The riot seemed to be the fault of everyone, and no one. It was the fault of Macready's father, for educating his son as a gentleman and going bankrupt. It was the fault of the theatre profession, for instilling vanity and insecurity in its practitioners. It was the fault of English writers, for stomping over American self-esteem. It was the fault of several American states, for causing Americans to be reviled as debt dodgers. It was the fault of journalists, for whipping up partisanship to sell papers. It was the fault of the British government, for its disastrous Irish policy. It was the fault of Jacksonian politics, for pandering to gang leaders. It was the fault of the Upper Ten, for building an opera house in a provocative location. It was the fault of the new mayor, unversed in crowd control. It was the fault of the irresistible flows of capital and population that had carved out a resentful and often violent underclass. And, yes, it was the fault of Forrest, for bullying his way to self-vindication, and of Macready, for defending his respectability to the bitter end.

EDWIN FORREST DID not mastermind the Astor Place riot, but neither had he tried to stop the b'hoys from avenging the wrong he imagined had been done him. That sin of omission was enough for society to treat him as an untouchable, and even former friends started to worry that his mind had become diseased by wounded egotism.

After the riot, his marriage deteriorated still further. He started prowling outside Kate's new home to see who went inside, and late one night he accosted a visitor as he left.

"Why are you sneaking away like a guilty man?" he demanded.

"Edwin Forrest," the caller replied, "you have waylaid me by night with a bludgeon. You want a pretence for attacking me, and I shall not give it you."

"Bludgeon!" Forrest growled. "I don't want a bludgeon to kill you.

Damn you, I can choke you to death with my hands! But you are not the man I am after now. If I catch that damned villain I'll rip his liver out. I'll cut his damned throat at the door. You may go this time, damn you. But I have marked you, all of you, and I'll have my vengeance."[15]

In 1851, after months of estrangement and legal maneuvers by her husband, Kate filed for divorce. Forrest immediately countersued. Charges of adultery flew around: nine counts were leveled at Forrest, six at Kate. It was a dangerous game: if both suits failed the spouses would be yoked together for life, whereas if one or both were found guilty of adultery, they would be prohibited from remarrying. The trial dragged on for a record thirty-eight days, dragged several socially prominent figures through the mud, and became one of the most notorious legal airings of dirty laundry in the nineteenth century.

When things were going Forrest's way, his goatee pointed outward in a show of dignified merriment, but most of the time he sat purple with rage, darting burning looks at his wife, the personification of an imperious nature that brooked no opposition. Despite suggestive evidence about Kate's dissolute friends and the best efforts of Forrest's counsel—the same John Van Buren who had defended Isaiah Rynders—to paint her as a *grande amoureuse,* Forrest lost. Once again, his friends had overreached themselves: the jury saw proof that they had plotted to extract a confession from a potential witness by getting him drunk, and heard testimony that they had tried to inveigle Kate into a brothel, though it reached its verdict on evidence that Forrest had himself been a regular visitor at a house of assignation. For fifteen years he appealed the case, admitting defeat only when the U.S. Supreme Court declined to hear it. The costs were high, financially and emotionally. Forrest never recovered his spirits, and he became convinced that he was the victim of a giant conspiracy. The American system, he wrote obsessively to his friends, had committed a great crime against him—a monstrous wrong, an unbearable mockery, an outrage of historical proportions. The witnesses, he fumed, had been bought off with diamond rings, the juries had been packed, and the judges were worse than pimps, panders, and bawds: they had robbed him of the results of an industrious life and lavished them on his wife, "a drunken female whose prostitutions and shameless acts have circled the world."[16] Whatever the murky rights and wrongs of the case, the vindictiveness with which Forrest pursued Kate finished his reputation with society; when, in 1852, he horsewhipped Nathaniel Parker Willis, the foppish editor of the *Home Journal* and a respondent in the trial—an assault that brought seven more years of libel suits, appeals, and countersuits—the lid was nailed shut. Society papers turned to abuse: one dubbed him, after the title of a popular play, "The Spoiled Child; or, Little Pickle of the American Stage."[17]

Yet after the shock of the riot had faded, and in the wake of a trial during which his supporters depicted him as the the victim—for the second time—of aristocratic vengeance, Forrest's true fans came back to him, their hero-worship redoubled. Immediately after the first trial was over, he began a record-breaking sixty-nine-day run at the Broadway Theatre. On the first night the orchestra struck up with "Hail Columbia" and "Yankee Doodle" as the audience arrived; cheers, applause, handkerchief and hat waving, cane rattling, and foot stamping greeted the star and continued for many minutes. As soon as the play ended, Isaiah Rynders sprang onto the stage to catch some of his friend's glory. The Stars and Stripes waved in the audience, bouquets fell on the stage, and a banner was unfurled in the pit:

"This is the people's verdict," it proclaimed.

The people, Forrest boomed, knew him to be a wronged man and would judge him rightly.

"Three groans for the jury!" Rynders cried.

On the fiftieth night, a jubilee attended by thousands lit up Broadway; on the last night, there were more bouquets and speeches, followed by a midnight serenade and supper.

For years afterward, Forrest's fans brought their sons and daughters to see the first American star. Yet he was no longer what he once was, the standard-bearer of his nation: he had become a historical curio while still at the height of his powers. He was more subdued now, more restrained, but however hard he worked to refine his Shakespearean interpretations, time and tastes overtook him. The b'hoys had largely disappeared into the orbit of the Bowery's vaudeville and variety shows, while to the middle classes he increasingly came to represent a primitive past: "the muscular school; the brawny art; the biceps aesthetics; the tragic calves; the bovine drama; rant, roar, and rigmarole."[18] One critic declared that Forrest showed how great Shakespeare was because his plays survived the actor's stupid and murderous assaults; another labeled him "a vast animal bewildered by a grain of genius."[19] Younger critics coined the adjective "Forrestonian" to describe a bad actor, and the great hero became the mark of burlesques.

Once he had been asked at a dinner whether he played King Lear: "Young man," he had bellowed, "I am Lear." He truly felt he was Lear now, at least as he played him: a noble hero beset by the chicanery of knavish men and women, a grand force of nature abandoned by the theatrical children to whom he gave his all, clinging to his crown and trying not to be left out in the cold. Perhaps flesh-and-blood children would have turned his mind to a more benevolent track—in old age he took to standing sadly at school gates at the end of the day—but instead he buried himself with his theatrical memorabilia behind a great brick wall, a lonely old man nursing his grievances, telling his few friends that he wished his sad life was over, vainly cursing the weak world that had dared to brook him, at his most misanthropic moments wishing annihilation on the whole wretched failure of human life.[20] The generous, eager face had aged into gnarled ruggedness: a walrus mustache and a muss of hair hiding a fierce, lined expression that made him look like a weary pug. Such was the effect of too much adulation, taken too much to heart, too young.

Soon, sooner than he could have expected, his iron frame was weakened by rheumatism and gout, but for all the agony he underwent in teeth-chatteringly cold theatres he could not quit the stage. He needed the applause: again like Lear, he had come to value himself by his reception. In 1860 he sent a friend an article that lauded him as the greatest actor in the world and added that he should never have considered Macready a rival. "It speaks the truth without flattery," his accompanying note read.[21] Great actors, he explained, were comparable only to the loftiest of mankind—or gods.

Sheer willpower kept him going. One night in 1865 he was seized by an attack of sciatica while he was playing in Washington; he struggled to the end, and dragged himself out of bed each day, but a second attack left him with a permanent drag in his right leg. In 1871, during one winter season, he was still able to travel seven thousand miles, acting in fifty-two places for a hundred and twenty-eight nights, but the crowds were becoming painfully thin, and he finally heeded his friends' entreaties and retired.

In 1872, shortly after struggling through a series of poorly attended Shakespeare readings, Edwin Forrest died alone in his bedroom while dressing, his hands clasping a pair of dumbbells, a red streak, the mark of a massive stroke, across his temple. Kate did not attend his funeral. He had sold Fonthill, his monument to love and acting, many years before: now Kate's claims ate away another chunk of his estate, and his will sank into litigation. The Edwin Forrest Home for retired actors, the legatee of the residue of his estate, opened its doors near Philadelphia four years after his death, the hallway overshadowed by a giant statue of its founder as Coriolanus, but it was never the grand memorial he had envisaged.

His real legacy was to have broken the hold that British actors had on America, and opened the way for new generations of American stars. He had forged from his world and his nature an American school of acting, a school that at its best was fresh, forthright, and vital, and though fashions would come and go, and though Forrest himself would be forgotten, his influence endured.

AFTER THE RIOTS, Macready arrived home to an outpouring of sympathy and enthusiasm. The shocking news had preceded him, and the papers were busy berating the lawless Yankees. Dickens wrote to Catherine proposing a dinner to give vent to "a reasonable expression of gentlemanly disgust," and added that the bestiality of the business astounded even him, though at least it took Macready out of "that damnable jumble . . . of false pretensions and humbugs, a week or so sooner."[22]*

Macready abandoned all thoughts of settling in a country whose brutal and beastly savages, he told his diary, had sought his life. The decision was made even easier when a friend sent him a circular published in the American papers, asking actors for tales of his ill-usage and lies which were being collected for a pamphlet. He was equally determined to retire

---

* Dickens finally reconciled himself to America: in 1867 he made a second visit, by which time the bad blood had been long forgotten.

as soon as possible: for all his newfound status as a national hero—one overexcited critic proclaimed that he towered over every previous actor, Garrick, Kemble, and Kean included, like Olympus over a molehill—the Astor Place riot put an end to any lingering doubts he had about leaving the vagabond stage. First, though, there was a lucrative farewell tour to be made, and for the last time, he set out on the road.

His plans were thrown to pieces by his agony at the death, at nineteen, of Nina, his firstborn child, after a long withdrawing bout of consumption. Macready sat alone with his heartache while Catherine was confined for the tenth time; and, coming on top of the tangle of bewildered thoughts left behind by the riot, and the buzz of self-doubt that had accompanied his whole puzzling life, it finally shattered his nerves. Suddenly, as he tossed sleeplessly with his dead child's image before him, the shock hit, and he felt as if he had stepped out of his body and was seeing himself for the first time. For days he shut himself away and reckoned with his soul. In the clear light of grief, he saw through the mask of rectitude that had made him believe he always behaved from just principles; he was seized by the conviction that vanity was the spring of all his actions. The purpose of adversity, he thought, had been made clear to him, and he vowed to atone for his crimes.

It was the reaction of a devout man who was desperately trying to retain his faith in God's goodness in the face of belief-numbing pain, and yet he failed to see the hubris of thinking that his child's death was designed to clarify the last act of his own turbulent drama. It was not just the business of performing that made Macready wonder where to find the center to life, that made him see men's behavior as a series of attitudes struck out of threadbare beliefs—though his assuming a different nature every night, and those natures belonging to Shakespearean characters who struggled to know themselves too, had dressed skepticism in a daily set of clothes. His dismay at the ways of the world had made his inner faith, sometimes desperately clung to, his only fixed point; now he saw that his prayers to be a better person had been empty words as well, and his guilt was as deeply felt and as deeply self-conscious as every other thought he had.

The revelation did not last for long. At the cemetery his usual distaste for the affected acting of churchmen turned to agony—the minister, he shuddered, was a platitudinous player who profaned the holiness of his suffering—and he turned his face away and clapped his ears shut, trying again to bring his God directly into his mind.

As soon as the funeral was over he sank into a long bout of illness, but when he recovered he gave some of the best performances of his life. Shakespeare's characters had become more real to him than his oldest friends: Hamlet, above all, had become a sort of love with him. "Beautiful Hamlet, farewell, farewell!" he mourned, though if he had known how ridiculous Thackeray thought he looked with a rich brown wig tumbling over his gnarled neck the parting would have been easier.[23] He even began to think of his audience with affectionate respect: in the end they had shown real attachment to him, and however forgetfully, he took his leave of them with something like gratitude.

On February 26, 1851, Macready awoke to the last day of his professional life. He turned over his thoughts, reassured himself that he had carried through his retirement in a seemly way at the height of his powers, and felt not the slightest regret. "I shall never have to do this again," he said to himself.[24] How could a sensitive man not feel that when, amid all the tributes, one paper printed a long article declaring he was a ridiculous, self-satisfied mannerist, a haughty, unsociable companion, mentally incompetent to grapple with Shakespeare's characters, and not fit to be classed with a single great actor of the past?[25]

The gallery and pit crowds started to gather outside Drury Lane at two o'clock, and another crowd gathered to see the crowd. For the first and last time, Macready had allowed his children to watch him act, and they took their seats, alongside Catherine, in a box.* He dressed in the room he had had fitted up when the theatre was his, listened to the cries of his fans, and gave thanks that they no longer held his livelihood in their throats.

Macbeth, of course, was the play. As he walked on stage the whole house rose to its feet, waving hats and handkerchiefs, stamping, shouting, and yelling: he thought of his children and was overcome, though he managed to stand stock-still as always, desperately trying to focus on

---

* He agreed to let his children watch his final performance at the urging of Dickens and Forster, but they were sufficiently well trained to be shocked by the poor standard of the supporting cast and glad their father had quit such an unbecoming sphere.

his first words. When the tumult died down there was utter quiet, and when, at the end, he fell pierced by Macduff's sword, his last look, his last moment on stage, struck the whole audience breathless until, what seemed like minutes later, choked tears gave way to deafening applause. After changing, he returned, dressed as a private gentleman, with a black crepe hatband and black studs offering a silent testament to his daughter's death, and the wild standing ovation went on and on, faintly echoed from outside, where hundreds who had not got in were still crowding the doors. He was glad of the delay, because he was shaking with emotion and incapable of speech. Eventually he collected himself and stood forward, calm, composed, and sad. His farewell address was formal, dignified, rehearsed, though his choked voice betrayed more than his words. He bowed repeatedly, gave one last, lingering look at the old arena, and walked slowly away, and though the audience shouted for him, and though the crowd milled outside until the early hours, he came no more.

"*Thank God!*" he wrote in his diary: his last words as an actor.[26]

There was one last public duty, a grand banquet held in the huge and drafty Hall of Commerce. Bulwer Lytton made a heartfelt speech that was strangulated by his lisp. Forster roared out a shockingly bad ode written for the occasion by Tennyson. Thackeray, whose task was to propose the health of the ladies, nearly broke down from nerves, which languidly amused Bulwer Lytton, who had fallen out with him. Thankfully Dickens, who had organized the night with some flustered help from Forster, was at his best. He stood up, resplendent in a blue dress coat faced with silk and brass buttons and a black satin vest, his curly hair and whiskers spreading over a white satin collar and an embroidered shirt, and launched into a speech half genial, half sad, and full of love for his dear friend.

When it was over Macready made his way through a sea of well-wishers who clutched at his hand and reached for his coat, crying, "God bless you, sir! God bless you, Mac!" and walked out into private life. He retired to the dignified pursuits of a country gentleman in Sherborne, a dozy town in Dorset—though the frostiness of his fellow countryfolk made him realize that his profession had followed him even there—and devoted himself to his family and a night school that he established for the poor boys of the town. It became a model for many institutions of its type, and he dragged down his London friends, Thackeray, Forster, and Dickens, the most frequent visitor of all, to give incongruously starry talks.

Tragedy dogged his last years. In 1852, his beloved Catherine died, like Nina from tuberculosis. The next year, their youngest son, Walter, followed her; in 1857, their son Henry succumbed to the same disease, shortly followed by their daughter Lydia. All the children were still in their teens.

At sixty-seven, after mourning Catherine for eight years, Macready remarried. Cecile was twenty-three and a friend of his daughter Katie; Forster, tactless as always, wrote to his old friend insinuating that she was a gold digger, and it took Dickens several years to patch up the rift. Cecile was intelligent, strong-minded, and patient, and it was a happy match: two years later, now a white-haired man with a gentle smile, he became a father again. To Macready's great satisfaction, Katie, his favorite daughter and a promising poet, announced her engagement to Bulwer Lytton's eldest son: they planned to marry after she returned from a health cure in Madeira. William and Cecile went down to the Plymouth docks to welcome her home; the captain took him aside and told him she had died on the voyage and had been buried at sea. It was a brutal shock, and the death of his eldest son, William, two years later, was the final blow.* He slowly slid into senility and died, peacefully, in his eighty-first year, having outlived even his dear Dickens. Only Forster was left to follow the coffin, and it was only then that Macready's young wife told his loyal, troublesome old friend how deeply isolated her husband had felt, sitting in his study until he could no longer read or hold a book, still trying out new interpretations of Shakespeare, far away from the congenial company of London and the applause of an audience— away from everything, however tormenting, that had given meaning to his life.[27]

Almost in concert with his retirement, the social standing of actors

---

* Seven of his and Catherine's ten children preceded Macready to the grave; an eighth, Edward, who had wanted to go on the stage but was dispatched with a commission into the army, boarded a ship at Bombay after his father recalled him to deal with his gambling debts and was never heard from again.

had at last begun to rise. Macready's own exertions had played a large part; so, too, had the sudden interest that Queen Victoria started to take in the English theatre after the 1848 revolutions. Barely two months after Macready's last performance, the Great Exhibition had opened in London, and as six million visitors poured into the Crystal Palace, Edmund Kean's son Charles took over the Princess's Theatre and purveyed Shakespeare for well-heeled tourists, complete with massive antiquarian sets, so many extras that the principals were almost lost from sight, and the queen in regular attendance. Kean's Shakespeare was the Shakespeare of Empire, a complacent show of heritage for a class that was smugly secure in its self-image. It was because Macready was the last in the old line of managers, the last heir to the great national theatres where men and women of every station in life went to be entertained and where clowns and chorus girls eked out a living among the stars, that he was deemed unfit to receive honors. With the establishment of unimpeachably middle-class theatres, respectable actors were finally allowed in from the cold, and at the end of the century Henry Irving, England's next great actor-manager, was knighted.

Macready's obituaries universally noted that he had outlived Forrest by four months, as if he had finally triumphed over his rival in death. The truth, as the Englishman knew well, was different. Both Macready and Forrest loomed so large over their worlds that their friends never doubted their fame would live as long as the theatre itself. But in an age before film ushered acting into immortality, the verdict of an audience was a hostage to the next day's billing, a momentary excitement tinged with melancholy because in the morning it was gone for good. It is one of the little quirks of history that these two hugely talented and hugely flawed men are best remembered and forever linked by a bloody riot that was only partly of their making, a judgment in which this book is guiltily complicit.

Epilogue

IN JANUARY 1848, gold was discovered in the Sierra foothills of California. The news spread east by September, and as the first prospectors snaked in ox-trains along the overland trail or braved the even more treacherous seagoing voyage around the Cape, the first actors were hard on their heels.

Gold rush California was a familiar prospect to actors who remembered the old west. They shared the miners' campfire dinners of charcoal-black coffee, slapjacks, salt pork, and flatbread, and put on shows in tent cities called Hell's Delight, Rat Trap Slide, and Skunk Gulch. By 1849, they had already knocked together the first theatre at the mouth of the Sacramento mines. A wooden frame building with a sheet-iron roof and canvas sides, it boasted a stage improvised from packing crates, a pit consisting of board benches on the bare ground, an outside ladder to the dress circle with its sides blocked off to preserve female modesty, and a ticket office in the next-door saloon where patrons poured gold dust into the treasurer's scales. When the Sacramento River burst its banks two months later, they watched with the same stoicism their forerunners had shown while the theatre was swept away.

The Chapmans were there. Old William had died on board his floating theatre in the midst of drawing up plans for an even bigger showboat (and while dressed as the Ghost from *Hamlet,* said one story). By 1851, though, George and Mary Chapman had made it across the country to Nevada City, which two years earlier had been a one-store outpost called Deer Creek Dry Diggings but was already so rich that the miners threw buckskin bags of gold dust on the stage, and the next March William and Caroline, the most gifted of the clan, arrived in San Francisco with their sister Sarah and her family.

Five years earlier, the California coast had been the preserve of mountain trappers and whaling ships restocking with wood and water; now San Francisco's dirt streets had been boarded over and department stores, bowling alleys, and a merchants' exchange had sprung up in showy buildings. So, too, had theatres, as sumptuous as any in the country, two-thousand-seaters plush with red velvet and gleaming with gilding. Most were built by an illiterate cabdriver turned gambler called Tom Maguire and all sported a bar at the entrance where newly dug fortunes were staked and lost every night; but they were too tame for the intrepid Chapmans, and the clan set off on a tour of the mines, lugging their baggage back and forth across the Sierras, playing in saloons, barns, and tents, and once on the stump of a giant sequoia. They became as legendary as their father had been, twenty years earlier, along the Mississippi, and before long they were joined by Julia Dean, the granddaughter of old Samuel Drake, the hardy pioneer who had led his tribe of actors to Kentucky all the way back in 1815. Julia quickly became the favorite actress of the new West, but soon another actress arrived with an even more famous name. She was called Catharine Forrest.

By 1852, Kate was broke. With Forrest's appeals pending she had no prospect of receiving alimony for years, and she decided to take up the only career she knew. Going on the stage was a risky move, a test not just of her talents but of her character, because acting was still a suspect profession for a gentlewoman, especially one who had been recently and scandalously divorced. She also had to reckon with the b'hoys. When she made her debut in New York, it was interrupted by hisses and curses, loud insinuations about her morality, and cheers for Forrest from the balcony; a large, menacing crowd gathered outside, but though it made plenty of noise, it was kept at bay by Chief Matsell and two regiments that were stationed around the corner. Yet with the help of her society friends, Kate made a sensational hit.* She was still only thirty-

---

* On the night of her debut, Kate was pointedly serenaded by the orchestra of the Astor Place Opera House, which had been hired by an anonymous admirer.

two, she was striking and accomplished, and though her stage voice was reedy and she had little of her husband's vivacity, her coolness and nerve astonished everyone: she looked as if she had been in the theatre all her life, which she nearly had. Soon, though, she discovered that almost none of the New York managers were willing to risk the wrath of the greater Forrest by taking her on, so in 1853 she set out west.

Kate's notoriety drew the crowds, but they took to her instantly. As well as being uncommonly ladylike, she was as good as most of the actresses who had made it to California, and diadems and tiaras, gold watches and jeweled brooches rained down on her curtain calls. Even so, she was made to work hard for her rewards. The new west wanted the best, and the best meant Shakespeare; within a few months, Kate had played Beatrice in *Much Ado About Nothing,* Queen Katherine in *Henry VIII,* Portia in *The Merchant of Venice,* Desdemona in *Othello,* and Ophelia in *Hamlet.*

Shakespeare was on the frontier again. Many of the Forty-niners were middle-class doctors, mechanics, lawyers, shopkeepers, artisans, farmers, and preachers, adventurers to a man—women were still a tiny minority—but thirsty for culture, and they knew their Bard. At an 1856 performance of *Richard III* in Sacramento, the notoriously inept Hugh McDermott was buried under a barrage of "cabbages, carrots, pumpkins, potatoes, a wreath of vegetables, a sack of flour and one of soot, and a dead goose" and finally driven from the stage by a burst of Chinese firecrackers, a well-directed pumpkin, and a potato that knocked off his cap.[1] But when accomplished actors like the Chapmans took the stage, even the roughest miners swarmed over from the saloons and fandango houses and whistled and cheered through *Hamlet* and *King Lear.* "There is hardly a butcher or a newspaper boy in the city who does not understand 'like a book,' the majority of the playable plays of Shakespeare, so often have they seen them acted, ranted, or slaughtered upon our boards," one San Francisco paper observed.[2]

For all her chutzpah, Kate was aware of her limitations as an actor, and she was aware, too, that the draw of her name would eventually wear thin. She decided to become a manager, and thanks to her contacts back east she briefly became the leading promoter of the legitimate drama in California. The cost of luring stars out west, though, was astronomical—ten times their price back east—and despite the outrageous price of admission the enterprise lost money. Kate abandoned management and set out on a tour of the mines.

Life in the gold fields was tough, lonely, and mind-blowingly monotonous, and to miners who had not seen a woman for months an elegant actress shimmered down the creeks looking like a mermaid to a drowning man. Few made it to the remotest camps: with trails barely marked and frequently impassable from snowfalls, flash floods, or high winds, mules that bolted and scattered costumes over hillsides, and the constant threat from grizzly bears, wolves, highwaymen, and gunfighters, the terrain was even tougher going than the backwoods of the Mississippi had been for the earlier pioneering troupes. Those who did reach places like Rough and Ready and Grass Valley, where Kate brought Shakespeare to hotels walled with paper and canvas, or to theatres with candles stuck in beer bottles for lights and kegs for seats, found that the miners would pay almost anything for a glimpse of civilization and ankle. Everywhere she went the rattle of the washing machines and the smack of picks, shovels, and pans ground to a halt and gave way to rounds of applause; and, having showered her with gold, the miners formed honor guards to escort her across the hills to her next stop. After little more than two years she had earned enough to support herself modestly for life, and it was just as well, because another eleven years went by before Forrest was forced to pay the arrears of her alimony, and most went straight to the lawyers.

Kate retired to private life in New York, but the appetite for Shakespeare was still going strong in the west when she left. On Sundays, between mending clothes and whittling shingles for cabin roofs, prospectors sat together and read his plays. Molly b'Damn, the most famous prostitute in Idaho, could quote from them at length. In tent cities they were performed alongside fights between grizzly bears and bulls. Travelers caught in snowdrifts recited *Hamlet* to stay awake, their predicament giving an authentic ring to the Prince's weighing of life and death.[3] Cowboys gathered around campfires and took a tilt at a dramatic episode from one of the histories or tragedies. When one ranch hand heard the "dogs of war" speech from *Julius Caesar* for the first time he was knocked over: "Gosh!" he cried. "That fellow Shakespeare could sure spill the real stuff. He's the only poet I ever seen what was fed on raw meat."[4]

Even Jim Bridger, the greatest scout, trapper, and Indian fighter in the far west, owned a copy of Shakespeare, and Bridger was illiterate. A tall, lean old man with sharp gray eyes, Bridger had exchanged a yoke of cattle for the precious volume, and he hired a boy to read the plays out loud for hours at a time. *Richard III* was too strong even for him: Shakespeare, he swore, must have been as devilish as a Sioux, and he threw the book in the fire. But by then he already knew the great speeches by heart. Bridger was a famous teller of tall tales—Ned Buntline got enough material from him to keep him supplied for years—and for the rest of his life he added Shakespeare to his repertoire. "W-a-a-l," he would drawl with an air of solemn gravity, before reeling off a soliloquy around the campfires. Every few lines he would throw in an oath of his own to spice things up, and he became so attuned to the rhythms of Elizabethan verse that his audience found it impossible to tell where Lear stopped and Bridger began.[5] However incongruous it seems today, to a lonely miner sick with scurvy or scrabbling for a strike through the bitter winter frost in the Sierras, Bridger's tales of madness, violence, and pitiless storms must have made all too much sense.

Everything went faster in California, and by 1856, as the gold rush petered out, so did the popular thirst for Shakespeare. Old-timers still read him, even in ghost towns like Two-Bit Gulch, where men had once buried gold in pickle jars under their cabin floors, gambling houses had blazed with light, and the fandango had shaken the bars. Turning to the worn, coverless edition of Shakespeare at his elbow, a whiskey-sodden hermit, once a store clerk in New England, would retreat into the time-honored plays for solace from the weed-covered scars left by the mines and the graveyards with their weathered headboards recording the premature deaths of strong, ambitious men.[6] But the Bard was no longer bound up in the everyday lives of ordinary Americans, and the Astor Place riot was one reason why.

THE VICTORY IN Astor Place went to the elite, but it was not a victory for Shakespeare. The segregation of audiences by class and taste which had provoked the riot was hastened by it, and as the West Coast cities grew more sophisticated they, too, sprouted exclusive theatres where the Bard was stripped of the old acrobatics and song-and-dance acts and performed with due deference to genius. The depopularizing of Shakespeare was completed in the schoolroom. As the great movement for universal education gathered pace, partly motivated by a desire to root out foreign influences and bind immigrants to the American way, English literature filled the role vacated by the classics. At the same time, oratory swung out of fashion, and Shakespeare became a perplexing puzzle of metrics and syntax, not a writer of familiar speeches to roll around the tongue.

First in England, and now in America, Bardolatry had become institutionalized. In 1872, on a shining spring day, six thousand people crowded into a specially built pavilion in Central Park to witness the unveiling of the great statue of Shakespeare. The social sympathies of the celebrants can be guessed from two familiar figures who were central to the proceedings: James Hackett, the manager of the Astor Place Theatre during the riot, had already laid the foundation stone, and Judge Charles Daly, Ned Buntline's nemesis, was the chair of the committee. It was a state occasion in all but name. The banners of thirty-eight countries fluttered from the roof; the flags of the United States and Great Britain waved side by side at the entrance. The orchestra played from the gallery, Judge Daly mounted the pulpit, and the Stars and Stripes slipped away to reveal Shakespeare ruminating in bronze. While the speakers struck familiar themes—Daly discoursed on that old favorite, America's common property in the Bard—a new note had crept into the ceremonies. At the dedication Hackett had declared that his own voice was "hushed in the performance of this reverential act" and cautioned that the moment was too solemn for applause, while in his oration at the unveiling William Cullen Bryant hailed Shakespeare as a genius sent by God to give mankind a glimpse of its immortal spirit.[7] Even this piece of star-hopping was outmatched when Emerson, yoking Thomas Gray into a moment of transcendental enthusiasm, wrote in his journal that in climes beyond the solar road they probably called the Earth Shakespeare.[8]

So much veneration did not make for good drama, and the Bard's streetwise fans knew it. Along the Bowery, as in the south and east of

London, the vaudeville and variety halls responded to the new high-flown style with burlesques. *Richard III* was camped up as *Bad Dicky; Julius Caesar* developed a cold and became *Julius Sneezer.* More explosive sneezing interrupted the balcony scene in one version of *Romeo and Juliet,* before Juliet performed a duet with a dog and fell asleep, in lieu of a potion, over a philosophy book, while *Hamlet* was punned into *Hamlet and Egglet* and "To be or not to be" was sung to the tune of "Three Blind Mice." Burlesques were an affectionate form of homage as well as a dig at the deadweight of Bardolatry, but the inevitable result was to push Shakespeare further into the realm of Culture, where academics armed with terrifying footnotes tilled the sacred ground, and soon everyone forgot that regular men and women had laughed and gasped at his plays more than two hundred years after they were written.[9]

By the end of the century, the theatre had changed out of all recognition from the anarchic, enterprising trade known to Samuel Drake, William Chapman, or even Edwin Forrest. Big business had moved in, and the Syndicate, a cartel of Broadway-based promoters that shipped prepackaged star vehicles around the country complete with sets, costumes, and cast, took control of virtually every major American theatre. Shakespeare's plays, which had become weighted down with huge casts and elaborate scenery, gave the Syndicate a logistical headache and a poor rate of return, and they all but vanished from sight.[10] The new monopoly finally killed off the old stock system, and with the death of repertory, actors began to forget the secret of delivering Shakespearean verse. As American playwrights, emboldened by the belated arrival of copyright laws, discovered that there was money to be made from the new long-running shows, cheap-to-produce domestic drama and drawing room comedy took over the stage, and for decades a growing obsession with realism sent Shakespeare firmly out of style.

Was there a deeper reason for America's waning infatuation with the Bard? Perhaps it was this. The pioneers had looked to Shakespeare to understand human nature, and what they found had echoed, nourished, and directed their own beliefs. The American Shakespeare was a free-thinker, scornful of dogma and undeceived by pretension, a guiding spirit who was luminously wise to men's driving passions, and passionately concerned about the ways in which societies served or failed their citizens; a man aware of human frailty, and alert to the dangers of tyranny and greed, but sustained by a belief in the value of sacrifice and love, and seized with an intense joy in the painful, mysterious, beautiful pageant of life. To the nation's builders, great and humble alike, Shakespeare was a light in the darkness, a voice that spoke directly to their hopes and fears.[11]

Yet as America matured and grew into itself, those raw, outreaching thoughts receded, and soon they seemed to belong to a bolder but more primitive past. What replaced them was a fascination with mapping the twists and turns of an increasingly complex society, and the novel was the right form for that. Though the nation's attachment to Shakespeare would revive, the time had long gone when ordinary Americans would take to the streets in their thousands to decide who owned the Bard.[12]

Shakespeare had served his purpose, but it was a purpose that no other storyteller had ever served. Once a voice carried a people across a continent and helped forge a brave new world. No other writer has been so powerful, and none ever will be again.

Acknowledgments

MY RESEARCH FOR *The Shakespeare Riots* took me on a tour of some of the great libraries, archives, and museums of the United States and Britain, where many kind and patient people helped me sift through their stacks. My grateful thanks to the librarians, curators, and staff of the following treasure houses:

The Humanities and Social Sciences and Performing Arts libraries of the New York Public Library, the Houghton Library and the Theatre Collection at Harvard University, the Annenberg Rare Books and Manuscripts Library at the University of Pennsylvania, the Princeton University Library, the Pierpont Morgan Library, the New-York Historical Society Library, the Rare Books and Manuscripts Library at Columbia University, and the Players Club Library.

The British Library, the National Arts Library and the Theatre Museum Library of the Victoria and Albert Museum, the Garrick Club Library, and the London Library.

For long-distance help: the Folger Shakespeare Library, the Huntington Library and Art Collections, and the Library of Congress.

What a pleasure to have worked with Nancy Miller, my editor at Random House, on my first book, and to have benefited from her kindness, enthusiasm, and incisive editing. My thanks, too, to the ever helpful Lea Beresford, and to word surgeon Jolanta Benal, whose knowledge of canine vocalizations is something else, and to Vincent La Scala.

My agent, Henry Dunow, was a champion of the book from the start, and he has been a sure guide ever since.

My thanks to Melanie Thernstrom for her invaluable guidance, to Marcia Biggs and Irina Prentice for generous hospitality, to Gillian Carey, who read a draft of the book, and to Grant Romer of Eastman House, who helped me track down the wonderful daguerreotype of Edwin Forrest in his Elvis period.

From beginning to end, Angelica von Hase gave me her unfailing advice, encouragement, and support, as always.

Notes

Prologue

1. The scramble for the Hoboken ferry was a much-remarked New York ritual; on a Sunday like that in 1849, the Fields commonly welcomed ten thousand visitors. See George Foster, *Fifteen Minutes Around New York* (New York, 1854), 27–30, 52–54, and *New York Naked* (New York, n.d.), 148; Fanny Trollope, *Domestic Manners of the Americans* (Harmondsworth, 1997), 272–74; Lydia Maria Francis Child, *Letters from New-York* (New York, 1843), 15–21; and Heath Schenker, "Pleasure Gardens, Theme Parks, and the Picturesque," in Terence Young and Robert Riley, eds., *Theme Park Landscapes: Antecedents and Variations* (Washington, D.C., 2002), 69–89. The Hudson shores are engraved across several feet of *Wade & Croome's Panorama of the Hudson River from New York to Albany* (New York, 1848).

2. The account is taken from Andrew Stevens's confession, published in the *Police Gazette,* April 1, 1852. Shortly before he wrote the piece, Stevens left town after Forrest accused him of fraudulently using his name to obtain a loan of fifteen hundred dollars. Although that episode supplied Stevens with a motive for revenge, this part of his testimony does not inculpate Forrest and was taken at face value by contemporary reporters. Stevens does not give a date for his trip to the Elysian Fields, but he says it took place several days before the May 7 riot. Since he recalls that the b'hoys already knew about Forrest's split with his wife, which took place on April 28, and since Sunday was the only day of leisure for workingmen, the date can be fixed as Sunday, April 30.

3. The May 1 removals were a constant source of astonishment to visitors: see Joe Cowell, *Thirty Years Passed Among the Players in England and America* (New York, 1845), 58, and Trollope, *Domestic Manners,* 271.

4. For Broadway, see George Foster, *New York in Slices* (New York, 1849), 3–13.

5. For the Broadway and other theatres, see George Foster, *New York by Gas-Light and Other Urban Sketches,* ed. Stuart M. Blumin (Berkeley, Los Angeles, and Oxford, 1990), 152–60, and Foster, *New York in Slices,* 89–93; for the Astor Place, see also Foster, *New York Naked,* 35–76.

6. For my sources for the May 7 riot see the headnote to Chapter 11. Macready's account is in *The Diaries of William Charles Macready 1833–1851,* ed. William Toynbee (London, 1912), II. 422–24; hereafter, *Diaries.*

7. In the acting version used by Macready, Macduff spoke Ross's lines in the second scene, and so came on before Macbeth.

8. Lester Wallack, *Memories of Fifty Years* (New York, 1889), 131.

9. English, rather than British; London was the great theatrical center, and it exported its stars and productions around Britain and Ireland as well as to the New World.

Chapter 1: A Shakespearean Ark

1. My account of the Drakes' odyssey is largely based on Noah Ludlow, *Dramatic Life as I Found It* (St. Louis, 1880), 5–78. Ludlow dedicated his book to Edwin Forrest: "No one," he wrote, "knew more thoroughly than Mr. Forrest the difficulties that had to be encountered by the pioneers of the Drama in the West."

2. "England, that never did us a single good office, accuses us of ingratitude; and through the whole history of her connexion with this country exhibits one uninterrupted series of the cold, haughty, and unfeeling selfishness of an unnatural parent; jealous of the growth and prosperity of her offspring, she is forever reproaching us with the crime of disobedience," Edwin Forrest's future friend James Kirke Paulding exclaimed in a pamphlet published during the war. See Paulding, "The United States and England: Being a Reply to the Criticism on Inchiquin's Letters Contained in the *Quarterly Review* for January, 1814" (New York, 1815), 5. The *Review*'s criticism was harsh indeed: the paper accused Americans of employing naked colored women to wait on their tables, kidnapping and enslaving Scotsmen, Irishmen, Welshmen, and Dutchmen, and fighting one another under rules which made it "allowable to peel the skull, tear out the eyes, and smooth away the nose."

3. Sol Smith, *Theatrical Management in the West and South for Thirty Years* (New York, 1868), 29.

4. Joseph Jefferson, *The Autobiography of Joseph Jefferson,* ed. Alan Downer (Cambridge, Mass., 1964), 23–45. Though the actors were innocent if foolhardy victims, the show of bloodthirstiness was not unprovoked: during the disastrous Seminole Wars, the U.S. Army had imported bloodhounds from Cuba to hunt fugitive Indians.

5. Cowell, *Thirty Years,* 59.

6. Anne Mathews, *Memoirs of Charles Mathews, Comedian* (London, 1839), III. 331.

7. Tyrone Power, *Impressions of America During the Years 1833, 1834, and 1835* (London, 1836), I. 66.

8. For Chapman's Ark, see Ludlow, *Dramatic Life,* 567–70; Smith, *Theatrical Management,* 89; John Hanners, *"It Was Play or Starve": Acting in the Nineteenth-Century Popular Theatre* (Bowling Green, Ohio, 1993), 12–13; Philip Graham, *Showboats: The History of an American Institution* (Austin, Tex., 1951), 9–21.

9. Hanners, *"It Was Play or Starve,"* 13–21. In 1849, Banvard finally made his fortune by exhibiting a panoramic painting of the Mississippi and Missouri Rivers in

London. The queen commanded a personal viewing at Windsor Castle; in one day four foreign princes, three foreign princesses, and a duchess called on him, and the enterprise was so successful that a group of American tricksters put a copy on display and accused Banvard of forgery.

10. Correspondence of the *Natchez Courier,* April 1837, quoted in George Prentiss, *A Memoir of S. S. Prentiss* (New York, 1855), 176–86.
11. Jefferson, *Autobiography,* 40.
12. David Grimsted, *Melodrama Unveiled: American Theater and Culture 1800–1850* (Chicago and London, 1968), appendices 1, 2; R. L. Rusk, *The Literature of the Middle Western Frontier* (New York, 1925), I. 413.
13. Alexis de Tocqueville, *Democracy in America* (London, 1968), II. 604.
14. Mark Twain, *Is Shakespeare Dead?* (New York, 1909), 5–7.
15. "Play the orator" appears at *3 Henry VI,* III. ii.
16. William Rounseville Alger, *Life of Edwin Forrest* (Philadelphia, 1877), I. 477. Forrest was the actor playing Iago.
17. Trollope, *Domestic Manners,* 101–103.
18. Ibid., 263.
19. Many of the most "immodest" scenes had been excised, though, which suggests even more strongly that something more fundamental was behind the West's fascination with Shakespeare.
20. Ralph Waldo Emerson, "Shakespeare; or, the Poet," from *Representative Men,* in *The Collected Works of Ralph Waldo Emerson,* ed. Wallace E. Williams, Douglas Emory Wilson (Cambridge, Mass., 1987), IV. 117.
21. James Fenimore Cooper, *Notions of the Americans: Picked Up by a Travelling Bachelor* (New York, 1850), II. 113, 100.

Chapter 2: The Western Star

1. Letter dated August 1, 1822, Folder 3, Box 1, Ms Coll 5, Annenberg Rare Book and Manuscript Library, University of Pennsylvania.
2. William and Rebecca only admitted to seven children: their first child was born and died before they married.
3. Richard Moody, *Edwin Forrest: First Star of the American Stage* (New York, 1960), 15.
4. Fanny Kemble, *Journal of a Residence in America* (Paris, 1835), 173.
5. The South Street was also known as the Southwark Theatre.
6. The incident was related by Forrest to the actor James Murdoch and recounted in Murdoch's *The Stage* (Philadelphia, 1880), 317–24.
7. Alger, *Life of Edwin Forrest,* 64. My account of Forrest's early years draws substantially on this source. Alger was Forrest's official biographer, and his book, for all its eccentric digressions and frequent inaccuracies, was in part based on interviews with his subject.
8. Ibid., 66–67.
9. Prune Street is now Locust Street.
10. Alger, *Life of Edwin Forrest,* 69.
11. Smith's early adventures are told in his *Theatrical Management,* 14–28.

12. Ibid., 27–28.
13. George Vandenhoff, *Leaves from an Actor's Note-book* (New York, 1860), 203–210.
14. Alger, *Life of Edwin Forrest,* 137.
15. The lines are at III.i.
16. Francis Courtney Wemyss, *Twenty-six Years of the Life of an Actor and Manager* (New York, 1847), 108.
17. Vandenhoff, *Leaves from an Actor's Note-book,* 22.
18. Alger, *Life of Edwin Forrest,* 150.
19. *Dramatic Mirror,* May 12, 1827.
20. Alger, *Life of Edwin Forrest,* 153.
21. Using a comparison of consumer prices; a conversion based on unskilled wages produces a sum of $45,000.

Chapter 3: Rogues and Vagabonds

1. A smaller theatre in the Haymarket was licensed for the summer season; only Drury Lane and Covent Garden were licensed for the legitimate drama, including Shakespeare, the year round.
2. My account of the O.P. riots draws substantially on Marc Baer, *Theatre and Disorder in Late Georgian London* (Oxford, 1992), 18–36, and John Bull [pseud.], *Remarks on the Cause of the Dispute Between the Public and Managers of the Theatre Royal, Covent Garden* (London, 1809), as well as Henry Saxe Wyndham, *The Annals of Covent Garden from 1732 to 1897* (London, 1906), I. 324–47, and contemporary newspaper reports.
3. William Prynne, *Histrio-mastix. The Players Scourge, or, Actors Tragaedie* (London, 1633), 133, 135, 140. The whole diatribe is the size of a large brick; it runs to more than a thousand pages and quotes many thousands of obscure authorities. Prynne made the mistake of listing actresses in his index as "notorious whores," and since his tome was published just as the queen was preparing to stage a pastoral at the palace, he was pilloried, imprisoned, fined, stripped of his degree and legal qualifications, shorn of his ears and branded on both cheeks with the letters "S.L." for Seditious Libeller. Yet within a decade he and his fellow Puritans had their way.
4. The term "Bardolatry," though, was coined much later, by George Bernard Shaw. Boswell's remarks appeared in *The London Magazine,* September 1769, 451–54.
5. Hamlet was the tutelary god of the pantheon: after Jesus he is the most cited figure in western culture. See Harold Bloom, *Shakespeare: The Invention of the Human* (London, 1999), xix.
6. *Macready's Reminiscences, and Selections from His Diaries and Letters,* ed. Sir Frederick Pollock (London, 1875), I. 23; hereafter, *Reminiscences.*
7. *Diaries,* II. 292.
8. *Reminiscences,* I. 14–15.
9. Vandenhoff, *Leaves from an Actor's Note-book,* 37. Vandenhoff was himself the son of a famous actor, though he trained as a barrister before he answered the call of the stage. His memoirs solemnly adjured others not to make the same mistake. "Actors in general, especially those who have attained eminence," he wrote,

have a dread, amounting almost to horror, of their young ones following in the same career. . . . The result of my experience is, that the Stage is the last occupation a young man of spirit and ambition should think of following. . . . The actor's individuality, as a citizen, seems lost in the fictitious world in which he lives and moves and has his being. He is king, governor, general, statesman, hero of a fantastic realm, but from the practical interests of this work-a-day world he seems to be segregated and apart. His ambition, if he have it, must be confined to the narrow circle and the unsubstantial honours of the mimic scene: from those nobler ones of the great stage of life, its civic laurels and political triumphs, he is silently shut out. . . . Besides, the novice's career is one of continual humiliations, and wounds to self-love; great uncertainty of employment; and, if employed, hard work and small pay. . . . Therefore, let no rash youth, "with a soul above buttons," adopt the stage as a means of elegant idleness; if he do, he will be woefully mistaken, when he finds that, after a hard week's work, even Sunday is not always a day of rest to his study-wearied brain.

The country actor Robert Dyer was another whose memoirs amount to a wake-up call to anyone stupid enough to think of going on the stage: his motivation in writing his autobiography, he explained, was the hope that "the aspiring young hero will be warned by my experience, to hold fast by whatever occupation he may be engaged in, rather than venture on a theatrical life in which honesty is a 'starving quality,' and virtue a thing of no report." Charles Mathews put it more succinctly: "A dog of mine," he said, "should not go upon the stage." See Vandenhoff, *Leaves from an Actor's Note-book,* 29–37; Dyer, *Nine Years of an Actor's Life* (London, 1833), 1; Leman Rede, *The Guide to the Stage* (New York, 1859), 3. Even in 1856, Henry Irving knew that taking up acting meant severing all ties with his devout mother.

10. Rede, *The Guide to the Stage,* 3.
11. Ibid., 18–42.
12. *Reminiscences,* I. 40.
13. William Archer, *William Charles Macready* (London, 1890), 20.
14. *The Examiner,* September 21, 1816.
15. *The Times,* September 17, 1816.
16. *The News,* September 17, 1816.
17. Adam Smith, *An Inquiry into the Nature and Causes of the Wealth of Nations* (Oxford, 1998), 438.
18. Pierce Egan, *Life in London* (London, 1821), 128–29.
19. Flora Tristan, *Flora Tristan's London Journal: A Survey of London Life in the 1830s,* trans. Dennis Palmer and Giselle Pinsett (London, 1980), 178–79, 75.
20. Jehangeer Nowrojee and Hirjeebhoy Merwanjee, *Journal of a Residence of Two Years and a Half in Great Britain* (London, 1841), 106.
21. *Diaries,* I. 406.
22. Prince Pückler-Muskau is quoted in *American Criticisms on Mrs Trollope's "Domestic Manners of the Americans"* (London, 1833), 46.
23. Nowrojee and Merwanjee, *Journal of a Residence,* 109–110.

24. James Grant, *The Great Metropolis* (London, 1837), I. 25.

25. Thomas Wright, *Some Habits and Customs of the Working Classes* (London, 1867), 220–21.

26. Charles Manby Smith, *Curiosities of London Life: or Phases, Physiological and Social of the Great Metropolis* (London, 1853), 102.

27. Henry Mayhew, *London Labour and the London Poor* (London, 1861–62), I. 15.

28. *Reminiscences,* I. 107.

29. Ibid., I. 131.

30. *The Morning Chronicle,* October 20, 1819.

31. Papers of Robert Elliston, TS 1091.192, Harvard Theatre Collection.

32. James Winston, *Drury Lane Journal: Selections from James Winston's Diaries 1819–1827,* ed. Alfred L. Nelson and Gilbert B. Cross (London, 1974), 4.

33. *Diaries,* I. 230.

34. Giles Playfair, *The Flash of Lightning: A Portrait of Edmund Kean* (London, 1983), 114, 116.

35. Matthew Mackintosh, *Stage Reminiscences* (Glasgow, 1866), 5–23.

36. Winston, *Drury Lane Journal,* 107.

37. The fullest estimates of the two actors were printed in the *New-York Mirror and Ladies' Literary Gazette,* beginning with its review of Forrest's debut on July 1, 1826; its general conclusion was that, while both were strikingly original and capable of taking the audience's breath away, Forrest was an astonishing but unpolished natural genius, while Macready's talent and taste created performances which approached perfection.

38. *Reminiscences,* I. 319–20.

Chapter 4: Boxing Mac and Hot Cross Bunn

1. *Diaries,* I. 15.

2. Macready to William McCready, n.d. [1819], William Charles Macready Collection, TC042, Manuscripts Division, Department of Rare Books and Special Collections, Princeton University Library.

3. *Reminiscences,* I. 289.

4. See Macready's letters to his father about the marriage, June 15 and 30, 1824, at Princeton.

5. *Diaries,* II. 45. See also his response to a young supplicant, January 20, 1837, bMS Thr 32, Harvard Theatre Collection. The would-be actor wants to desert the family business for the stage: Macready tells him that he wishes to save him "from the lamentable consequences, which his folly & inexperience may bring upon him . . . of the fatal step he was, in ignorance, and rashness, desirous of taking." He would receive no encouragement in his ambition from him, he declares: "It is one, that no well regulated mind would adopt for choice." Respect, he adds, was "almost IMPOSSIBLE on the Stage, where temptation is constantly around," and he earnestly hopes that his warnings will make the young man "sensible of the danger, into which he would have precipitated himself—by following a wretched and disreputable life." He should go back to his parents, Macready concludes, and

if, after all this, he persists in his folly and disobedience, his ruin, which is certain, will be on his own head.

6. See, for example, his lengthy and heavily underlined instructions to his step-mother, who took over the Bristol theatre when his father died in 1829. TC042, Princeton.

7. *Diaries,* I. 212, 288.

8. Ibid., I. 218.

9. Ibid., I. 343, 106.

10. Ibid., I. 215.

11. Cowell, *Thirty Years,* 47.

12. Quoted in *The Quarterly Review,* April 1875.

13. *Oxberry's Dramatic Biography and Histrionic Anecdotes,* ed. Catherine E. Oxberry (London and Bristol, 1825, 1826), V. 42.

14. Unattributed clipping, MWEZ+ n.c. 6476, New York Public Library for the Performing Arts.

15. *Diaries,* I. 241.

16. Ibid., II. 50.

17. Ibid., I. 296.

18. Ibid., I. 398.

19. Ibid., I. 31.

20. Ibid., II. 140.

21. Ibid., II. 40.

22. In 1843, Edward Bulwer added Lytton, his mother's maiden name, to his surname; later he was created Baron Lytton. For clarity I have used Bulwer Lytton throughout.

23. Harold Perkin, *The Origins of Modern English Society 1780–1880* (London, 1969), 280.

24. Willert Beale (Walter Maynard), *The Light of Other Days* (London, 1850), 122.

25. Mackintosh, *Stage Reminiscences,* 205.

26. Clifford John Williams, *Madame Vestris—A Theatrical Biography* (London, 1973), 151–52.

27. Wyndham, *Annals of Covent Garden,* 336–37.

28. James Robinson Planché, *Recollections and Reflections* (London, 1901), 170–71.

29. Ibid., 171.

30. Sara Hudston, *Victorian Theatricals: From Menageries to Melodrama* (London, 2000), 81.

31. Alfred Bunn, *The Stage: Both Before and Behind the Curtain, from "Observations Taken on the Spot"* (London, 1840), I. 286–87.

32. See Macready's exchange of letters with Bunn's deputy Thomas Cooper in TS 143.6F, v. 4 facing p. 314 and v. 5 facing p. 5, Harvard Theatre Collection.

33. *Diaries,* I. 261.

34. Ibid., I. 299.

35. Ibid., I. 301.

36. The episode is recounted from Bunn's viewpoint in his *The Stage,* II. 33–34.

37. *Diaries,* I. 303.

38. Ibid, I. 308–309, 317, 331–32.
39. Ibid., I. 312–13.

Chapter 5: An American in London

1. One American-born actor preceded him—James Hackett, a light comedian and Falstaff specialist who was the comanager of the Astor Place Theatre during the riot—but Forrest was the first true American star, and the first to visit Britain.
2. Quoted in Moody, *Edwin Forrest*, 92.
3. Walt Whitman, "The Old Bowery" (from "November Boughs"), in *Complete Prose Works* (Philadelphia, 1892), 426.
4. Vandenhoff, *Leaves from an Actor's Note-book*, 201.
5. *The Times*, October 18, 1836.
6. Bruce McConachie has cleverly suggested that the tragic endings of Forrest's American plays expose a subconscious awareness of the fault line in Jacksonian democracy: the paradox of one hero trying to return America to an agrarian past already doomed by the new individualism of which Jackson was the leading exemplar. After all, at the end of *Metamora* and *The Gladiator* the stage was strewn with dead Indians and slaves, but the audience wept only when Forrest grandly expired. See McConachie, "The Theatre of Edwin Forrest and Jacksonian Hero Worship," in *When They Weren't Doing Shakespeare: Essays on Nineteenth-Century British and American Theatre*, ed. Judith L. Fisher, Stephen Watt (Athens, Ga., 1989), 3–18.
7. The reviews are quoted in Alger, *Life of Edwin Forrest*, 299–305.
8. *Richard III*, I. i.
9. *Diaries*, I. 349.
10. *The Age*, October 16, 1836.
11. Wemyss, *Twenty-six Years*, 112; *Diaries*, I. 353.
12. *Diaries*, I. 350.
13. Ibid., I. 247, 405.
14. Ibid., I. 176, 148.
15. Ibid., I. 336.
16. Draft of letter in Macready's hand, October 18, [1836], TC042, Princeton.
17. *Diaries*, I. 350, 351.
18. Ibid., I. 352–53.
19. Podsnap in *Our Mutual Friend* has a good deal of Forster about him.
20. *Diaries*, I. 353.
21. The diary is in Ms Thr 131, Harvard Theatre Collection.
22. *The Examiner*, October 30, 1836 (*Othello*); February 12, 1837 (*Macbeth*); March 5, 1837 (*Richard III*).
23. Ibid., October 30, 1836.
24. Alger, *Life of Edwin Forrest*, 316–17.
25. Edwin Forrest to Rebecca Forrest, April 29, 1837, Ms Add. 1211, Folger Shakespeare Library.
26. Alger, *Life of Edwin Forrest*, 316–18.
27. Henry Wikoff, *The Reminiscences of an Idler* (New York, 1880), 196.
28. Alger, *Life of Edwin Forrest*, 321.

29. Bunn, *The Stage,* II. 268–73.

30. Victoria's theatrical tastes are discussed in Richard Schoch, *Queen Victoria and the Theatre of Her Age* (Basingstoke, 2004).

31. See Sir George Scharf, *Recollections of the Scenic Effects of Covent Garden Theatre During the Season 1838–9* (London, 1839).

32. Thomas Carlyle, *On Heroes, Hero-worship, and the Heroic in History,* ed. Carl Niemeyer (Lincoln, Neb., 1966), 113.

33. *Romeo and Juliet . . . with Alterations, and an Additional Scene: by D. Garrick* (London, 1753), 65–66.

34. Quoted in *Shakespeare Made Fit: Restoration Adaptations of Shakespeare,* ed. Sandra Clark (London, 1997), 295–96.

35. Garrick had cut some of Tate's lines; Kean briefly tried out the original ending, but it was not a success and he went back to Tate. Neither restored the Fool.

36. *The Examiner,* February 4, 1838.

37. *The Stage-Manager,* October 11, 1849.

38. *The Times,* January 15, 1842.

39. Alan Downer, *The Eminent Tragedian* (Cambridge, Mass., 1966), 214.

40. Quoted in Archer, *William Charles Macready,* 211–12.

41. Dickens to Macready, [April 7, 1839], MA 106, Pierpont Morgan Library Dept. of Literary and Historical Manuscripts.

42. Planché, *Recollections and Reflections,* 286–314.

43. Macready, Dickens once said, was "an impetuous passionate sort of fellow—devilish grim upon occasion—and of an iron purpose." November 1, 1854, MA 109, Pierpont Morgan Library.

44. Dickens to Macready, November 23, 1847, MA 106, Pierpont Morgan Library.

45. Dickens to Macready, September 1, 1843, MA 106, Pierpont Morgan Library.

Chapter 6: Cross Currents

1. Charles Dickens, *The Pickwick Papers* (Oxford, 1986), 572.

2. Kemble, *Journal,* 67; see also Mathews, *Memoirs of Charles Mathews,* III. 322–23, 382–83, for similar comments.

3. Frederick Marryat, *Second Series of A Diary in America, with Remarks on Its Institutions* (Philadelphia, 1840), 7.

4. Cowell, *Thirty Years,* 91–93.

5. Trollope, *Domestic Manners,* 20.

6. Charles William Janson, *The Stranger in America, 1793–1806* (New York, 1935), 86.

7. George Nettle, *A Practical Guide for Emigrants to North America by a Seven Year Resident in North America* (London, 1850), 53.

8. Basil Hall, *Travels in North America in the Years 1827 and 1828* (Edinburgh, 1829), I. 110.

9. Washington Irving, "English Writers on America," in *The Sketch Book of Geoffrey Crayon* (London, 1820), 105.

10. Trollope, *Domestic Manners,* 232.

11. Ibid., 96.

12. Ibid., 314. One of the travel writers' most invidious arguments was that many

Anglo-Americans came from criminal stock: England had transported fifty thousand convicts to its American colonies between 1718 and 1775, half of all the English (as distinct from Irish or Scots) who arrived during those years. Trollope made the point loudly; so did George Nettle, who charged the transportees, together with the political dissidents and fugitive felons whom he identified as making up most of the remaining English emigrants, with whipping up Anglophobia. The result, he claimed, was that "of all the nations on the face of the earth, the English is the most disliked by Yankees." Nettle, *A Practical Guide for Emigrants,* 54.

13. Marryat, *A Diary in America,* 184, 293.

14. Ibid., 133–34. Marryat was not alone. Gustave de Beaumont, Tocqueville's traveling companion, thought Americans regarded Britain with a "venomous hatred" and "detested the English." Kim C. Sturgess, *Shakespeare and the American Nation* (Cambridge, 2004), 24.

15. Quoted in Marryat, *A Diary in America,* 147.

16. "The young Queen of England is a plain-looking girl of eighteen, without any personal attractions," the *New York Herald* declared on Victoria's coronation. "Let them say what they please about Europe—her old towers and palaces—her bloated aristocracy—her ancient institutions—let them look at her miserable subjects, more than half dying of hunger—her ancient edifices and her institutions tumbling to the ground—her debauched priesthood—and miserably ignorant population . . . look at the beautiful republic of fifteen millions of happy Americans. We ought to love our country—it is a glorious one. I do not care what all the Martineaus, Trollopes, &c., say about our 'thin-skinnedness.' We have a right to be jealous of our dear country—it has no rival—she stands alone—beautiful and cloudless as a summer's day." September 23, 1837.

17. Edwin Forrest, "Oration Delivered at the Democratic Republican Celebration of the Sixty-second Anniversary of the Independence of the United States: In the City of New-York, Fourth July, 1838" (New York, 1838), 5, 14–15, 23.

18. Irving, *Geoffrey Crayon,* 108–116.

19. See, for instance, Cooper's *Notions of the Americans: Picked Up by a Travelling Bachelor* (1828) for the defense and *The American Democrat* (1838) for the critique.

20. *The Sun,* September 5, 1833.

21. Marryat, *A Diary in America,* 65.

22. *Cincinnati Gazette,* June 19, 1832.

23. Ralph Waldo Emerson, "The Young American," in *The Collected Works,* I. 222.

24. See Sturgess, *Shakespeare and the American Nation,* 56.

25. *Diaries,* II. 181.

26. Dickens to Macready, January 31, 1842, MA 106, Pierpont Morgan Library.

27. Dickens, *American Notes for General Circulation* (London, 2000), 133–34.

28. Dickens to Macready, January 3, 1844, MA 106, Pierpont Morgan Library.

29. Quoted in Joseph Leach, *Bright Particular Star: The Life and Times of Charlotte Cushman* (New Haven and London, 1970), 135.

30. *New Englander,* January, 1843.

31. Charles Dickens, *Martin Chuzzlewit* (London, 1999), 576. The hope which Martin expresses in reply—"And like a Phoenix, for its power of springing from the ashes

of its faults and vices, and soaring up anew into the sky!"—clearly did not mitigate the insult.

32. *Diaries,* II. 218–19.

33. *Reminiscences,* I. 321.

34. Dickens to Macready, September 1, 1843, MA 106, Pierpont Morgan Library. This letter is wrongly dated in Macready's *Diaries,* ed. Toynbee, to 1848, and consequently has often been taken to refer to Macready's later trip.

35. See *The Sun,* July 8, 1834, and the *New-York American,* July 10, 1834.

36. *The Sun,* July 11, 1834.

37. *Boston Gazette,* May 28, 1821, quoted in Grimsted, *Melodrama Unveiled,* 66.

38. *Commercial Advertiser,* quoted in Playfair, *The Flash of Lightning,* 126.

39. *Evening Post,* November 17, 1825, quoted in Wemyss, *Twenty-six Years,* 97–8.

40. Wemyss, *Twenty-six Years,* 117–18.

Chapter 7: The Paper War

1. *Diaries,* II. 224.

2. Ibid., II. 226.

3. Forrest to Catharine Forrest, both no date, quoted in *Report of the Forrest Divorce Case* (New York, 1852), 123, 124, 126.

4. Alger, *Life of Edwin Forrest,* 328–37.

5. *Diaries,* II. 227.

6. Ibid., II. 228.

7. Ibid., II. 228–30.

8. Murdoch, *The Stage,* 300–301.

9. *New York Herald,* October 26, 1843.

10. *Diaries,* II. 230–31.

11. Ibid., II. 231.

12. Macready to Letitia Macready, October 27, 1843, quoted in Downer, *The Eminent Tragedian,* 258.

13. Catherine Macready to Edwin Forrest, November 3, [1843], Y.c.406 (2a), Folger Shakespeare Library.

14. Smith, *Theatrical Management,* 179.

15. Unattributed clipping, Box 33, p. 13F, Ms Coll 5, University of Pennsylvania; from the context it can be dated to early November 1843. Even Walt Whitman, who was convinced that English managers, actors, and plays needed to die away before the American theatre could address American needs, began to worry about Forrest's acting: he characterized it as "the loud mouthed ranting style—the tearing of every thing to shivers" accompanied by "the loudest exhibition of sound, and the most distorted gesture" and "all kinds of unnatural and violent jerks, swings, screwing of the nerves of the faces, rolling of the eyes, and so on." Quoted in David Reynolds, *Walt Whitman's America: A Cultural Biography* (New York, 1995), 65. Conversely Macready, said Whitman, inhabited his roles: "We have known the time when an actual awe and dread crept over a large body assembled in the theatre, when Macready merely appeared, walking down the stage, a king. He was a king—not because he had a tinsel-gilded crown, and the counterfeit

robe, but because he then dilated his heart with the attributes of majesty, and they looked forth from his eyes, and appeared in his walk" (*Brooklyn Eagle,* August 20, 1846).

16. *Diaries,* II. 263.
17. Ibid., II. 266.
18. *Republican,* June 14, 1844, quoted in Moody, *Edwin Forrest,* 210.
19. *New York Herald,* March 18, 1844.
20. See London *Morning Post,* January 9, 1843, and *Sun,* January 13, 1843.
21. March 6, 1845, MM Walker, Robert J., New-York Historical Society Library.
22. *New York Herald,* December 11, 1843.
23. *The Times,* November 14, 1843.
24. *New York Herald,* January 29, 1844.
25. Macready to Horace Twiss, September 14, 1844, TC042, Princeton.
26. *Diaries,* II. 274.
27. *American Advocate,* September 10, 1844.
28. Quoted in Downer, *The Eminent Tragedian,* 268.
29. Macready to Thomas Noon Talfourd, July 5, 1844, Ms Eng 883 (II.116 facing), Houghton Library, Harvard University.

Chapter 8: The Man in the Box

1. The English actors who visited Paris in 1827–28 sent the young Parisian radicals—among them Alexandre Dumas, Victor Hugo, and Hector Berlioz—into transports over the wild passions of Shakespeare, and it was Macready, more than Kean or his other colleagues, who enthralled the city. Suddenly Shakespeare's barbaric blend of tragedy and comedy seemed right for the age. "After God," said the thoroughly converted Dumas, "Shakespeare created most," and Hugo wrote a typically hefty book in which he proposed that the Bard be appointed poet laureate of Europe. "Shakespeare," recalled Berlioz, "coming upon me unawares, struck me like a thunderbolt. The lightning flash of that discovery revealed to me at a stroke the whole heaven of art. . . . I recognized the meaning of grandeur, beauty, dramatic truth, and I could measure the utter absurdity of the French view of Shakespeare which derives from Voltaire—'That ape of genius, sent / By Satan among men to do his work'—and the pitiful narrowness of our own worn-out academic, cloistered traditions of poetry. I saw, I understood, I felt . . . that I was alive and that I must arise and walk" (Bate, *The Genius of Shakespeare,* 34, 232–33). Berlioz fell so deeply in love that he pursued and married the actress who played Juliet and Ophelia. It is impossible to overestimate the extent to which Shakespeare trampled over eighteenth- and nineteenth-century creeds.
2. Leach, *Bright Particular Star,* 150.
3. *The Spectator,* February 22, 1845.
4. Ibid., March 8, 1845. Forrest's friends later claimed that the *Spectator*'s review of *Lear* was written by Forster, though their only evidence was a perceived congruity of style with his earlier reviews. See *A Rejoinder to "The Replies from England, etc. to Certain Statements Circulated in This Country, Respecting Mr. Macready"* (New York, 1849), 66; hereafter, *A Rejoinder.*

5. Quoted in Moody, *Edwin Forrest*, 217.
6. The *Times* and *Sun* reviews were published on March 9, 1845.
7. *Punch,* VIII (1845), 138.
8. *Diaries,* II. 289.
9. Ibid., II. 412.
10. Ibid., II. 290.
11. Forrest to James Oakes, December 22, 1867, C0721, Princeton.
12. *The Examiner,* February 22, March 1, 1845.
13. Letter from Bulwer Lytton to Forrest, March 4, 1845, in extra-illustrated Gabriel Harrison, *Edwin Forrest,* THX 35702.354.43.11q, Princeton University Library.
14. *The Replies from England, etc., to Certain Statements Circulated in This Country Respecting Mr. Macready* (New York, 1849), 12.
15. Quoted in Downer, *The Eminent Tragedian,* 275.
16. *The Times,* March 12, 1846.
17. *Punch,* VIII (1845), 223.
18. Quoted in Montrose J. Moses, *The Fabulous Forrest* (Boston, 1929), 210.
19. See *Charlotte Cushman: Her Letters and Memories of Her Life,* ed. Emma Stebbins (Boston, 1878), 51–60. Stebbins was Cushman's long-term partner.
20. Leach, *Bright Particular Star,* 150.
21. *The Replies from England,* 19.
22. John Coleman, *Fifty Years of an Actor's Life* (London, 1904), I. 336.
23. Leach, *Bright Particular Star,* 150.
24. Moody, *Edwin Forrest,* 232–33.
25. Coleman, *Fifty Years,* II. 344.
26. The lines are at III.ii.
27. Coleman, *Fifty Years,* II. 345.
28. *The Replies from England,* 14, 15.
29. *The Scotsman,* March 4, 1846, quoted in *A Rejoinder,* 56.
30. *The Replies from England,* 14.
31. *Diaries,* II. 327.
32. Alger, *Life of Edwin Forrest,* 412.
33. *The Times,* March 12, 1846.
34. Ibid., April 4, 1846.
35. Ibid.
36. *Diaries,* II. 334.
37. Alger, *Life of Edwin Forrest,* 419–21.

Chapter 9: Of Men and Sheep

1. *Diaries,* II. 408–409; *Public Ledger and Daily Transcript,* November 21, 1848.
2. *Public Ledger,* November 22, 1848.
3. Quoted in *The Replies from England,* 5–8.
4. Ibid., 6. See also Forrest's letter to his close friend James Lawson thanking him for publishing a similar piece and rebutting "the venom of the penny a liners" who took Macready's side: November 28, [1848], Folder 25, Box 2, Ms Collection 5, University of Pennsylvania.

5. *The United States Magazine and Democratic Review,* January 1849; *The Literary World,* March 31, 1849.

6. Forrest to Catharine Forrest, November 25, 1848, quoted in *Report of the Forrest Divorce Case,* 121.

7. Quoted in *The Replies from England,* 38.

8. Dickens to Macready, February 2, 1849, MA 106, Pierpont Morgan Library.

9. *Diaries,* II. 411.

10. Reprinted in *The Replies from England,* 9–10.

11. See Macready's lengthy correspondence with Charles Sumner, Ms Am 1 (4040), Houghton Library, Harvard University, and also with Samuel Ruggles. Macready discusses questions of servants, manners, and the social position of his children. "England," he wrote to Ruggles, "will right herself yet, I think, and the abuses of the aristocratic classes will be swept away: —the question with me is, can I afford for my children's sake to wait the chances of the struggle, that must precede it? — I think not." June 2, 1848, TS 933.9, v. 1, facing p. 18, Harvard Theatre Collection.

12. *Diaries,* II. 414.

13. Quoted in *A Rejoinder,* 43–44.

14. Quoted in Downer, *The Eminent Tragedian,* 295.

15. *Spirit of the Times* (New York), April 7, 1849. For all his awareness of slavery and Native American issues, Macready was of his time.

16. *Diaries,* II. 420.

17. Archer, *William Charles Macready,* 177.

18. *Diaries,* II. 421.

19. Philadelphia *Sun,* quoted in *New York Herald,* May 16, 1849.

20. *Diaries,* II. 421.

21. *New York Herald,* August 17, 1848.

22. Trollope, *Domestic Manners,* 217–19.

23. Quoted in Alger, *Life of Edwin Forrest,* 506–508.

24. See Donald M. Reynolds, Jane Nobest Brennan, Sister Mary David Barry, *Fonthill Castle: Paradigm of Hudson-River Gothic* (New York, 1976).

25. *Report of the Forrest Divorce Case,* 75.

26. Ibid., 76.

27. Ibid., 71.

28. Forrest to William Rounseville Alger, August 28, 1870, ALS Box 32 P2 R09.01.06, Harvard Theatre Collection.

Chapter 10: A Night at the Opera, and Another in Hell

1. *New York Herald,* January 6, September 3, 1849.

2. *The Evening Post,* May 2, May 4, 1849.

3. See Herbert Asbury, *The Gangs of New York* (New York, 1928), 13–16.

4. George Foster describes such scenes at length. In his *Semi-annual Report of the Chief of Police from May 1, to October 31, 1849* (New York, 1850), George Matsell identified two thousand female thieves, beggars, and prostitutes between eight and sixteen years of age in eleven wards alone, a figure that he believed was far short of the true number; most, he added, spent the proceeds "in visiting the galleries of

the minor theatres, or in the lowest dens of drunkenness and disease which abound in the 'Five Points' and its vicinity; and they oftentimes waste large sums of money, amid half-grown boys of similar stamp, in the most disgusting scenes of precocious dissipation and debauchery."

5. Davy Crockett, *An Account of Col. Crockett's Tour to the North and Down East* (Philadelphia, 1835), 49.

6. Most of the nativist b'hoys were proslavery as well as antiforeigner, though most Tammany Democrats were against emancipation, too.

7. Foster, *New York Naked,* 121–22.

8. Quoted in *New York Herald,* August 12, 1844.

9. Edwin G. Burrows and Mike Wallace, *Gotham: A History of New York City to 1898* (New York, 1999), 753.

10. Foster, *New York by Gas-Light,* 171.

11. Quoted in Michael Feldberg, *The Philadelphia Riots of 1844: A Study of Ethnic Conflict* (Westport, Conn., and London, 1975), 60.

12. Peter Buckley's researches suggest that in reality Judson spent most of his naval career in harbor, and that his Seminole War service consisted mainly of coastal patrols.

13. Abingdon Place is now West Twelfth Street between Hudson and Greenwich.

14. *Edward J. C. Judson vs. Kate Hastings,* Police Court Cases Dismissed, 1807–1848: March 11, 1849, to May 31, 1849, roll no. 139, New York City Municipal Archives. A second equally scurrilous letter quoted by Peter Buckley has disappeared from the record.

15. The inventory is from Ned Buntline's *The Mysteries and Miseries of New York,* quoted in Jay Monaghan, *The Great Rascal: The Life and Adventures of Ned Buntline* (Boston, 1952), 154.

16. *New York Herald,* October 1, 1844.

17. *Morning Courier and New-York Enquirer,* April 9, 1834.

18. *The Evening Post,* July 12, 1834; the city's recorder is quoted in Paul Weinbaum, *Mobs and Demagogues: The New York Response to Collective Violence in the Early Nineteenth Century* (Ann Arbor, Mich., 1979), 48.

19. As Washington Irving had at the Park Theatre: he suggested an umbrella as necessary equipment for a pit seat, though he also complained about the heedlessly loud conversations in the boxes. Despite its reputation, the old Park had never been a salubrious place. The benches were muddy from the boots of pittites who insisted on standing on them to get a better view, rats ran across the floor, and one evening an elephant urinated over the orchestra from the stage. See Irving's *Letters of Jonathan Oldstyle, Gent.* (London, 1824), 17–18, 26, 32; Cowell, *Thirty Years,* 64.

20. Foster, *New York Naked,* 146.

21. Chas. H. Haswell, *Reminiscences of an Octogenarian of the City of New York (1816 to 1860)* (New York, 1897), 356–65.

22. Whitman is quoted in Reynolds, *Walt Whitman's America,* 166; Foster, *New York Naked,* 144.

23. *New York Mirror,* December 29, 1832, quoted in Lawrence Levine, *Highbrow/Lowbrow: The Emergence of Cultural Hierarchy in America* (Cambridge, Mass., 1988), 29. My reading of Shakespeare's shifting role in American culture gained much from Levine's groundbreaking study.

24. Chatham Street is now the stretch of Park Row that runs from City Hall Park to the Bowery. In Mrs. Trollope's time, the National Theatre was called the Chatham.

25. Trollope, *Domestic Manners,* 263.

26. Quoted in Eric Lott, *Love and Theft: Blackface Minstrelsy and the American Working Class* (New York, 1993), 83.

27. Burrows and Wallace, *Gotham,* 762.

28. *Spirit of the Times,* March 4, 1848.

29. *A Rejoinder,* 119.

30. Quoted in Monaghan, *The Great Rascal,* 172.

31. John Wallace Hutchinson, *Story of the Hutchinsons,* ed. Charles E. Mann (Boston, 1896), I. xvi, 262–63.

32. *New York Herald,* September 19, 1849.

33. Ibid., May 12, 1849.

Chapter 11: America Rules England Tonight!

My account of the riots is largely based on contemporary reports in the *New York Herald, Morning Courier and New-York Enquirer, New-York Tribune, Morning Express, The Evening Post,* and to a lesser extent *The Daily Globe, The Home Journal, The Albion, The United States Magazine and Democratic Review,* and other local and national papers. Vital testimony was also given in the coroner's trial, transcripts of which were widely published in the days following the riots, and the trials of the rioters, published on September 13–29, 1849, and January 15–20, 1850. As well as Macready's *Diaries,* the diaries of Philip Hone and George Templeton Strong and the recollections of George Walling and John Ripley are also important. To avoid weighing down the text with footnotes, and the footnotes with inventories of overlapping and often inconsistent sources, I have referenced only unique quotations.

1. Forty-eight names were listed in the *Morning Courier and New-York Enquirer,* the *Morning Express* and *The Evening Post* on May 9, 1849; the *New York Herald* omitted one name.

2. Philip Hone, *The Diary of Philip Hone 1828–1851,* ed. Allan Nevins (New York, 1936), 876.

3. *New-York Tribune,* May 9, 1849.

4. *Morning Courier and New-York Enquirer,* May 8, 1849. Andrew Stevens, in his confession in the *Police Gazette* of April 1, 1852, insisted that the *Courier*'s allegations were true to the letter, thus implying that Forrest funded the May 7 protests. The same caution, though, applies as to Stevens's other claims; see note to the Prologue. Elsewhere in the same piece, Stevens refuses to specify where the money came from; in the absence of hard evidence, it remains most likely that Forrest's friends acted on their own initiative.

5. *New York Herald,* May 9, 1849.

6. George W. Walling, *Recollections of a New York Chief of Police* (New York, 1887), 46; *New York Herald,* January 16, 1850.

7. *New York Herald,* May 10, 1849.

8. In one year, 163 conveyances were deeded to Matsell and his partner, and he was

also alleged to have received backhanders from a hundred gentlemen clients of Madame Restell (the pseudonym of the English-born Ann Lohman), the notorious Greenwich Street abortionist. See Gustavus Myers, *The History of Tammany Hall* (New York, 1901), 202.

9. Quoted in testimony to the Coroner's Court: see *A Rejoinder*, 79.

10. *Police Gazette*, April 1, 1852.

11. The estimate was given to the Coroner's Inquest by General Sandford. The *Globe* and *Post* estimated the crowd at ten thousand; in his *Account of the Terrific and Fatal Riot at the New-York Astor Place Opera House* (New York, 1849), H. M. Ranney put the figure at ten thousand to fifteen thousand. By any measure, in a time before professional sports stadia had begun to attract a mass public, it was a striking and alarming number.

12. *Diaries*, II. 425.

13. Ibid., II. 426.

14. *Morning Express*, May 11, 1849.

15. Thomas Addis Emmet had been a prominent figure among the United Irishmen during the 1798 rising: he had been imprisoned under unpleasant conditions by the British on a count of treason, held without evidence for four years, and released only to see his brother Robert executed for his part in the 1803 attempt to storm Dublin Castle. He finally made his way to America and became a leading advocate. Macready had made fast friends with him in 1826.

16. *Diaries*, II. 428.

Chapter 12: Exit, Pursued by a B'hoy

1. Forrest to James Oakes, May 11, 1849, C0721, Princeton.

2. Accounts of the numbers at the meeting varied widely: the *Courier* estimated fifteen thousand, Ranney in the *Review* twenty-five thousand, but the *Evening Post* only a thousand.

3. Each speaker was careful to warn against proximate violence, but the crowd gave their admonitions the credence they expected.

4. Again the range of estimates was wide, from the *Herald*'s fifteen hundred to the *Courier*'s six thousand or seven thousand.

5. George Templeton Strong, *The Diary of George Templeton Strong, Young Man in New York, 1835–1849*, ed. Allan Nevins and Milton Halsey Thomas (New York, 1952), 353.

6. *Morning Express*, May 15, 1849.

7. Eighteen—George A. Curtis, John McDonald, George Lincoln, Thomas Aylwood, Timothy Burns, Henry Otten, George W. Brown, William Butler, George W. Taylor, Owen Burns, Thomas Bulman, Neil Gray Mellis, Asa F. Collins, William Harman, Thomas Kearnin, Matthew Cahill, Timothy McGuin, and George W. Gedney—were listed as dead at the first coroner's inquest. Five more—Robert Macleurgen, Bridget Fagan, John Dalzell, John McKinley, and Stephen Kehoe—were widely reported as dead within a few days. Henry Burguist was listed among the dead in Ranney's generally reliable *Account of the Terrific and Fatal Riot,* which was published shortly after the event. The twenty-fifth, S. F. Cornell, is listed among

the dead in two newspaper accounts, and his death was attested to by a witness at the coroner's trial. The figure of twenty-five tallies with that given in the *Herald,* both in its review of the year 1849, published on January 1, 1850, and in its reports of the trials of the rioters. My twenty-sixth fatality is the boy killed in the May 11 meeting at the park. Of the other names given in the newspapers, several look like variant spellings. The *Herald*'s George A. Charles may be others' George A. Curtis; Messrs. Kelly, Cahan, and Cahart are probably Kehoe or Cahill; Andrew McKinley is probably John McKinley; Thomas Brennan is probably Thomas Bulman, Frederick Burns may be Timothy or Owen Burns, and William Parker may be William Butler or William Harman (also spelled Harmer). There are four persons listed with names distinct from those whose deaths were better documented but which appear in only one report: Frederick Gilpin, H. Mansfield, and Messrs. McGrange and Maitland. Peter Buckley in "To the Opera House: Culture and Society in New York City, 1820–1860" (unpublished Ph.D. diss., SUNY Stony Brook, 1984) lists twenty-one names but excludes three from the first coroner's trial; Richard Moody in *The Astor Place Riot* (Bloomington, 1958) claims thirty-one dead.

8. Michael Feldberg, in *The Philadelphia Riots of 1844,* identifies six rioters who were shot by troops; the *Public Ledger* claimed the higher figure. Perhaps twelve rioters were killed in 1835 during the Baltimore Bank riot, but by vigilante citizens rather than soldiers.

9. Portfolio 120, Folder 23, Printed Ephemera Collection, Library of Congress.

10. Monaghan, *The Great Rascal,* 183.

11. *Public Ledger and Daily Transcript,* May 16, 1849.

12. *The Home Journal,* May 26, 1849.

13. The Nuns of St. Vincent were also evicted from their retreat; they moved into Fonthill Castle, which they purchased from Forrest after lengthy negotiations.

14. A theme that never went away: Teddy Roosevelt was still worrying about the creation of a decadent American aristocracy at the turn of the century.

15. Quoted in Alger, *Life of Edwin Forrest,* 497.

16. Forrest to James Oakes, July 16, 1867, June 4, 1868, November 19, 1868, C0721, Princeton.

17. Unattributed clipping, Box 33, p. 13F, Ms Coll 5, University of Pennsylvania.

18. George William Curtis, "Editor's Easy Chair," *Harper's New Monthly Magazine,* December 1863, quoted in Levine, *Highbrow/Lowbrow,* 57.

19. William Winter, *The Wallet of Time* (New York, 1913), I. 124. Winter's analysis is exemplary of the jaundiced reevaluations of Forrest that followed his death.

20. One glimmer of his old self, and his theatrical isolation, came one day when he was seen early in the morning wheeling one of his few remaining friends around his garden; the friend was wearing George Frederick Cooke's gown, John Kemble's wig, and Edmund Kean's sword.

21. Forrest to James Lawson, August 29, 1860, Folder 21, Box 2, Ms Coll 5, University of Pennsylvania.

22. Dickens to Catherine Macready, n.d. [1849], MA 109, Pierpont Morgan Library.

23. *Diaries,* II. 490; Downer, *William Charles Macready,* 316.

24. *Diaries,* II. 495.

25. *Tallis's Dramatic Magazine and General Theatrical and Musical Review,* April 1851.

26. *Diaries,* II. 498.
27. See Cecile's letter to Forster, FD 18.33, National Art Library, London.

Epilogue

1. *Sacramento Daily Union,* December 8, 1856, quoted in Levine, *Highbrow/ Lowbrow,* 28.
2. *Golden Era,* February 15, 1857, quoted in Helene Wickham Koon, *How Shakespeare Won the West: Players and Performances in America's Gold Rush, 1849–1865* (Jefferson, N.C., 1989), 88.
3. Prentice Mulford, *Life by Land and Sea* (New York, 1889), 224.
4. Philip Ashton Rollins, *The Cowboy: An Unconventional History of Civilization on the Old-time Cattle Range* (Norman, Okla., 1997), 171.
5. The story of how Bridger encountered Shakespeare is in J. Lee Humfreville, *Twenty Years Among Our Hostile Indians* (New York, 1903), 462–70. Humfreville's memoir is first-hand, but several other versions of the story exist. One holds that an Irish baronet introduced Bridger to Shakespeare while the guide was leading his industrial-scale hunting expedition. Another adds that at first Bridger thought Shakespeare was "a little too high falutin'" for him, and he "rather calculated that thar big Dutchman, Mr. Full-stuff was a leetle bit too fond of lager beer" and would have been better off taking the same amount of alcohol in the more condensed medium of Bourbon whisky. A third claims that Bridger saw a soldier act Shakespeare and hired him to read to him; he listened to Shakespeare, a colonel's wife said, "with unfeigned pleasure." It is possible that all the stories are true, though it is curious that in each one he was said to have balked at *Richard III.* See Eugene Lee Caesar, *King of the Mountain Men* (New York, 1961), 242; J. Cecil Alter, *Jim Bridger* (Norman, Okla., 1962); Peter Lamb, *The Sign of the Buffalo Skull* (New York, 1932), 265–70.
6. Mulford, *Life by Land and Sea,* 256–61.
7. See *The New York Times,* April 24, 1864, and May 24, 1872; *New York Tribune,* May 23, 1872; *Shakespeare: Ward's Statue in the Central Park, New York* (New York, 1873).
8. *Emerson in His Journals,* ed. Joel Porte (Cambridge, Mass., 1982), 521. The elitist tendencies of American Shakespeare can also be judged from the fact that Americans were among the first to wade into the dreaded authorship question—on the anti-Stratfordian side. In 1857 Delia Bacon, an amateur literary sleuth, published a 675-page book entitled *The Philosophy of the Plays of Shakespeare Unfolded,* in which she dismissed William Shakespeare of Stratford as "a stupid, ignorant, illiterate, third-rate play-actor" and claimed that her namesake Francis Bacon was the true author of the plays. She attracted numerous disciples, including Henry James and, bizarrely, Walt Whitman and Mark Twain, though the year her book was published, having been caught poking suspiciously around Shakespeare's grave, she was committed to an insane asylum just outside Stratford; she died in an American institution two years later. In *Is Shakespeare Dead?* Twain, the boy from Hannibal, Missouri, insisted that a simple country lad like William Shakespeare could not possibly have gleaned the recondite knowledge wielded by the writer of the plays; perhaps it was a way to loosen the anxiety of influence. One of Twain's main contentions is that Shakespeare must have been a lawyer to represent the forms of legal

process with due accuracy (in terms of Elizabethan jurisprudence) in plays like *The Merchant of Venice*, though he does not ask whether, conversely, a lawyer could have written Shakespeare's plays with their flocks of neologisms, their little Latin and their less Greek. The book contains a number of striking logical non sequiturs. For instance, Twain wonders why no one important attended the funeral of England's greatest poet. Quite apart from the fact that Shakespeare was a mere dramatist who retired obscurely to Stratford, and so a figure of scant social standing—and that his end was rather better than that of many contemporary writers, or, for that matter, of Molière or Mozart—had a cabal of prominent figures known that Shakespeare was not the man he was supposed to be, and had they wanted to keep up the pretense, they would presumably have turned out; whereas the fact that the entire English establishment stayed away suggests, on Twain's terms, a conspiracy of such giant dimensions that it could surely not have been hushed up.

9. Some thought that was a good thing. Americanizing Shakespeare, they argued, had made it hard to Americanize the theatre. He was the poet of feudalism, tyranny, and superstition, said Walt Whitman, things America had come on this earth to destroy: now it was time for Yellowstone geysers and Colorado ravines. Whitman conceded that some of the tragedies and histories might, as an earlier generation of Americans had believed, contain a covert critique of feudalism and even foreshadow the inauguration of democracy. But the comedies, he declared, were divertissements for the elite of the castle, altogether unacceptable to America, and they needed to be replaced with inspiring poems of freedom to brother democracies. Herman Melville went further: Shakespeare, he said, was sure to be surpassed by an American, but that could only happen if the superstition of Bardolatry was allowed to die away so that America could carry republicanism into literature. Things did not turn out as either Whitman or Melville hoped: it is not a coincidence that *Moby-Dick* is the most Shakespearean of American novels, nor that it turned Melville into a prophet in the wilderness.

10. "Two of our best tragedians are obliged to make up strolling companies," Sol Smith lamented as early as 1868, "and roam through the rural districts, in hopes of finding some lovers of the good old drama in villages which have not yet had the love of Shakespeare fumigated out of them by red fires and blue blazes." *Theatrical Management*, 238.

11. Not everyone agreed on the answers to the questions Shakespeare raised; it was the fact that Shakespeare meant different things to different people that gave fuel to the supporters of Macready and Forrest, and to the Astor Place riots. Undeniably, too, some Americans read their Shakespeare selectively. The Prince of Morocco's plea, in *The Merchant of Venice*, that Portia should "Mislike me not for my complexion, / The shadowed livery of the burnish'd sun," is a particularly plangent example.

12. The twentieth century's gathering Shakespeare revival had several inspirations: the stars who rebelled against the monopoly system; the brave souls who set out to revive repertory; and the downfall of realism, as writers and directors once again sought more imaginative forms, in particular to grapple with shattering new ideologies. In New York, the revival is linked especially with the name of Joseph Papp, who staged bare-boards Shakespeare festivals in a Lower East Side church basement, on a truck, and, famously, in Central Park.

Bibliography

Much of the source material for *The Shakespeare Riots* is drawn from a wide range of contemporary newspapers: the titles are given at the relevant points in the notes.

1. Unpublished Sources

The collections of clippings, scrapbooks, prompt books, and playbills held at the New York Public Library for the Performing Arts, the Harvard Theatre Collection, the Rare Book and Manuscript Library at the University of Pennsylvania, and the Garrick Club in London have been heavily used. Forrest's and Macready's letters and papers are widely dispersed; the following is a list of the main collections.

The Edwin Forrest Collection of the Annenberg Rare Book and Manuscript Library of the University of Pennsylvania: letters and other papers of Forrest.

The Manuscripts Division of the Department of Rare Books and Special Collections of Princeton University Library: letters of Forrest and Macready, and the manuscript of Macready's *Reminiscences and Confessions*.

The Harvard Theatre Collection and the Houghton Library, Harvard University: letters of Forrest and Macready, the papers of Robert Elliston, and the manuscript diary of Forrest's grand tour.

The Pierpont Morgan Library Department of Literary and Historical Manuscripts: letters from Charles Dickens to Macready and other letters of Macready.

The British Library: letters of Macready.

The Folger Shakespeare Library: letters of Forrest and Macready.

The National Art Library and Theatre Museum of the Victoria and Albert Museum: papers of Macready. The National Art Library also houses the John Forster Collection.

The Manuscripts and Archives Division, New York Public Library: Charles P. Daly and Samuel B. Ruggles papers.

The New-York Historical Society Library: journals of Robert McCoskry Graham and Edward Neufville Tailer, Jr.; John W. Ripley's account of the riot; letter of Edward Everett.

2. Forrest, Macready, and the Riots

Alger, William Rounseville. *Life of Edwin Forrest, the American Tragedian.* 2 vols. (Philadelphia, 1877).

Anon. *A Rejoinder to "The Replies from England, etc. to Certain Statements Circulated in This Country, Respecting Mr. Macready." Together with an Impartial History and Review of the Lamentable Occurrences at the Astor Place Opera House, on the 10th of May, 1849. By An American Citizen.* (New York, 1849).

Anon. *The Replies from England, etc., to Certain Statements Circulated in This Country Respecting Mr. Macready* (New York, 1849).

Anon. *Report of the Forrest Divorce Case, Containing the Full and Unabridged Testimony of All the Witnesses, the Affidavits and Depositions, Together with the Consuelo and Forney Letters* (New York, 1852).

Archer, William. *William Charles Macready* (London, 1890).

Barrett, Lawrence. *Edwin Forrest* (Boston, 1881).

Buckley, Peter George. "To the Opera House: Culture and Society in New York City, 1820–1860" (unpublished Ph.D. diss., SUNY Stony Brook, 1984).

Downer, Alan S. *The Eminent Tragedian: William Charles Macready* (Cambridge, Mass., 1966).

Forrest, Edwin. "Oration Delivered at the Democratic Republican Celebration of the Sixty-second Anniversary of the Independence of the United States: In the City of New-York, Fourth July, 1838" (New York, 1838).

Harrison, Gabriel. *Edwin Forrest: The Actor and the Man* (Brooklyn, N.Y., 1889).

Macready, William Charles. *Macready's Reminiscences, and Selections from his Diaries and Letters.* Ed. Sir Frederick Pollock. 2 vols. (London, 1875).

———. *The Diaries of William Charles Macready 1833–1851.* Ed. William Toynbee. 2 vols. (London, 1912).

Moody, Richard. *The Astor Place Riot* (Bloomington, Ind., 1958).

———. *Edwin Forrest: First Star of the American Stage* (New York, 1960).

Moses, Montrose J. *The Fabulous Forrest* (Boston, 1929).

Pollock, [Juliet Creed], Lady. *Macready as I Knew Him* (London, 1884).

[Ranney, H. M.] *Account of the Terrific and Fatal Riot at the New-York Astor Place Opera House, on the Night of May 10th, 1849 : With the Quarrels of Forrest and Macready, Including All the Causes Which Led to That Awful Tragedy! Wherein an Infuriated Mob Was Quelled by the Public Authorities and Military, with Its Mournful Termination in the Sudden Death or Mutilation of More Than Fifty Citizens, with Full and Authentic Particulars* (New York, 1849).

Rees, James. *The Life of Edwin Forrest* (Philadelphia, 1874).

Trewin, J. C. *Mr. Macready: A Nineteenth-Century Tragedian and His Theatre* (London, 1955).

3. Theatrical Memoirs

Anderson, James R. *An Actor's Life* (London, 1902).

Beale, Willert (Walter Maynard), *The Light of Other Days* (London, 1850).

Belton, Fred. *Random Recollections of an Old Actor* (London, 1880).

Bunn, Alfred. *The Stage: Both Before and Behind the Curtain, from "Observations Taken on the Spot."* 3 vols. (London, 1840).

Coleman, John. *Fifty Years of an Actor's Life.* 2 vols. (London, 1904).

Cowell, Joe. *Thirty Years Passed Among the Players in England and America* (New York, 1845).

Dyer, Robert. *Nine Years of an Actor's Life* (London, 1833).

Fitzball, Edward. *Thirty-five Years of a Dramatic Author's Life.* 2 vols. (London, 1859).

Goodwin, Thomas. *Sketches and Impressions Musical, Theatrical, and Social (1799–1885)* (New York and London, 1887).

Hackett, James Henry. *Notes and Comments upon Certain Plays and Actors of Shakespeare, with Criticisms and Correspondence* (New York, 1863).

Jefferson, Joseph. *The Autobiography of Joseph Jefferson.* Ed. Alan Downer (Cambridge, Mass., 1964).

Kemble, Fanny. *Further Records 1848–1883* (New York, 1891).

——— *Records of Later Life* (New York, 1882).

Leman, Walter M. *Memories of an Old Actor* (New York, 1886).

Logan, Olive. *Apropos of Women and Theatres* (New York, 1869).

———. *Before the Footlights and Behind the Scenes* (Philadelphia, 1870).

Ludlow, Noah M. *Dramatic Life as I Found It* (St. Louis, 1880).

Mackintosh, Matthew. *Stage Reminiscences* (Glasgow, 1866).

Mathews, Anne. *Memoirs of Charles Mathews, Comedian.* 4 vols. (London, 1839).

Mowatt, Anna Cora. *Autobiography of an Actress; or, Eight Years on the Stage* (Boston, 1854).

Murdoch, James. *The Stage* (Philadelphia, 1880).

Parke, W. T. *Musical Memoirs* (London, 1830).

Planché, James Robinson. *Recollections and Reflections* (London, 1901).

Sala, George Augustus. *The Life and Adventures of George Augustus Sala.* 2 vols. (London, 1895).

Smith, Sol. *Theatrical Management in the West and South for Thirty Years* (New York, 1868).

Stirling, Edward. *Old Drury Lane: Fifty Years' Recollections of Author, Actor, and Manager.* 2 vols. (London, 1881).

Vandenhoff, George. *Leaves from an Actor's Note-book* (New York, 1860).

Wallack, Lester. *Memories of Fifty Years* (New York, 1889).

Wemyss, Francis Courtney. *Twenty-six Years of the Life of an Actor and Manager.* 2 vols. (New York, 1847).

Winston, James. *Drury Lane Journal: Selections from James Winston's Diaries 1819–1827.* Ed. Alfred L. Nelson and Gilbert B. Cross (London, 1974).

Winter, William. *The Wallet of Time.* 2 vols. (New York, 1913).

Yates, Edmund. *Fifty Years of London Life* (New York, 1885).

4. Theatre History

Archer, William and Robert W. Lowe, eds. *Dramatic Essays*. 3 vols. (London, 1894–96).

Baer, Marc. *Theatre and Disorder in Late Georgian London* (Oxford, 1992).

Baker, Michael. *The Rise of the Victorian Actor* (London, 1978).

Bank, Rosemarie K. *Theatre Culture in America, 1825–1860* (Cambridge and New York, 1997).

Booth, Michael R. *Theatre in the Victorian Age* (Cambridge, U.K., and New York, 1991).

Chaulin, N. P. *Biographie dramatique des principaux artistes anglais venus à Paris; précédée de souvenirs historiques du théâtre anglais à Paris en 1827 et 1828* (Paris, 1828).

Davis, Jim, and Victor Emeljanow. *Reflecting the Audience: London Theatregoing, 1840–1880* (Iowa City, 2001).

Fisher, Judith L., and Stephen Watt, eds. *When They Weren't Doing Shakespeare: Essays on Nineteenth-Century British and American Theatre* (Athens, Ga., 1989).

Genest, John. *Some Account of the English Stage, from the Restoration in 1660 to 1830*. 10 vols. (Bath, 1832).

Grimsted, David. *Melodrama Unveiled: American Theater and Culture, 1800–1850* (Chicago, 1968).

Hanners, John. *"It Was Play or Starve": Acting in the Nineteenth-Century Popular Theatre* (Bowling Green, Ohio, 1993).

Hudston, Sara. *Victorian Theatricals: From Menageries to Melodrama* (London, 2000).

Jackson, Russell, ed. *Victorian Theatre* (London, 1989).

"John Bull." *Remarks on the Cause of the Dispute Between the Public and Managers of the Theatre Royal, Covent Garden* (London, 1809).

Johnson, Claudia D. "That Guilty Third Tier: Prostitution in Nineteenth-Century American Theaters." *American Quarterly* 27 (1975), 575–84.

————and Vernon E. Johnson. *Nineteenth-Century Theatrical Memoirs* (Westport, Conn., 1982).

Leach, Joseph. *Bright Particular Star: The Life and Times of Charlotte Cushman* (New Haven and London, 1970).

Lewes, George Henry. *On Actors and the Art of Acting* (London, 1875).

Lott, Eric. *Love and Theft: Blackface Minstrelsy and the American Working Class* (New York, 1993).

McConachie, Bruce A., and Daniel Friedman, eds. *Theatre for Working-Class Audiences in the United States, 1830–1980* (Westport, Conn., 1985).

Moody, Jane. *Illegitimate Theatre in London, 1770–1840* (London and New York, 2000).

Martin, Sir Theodore. *Helen Faucit* (Edinburgh and London, 1900).

————. *Monographs: Garrick, Macready, Rachel, and Baron Stockmar* (New York, 1906).

Nathans, Heather S. *Early American Theatre from the Revolution to Thomas Jefferson: Into the Hands of the People* (New York, 2003).

Odell, George C. D. *Annals of the New York Stage*. 15 vols. (New York, 1927–49).

Playfair, Giles. *The Flash of Lightning: A Portrait of Edmund Kean* (London, 1983).

Prynne, William. *Histrio-mastix. The Players Scourge, or, Actors Tragaedie* (London, 1633).

Rede, Leman Thomas. *The Guide to the Stage*. American edition, ed. Francis C. Wemyss (New York, 1859).

Richards, Sandra. *The Rise of the English Actress* (London, 1993).

Rowell, George. *Queen Victoria Goes to the Theatre* (London, 1978).
———. *The Victorian Theatre, 1792–1914: A Survey* (Cambridge, 1978).
Schoch, Richard. *Queen Victoria and the Theatre of Her Age* (Basingstoke, 2004).
Shattuck, Charles H. *Bulwer and Macready: A Chronicle of the Early Victorian Theatre* (Urbana, Ill., 1958).
Stebbins, Emma, ed. *Charlotte Cushman: Her Letters and Memories of Her Life* (Boston, 1878).
Wilmeth, Don B., and Christopher Bigsby. *The Cambridge History of American Theatre.* 3 vols. (Cambridge, 1998–2000).
Woolcott, Alexander. *Mr. Dickens Goes to the Play* (New York and London, ca. 1922).
Wyndham, Henry Saxe. *The Annals of Covent Garden Theatre from 1732 to 1897.* 2 vols. (London, 1906).

5. Contemporary American Writings

Anon. *American Criticisms on Mrs Trollope's "Domestic Manners of the Americans"* (London, 1833).
Badeau, Adam. *The Vagabond* (New York, 1859).
"Buntline, Ned" (E.Z.C. Judson). *The Convict, or, the Conspirators' Victim* (New York, 1863).
———. *The Mysteries and Miseries of New York* (New York, 1848).
———. "Ned Buntline's Life-Yarn." *Knickerbocker,* November 1844, January, 1845.
Child, Lydia Maria Francis. *Letters from New-York* (New York, 1843).
Cooper, James Fenimore. *Notions of the Americans: Picked Up by a Travelling Bachelor.* 2 vols. (New York, 1850).
Crockett, Davy. *An Account of Col. Crockett's Tour to the North and Down East* (Philadelphia, 1835).
Emerson, Ralph Waldo. *The Collected Works of Ralph Waldo Emerson.* Ed. Robert E. Spiller, Alfred R. Ferguson, et al. 6 vols. (Cambridge, Mass., 1971).
———. *Emerson in His Journals.* Ed. Joel Porte (Cambridge, Mass., 1982).
Foster, George G. *Fifteen Minutes Around New York* (New York, 1854).
———. *New York by Gas-Light and Other Urban Sketches.* Ed. Stuart M. Blumin (Berkeley, Los Angeles, and London, 1990).
———. *New York in Slices* (New York, 1849).
———. *New York Naked* (New York, n.d.).
Haswell, Chas. H. *Reminiscences of an Octogenarian of the City of New York (1816 to 1860)* (New York, 1897).
Hone, Philip. *The Diary of Philip Hone 1828–1851.* Ed. Allan Nevins (New York, 1936).
Humfreville, J. Lee. *Twenty Years Among Our Hostile Indians* (New York, [1903]).
Irving, Washington. *The Letters of Jonathan Oldstyle, Gent.* (New York, 1824).
———. *The Sketch Book of Geoffrey Crayon* (London, 1820).
Mulford, Prentice. *Life by Land and Sea* (New York, 1889).
Paulding, James Kirke. *John Bull in America; or, the New Munchausen* (New York, 1825).
[Paterson, Thomas V]. *The Private Life, Public Career, and Real Character of That Odious Rascal Ned Buntline!! etc.* (New York, 1849).
Prentiss, George. *A Memoir of S. S. Prentiss* (New York, 1855).

Schaeffer, Luther Melanchthon. *Sketches of Travels in South America, Mexico and California* (New York, 1860).

Strong, George Templeton. *The Diary of George Templeton Strong, Young Man in New York, 1835–1849.* Ed. Allan Nevins and Milton Halsey Thomas (New York, 1952).

Twain, Mark. *Life on the Mississippi* (Boston, 1883).

Walling, George W. *Recollections of a New York Chief of Police* (New York, 1887).

Walsh, Robert. *An Appeal from the Judgments of Great Britain Respecting the United States of America. Part First. Containing an Historical Outline of their Merits and Wrongs as Colonies, and Strictures on the Calumnies of British Writers* (Philadelphia and London, 1819).

Whitman, Walt. *Complete Prose Works* (Philadelphia, 1892).

Wikoff, Henry. *The Reminiscences of an Idler* (New York, 1880).

6. Travelers' Accounts of America

Dickens, Charles. *American Notes for General Circulation* (London, 2000).

Hall, Captain Basil. *Travels in North America in the Years 1827 and 1828.* 3 vols. (Edinburgh, 1829).

Janson, Charles William. *The Stranger in America, 1793–1806* (New York, 1935).

Kemble, Fanny. *Journal of a Residence in America* (Paris, 1835).

Lieber, Francis. *The Stranger in America.* 2 vols. (London, 1835).

Marryat, Frederick. *Second Series of A Diary in America, with Remarks on Its Institutions* (Philadelphia, 1840).

Martineau, Harriet. *Society in America.* 3 vols. (London, 1837).

Nettle, George. *A Practical Guide for Emigrants to North America by a Seven Year Resident in North America* (London, 1850).

Power, Tyrone. *Impressions of America During the Years 1833, 1834, and 1835.* 2 vols. (London, 1836).

Tocqueville, Alexis de. *Democracy in America.* 2 vols. (London, 1968).

Trollope, Frances. *Domestic Manners of the Americans* (Harmondsworth, 1997).

7. U.S. History

Alter, John Cecil. *Jim Bridger* (Norman, Okla., 1962).

Anbinder, Tyler. *Five Points: The Nineteenth-Century New York City Neighborhood That Invented Tap Dance, Stole Elections, and Became the World's Most Notorious Slum* (New York, 2002).

Asbury, Herbert. *The Gangs of New York* (New York, 1928).

Burrows, Edwin G., and Mike Wallace. *Gotham: A History of New York City to 1898* (New York, 1999).

Caesar, Eugene Lee. *King of the Mountain Men* (New York, 1961).

Clark, Emmons. *History of the Seventh Regiment of New York, 1806–1889* (New York, 1890).

Emmet, Thomas Addis. *The Emmet Family* (New York, 1898).

Ernst, Robert. *Immigrant Life in New York City 1825–1863* (New York, 1949).

Feldburg, Michael. *The Philadelphia Riots of 1844: A Study of Ethnic Conflict* (Westport, Conn., and London, 1975).

————. *The Turbulent Era: Riot and Disorder in Jacksonian America* (New York and Oxford, 1980).

Graham, Philip. *Showboats: The History of an American Institution* (Austin, Tex., 1951).

Hall, Peter Dobkin. *The Organization of American Culture, 1700–1900: Private Institutions, Elites and the Origins of American Nationality* (New York, 1982).

Hammond, Harold Earl. *A Commoner's Judge: The Life and Times of Charles Patrick Daly* (Boston, 1954).

Himmelfarb, Gertrude. *One Nation, Two Cultures* (New York, 1999).

Hutchinson, John Wallace. *Story of the Hutchinsons.* Ed. Charles E. Mann. 2 vols. (Boston, 1896).

Lamb, Peter O. *The Sign of the Buffalo Skull: The Story of Jim Bridger, Frontier Scout* (New York, 1932).

Levine, Bruce C. *The Spirit of 1848: German Immigrants, Labor Conflict and the Coming of the Civil War* (Urbana, Ill., 1992).

Levine, Lawrence. *Highbrow/Lowbrow: The Emergence of Cultural Hierarchy in America* (Cambridge, Mass., 1988).

Monaghan, Jay. *The Great Rascal: The Life and Adventures of Ned Buntline* (Boston, 1952).

Moss, Sidney P. *Charles Dickens' Quarrel with America* (New York, 1984).

Myers, Gustavus. *The History of Tammany Hall* (New York, 1901).

Nye, Russell Blaine. *Society and Culture in America, 1830–1860* (New York, 1974).

Reynolds, David S. *Walt Whitman's America: A Cultural Biography* (New York, 1995).

Rollins, Philip Ashton. *The Cowboy: An Unconventional History of Civilization on the Old-time Cattle Range* (Norman, Okla., and London, 1997).

Rosenzweig, Roy, and Elizabeth Blackmar. *The Park and the People: A History of Central Park* (Ithaca, N.Y., 1992).

Rusk, R. L. *The Literature of the Middle Western Frontier.* 2 vols. (New York, 1925).

Stansell, Christine. *City of Women: Sex and Class in New York, 1789–1860* (Urbana, Ill., 1987).

Streeby, Shelley. *American Sensations: Class, Empire, and the Production of Popular Culture* (Berkeley, 2002).

Sween, Gretchen. "Rituals, Riots, Rules, and Rights: The Astor Place Theater Riot of 1849 and the Evolving Limits of Free Speech." *Texas Law Review* 81 (2002), 679–713.

Temin, Peter. *The Jacksonian Economy* (New York, 1969).

Turner, Frederick Jackson. *The Frontier in American History* (New York, 1920).

Weinbaum, Paul O. *Mobs and Demagogues: The New York Response to Collective Violence in the Early Nineteenth Century* (Ann Arbor, Mich., 1979).

Wilentz, Sean. *Chants Democratic: New York City and the Rise of the American Working Class, 1788–1850* (New York, 1984).

Young, Terence, and Robert Riley, eds. *Theme Park Landscapes: Antecedents and Variations* (Washington, D.C., 2002).

8. Britain

Ackroyd, Peter. *Dickens* (London, 1990).

Beames, Thomas. *The Rookeries of London: Past, Present, and Prospective* (London, 1852).

Brewer, John. *The Pleasures of the Imagination: English Culture in the Eighteenth Century* (London, 1997).

Davies, James A. *John Forster: A Literary Life* (Leicester, 1983).

Egan, Pierce. *Life in London; or, the Day and Night Scenes of Jerry Hawthorn, Esq., and His Elegant Friend Corinthian Tom, Accompanied by Bob Logic, the Oxonian, in Their Rambles and Sprees Through the Metropolis* (London, 1821).

Forster, John. *The Life of Charles Dickens.* 3 vols. (London, 1872–74).

Grant, James. *The Great Metropolis* (London, 1837).

Mayhew, Henry. *London Labour and the London Poor.* 4 vols. (London, 1968).

Nowrojee, Jehangeer, and Hirjeebhoy Merwanjee. *Journal of a Residence of Two Years and a Half in Great Britain* (London, 1841).

Perkin, Harold. *The Origins of Modern English Society, 1780–1880* (London, 1969).

Porter, Roy. *London: A Social History* (Harmondsworth, 1994).

Reid, J. C. *Bucks and Bruisers: Pierce Egan and Regency England* (London, 1971).

Smith, Charles Manby. *Curiosities of London Life, or Phases, Physiological and Social of the Great Metropolis* (London, 1853).

Tristan, Flora. *Flora Tristan's London Journal: A Survey of London Life in the 1830s.* Trans. Dennis Palmer and Giselle Pinsett (London, 1980).

Wright, Thomas. *Some Habits and Customs of the Working Classes* (London, 1867).

9. Shakespeare

Bate, Jonathan. *The Genius of Shakespeare* (London, 1997).

Bristol, Frank M. *Shakespeare and America* (Chicago, 1898).

Carlyle, Thomas. *On Heroes, Hero-worship, and the Heroic in History.* Ed. Carl Nieyemer (Lincoln, Neb., 1966).

Clark, Sandra. *Shakespeare Made Fit: Restoration Adaptations of Shakespeare* (London, 1997).

Dobson, Michael. *The Making of the National Poet: Shakespeare, Adaptation and Authorship 1660–1769* (Oxford, 1992).

Dunn, Esther Cloudman. *Shakespeare in America* (New York, 1939).

Foulkes, Richard. *Performing Shakespeare in the Age of Empire* (Cambridge, 2002).

Gayley, Charles Mills. *Shakespeare and the Founders of Liberty in America* (New York, 1917).

Greenblatt, Stephen. *Will in the World* (London, 2004).

Koon, Helene Wickham. *How Shakespeare Won the West: Players and Performances in America's Gold Rush, 1849–1865* (Jefferson, N.C., 1989).

Kujawińska Courtney, Krystyna, and John M. Mercer, eds. *The Globalization of Shakespeare in the Nineteenth Century* (Lewiston, N.Y., 2003).

Odell, George C. D. *Shakespeare from Betterton to Irving.* 2 vols. (London, 1920).

Schoch, Richard W. *Not Shakespeare: Bardolatry and Burlesque in the Nineteenth Century* (Cambridge, 2002).

Shattuck, Charles H. *Shakespeare on the American Stage: From the Hallams to Edwin Booth* (Washington, D.C., 1976).

Sturgess, Kim C. *Shakespeare and the American Nation* (Cambridge, 2004).

Taylor, Gary. *Reinventing Shakespeare: A Cultural History from the Restoration to the Present* (London, 1990).

Twain, Mark. *Is Shakespeare Dead?* (New York, 1909).

Webb, Nancy, and Jean Francis Webb. *Will Shakespeare and His America* (New York, 1964).

Wells, Stanley. *Nineteenth-Century Shakespeare Burlesques.* 5 vols. (London, 1977).

Index

Page numbers in *italics* refer to illustrations.

NIGEL CLIFF was educated at Oxford University, where he was awarded a double first in English and the Beddington Prize for English literature. He is a former theatre and film critic for the *Times* (London) and contributor to *The Economist*. This is his first book.

ABOUT THE TYPE

This book was set in Garamond No. 3, a variation of the classic Garamond typeface originally designed by the Parisian type cutter Claude Garamond (1480–1561).

Claude Garamond's distinguished romans and italics first appeared in *Opera Ciceronis* in 1543–44. The Garamond types are clear, open, and elegant.